Gustave Doré

Masterpieces of Art

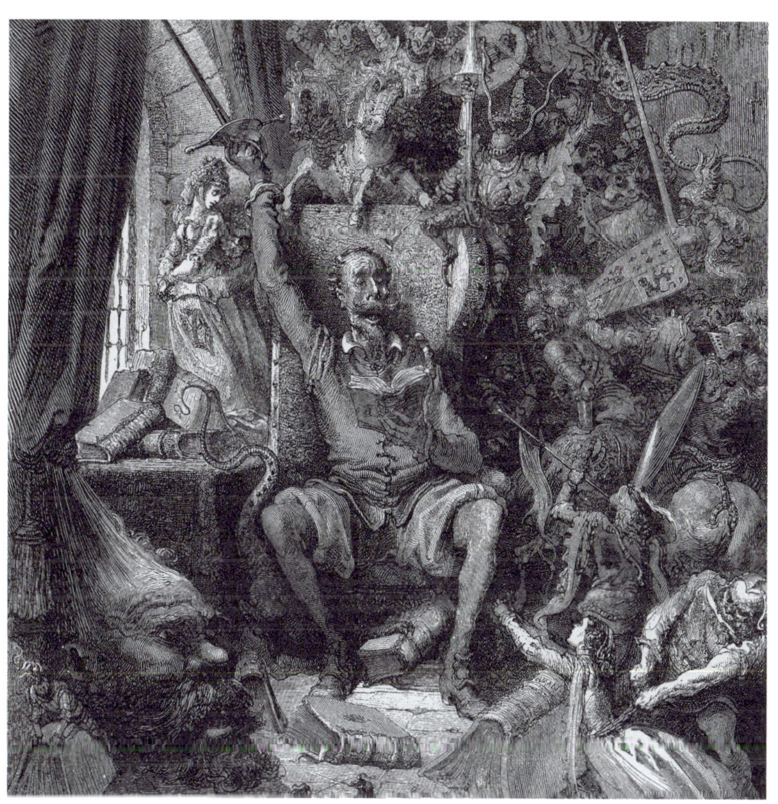

Publisher & Creative Director: Nick Wells
Senior Project Editor: Catherine Taylor
Copy Editor: Daniela Nava
Art Director: Mike Spender
Layout Design: Jane Ashley
Digital Design & Production: Chris Herbert
Proofreader: Dawn Laker

Special thanks to Angelica Stevenson, Frances Bodiam.

FLAME TREE PUBLISHING
6 Melbray Mews
Fulham, London SW6 3NS
United Kingdom

www.flametreepublishing.com

First published 2019

24 26 28 27 25
3 5 7 9 10 8 6 4 2

A copy of the CIP data for this book is available from the British Library.

All images courtesy of Dan Malan, except that on page 27
which is courtesy of and © Kristen Lawrence (HalloweenCarols.com).

ISBN: 978-1-80417-786-0

Printed in China | Created, Developed & Produced in the United Kingdom

Gustave Doré

Masterpieces of Art

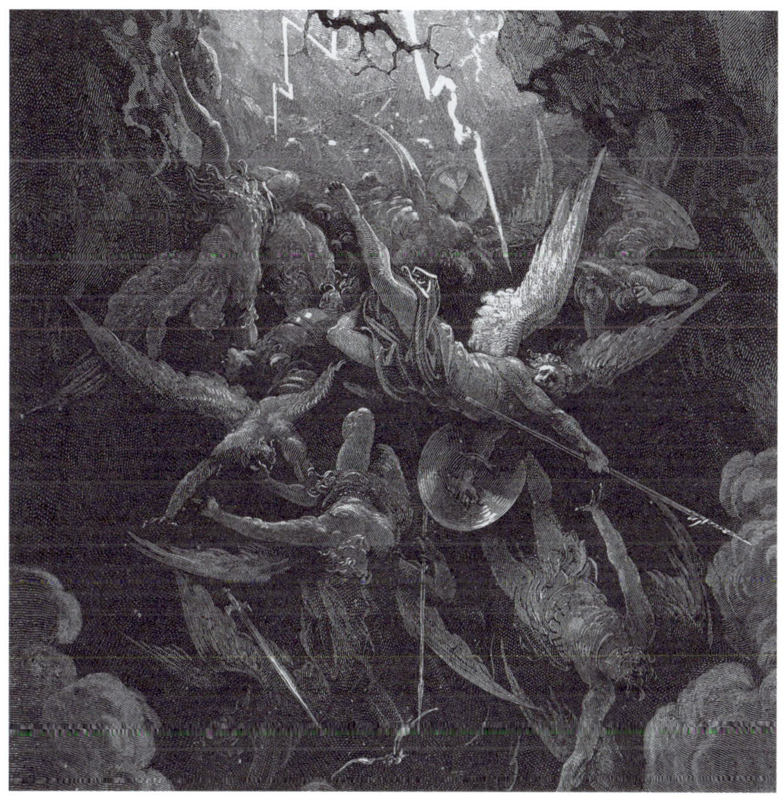

Dan Malan

FLAME TREE
PUBLISHING

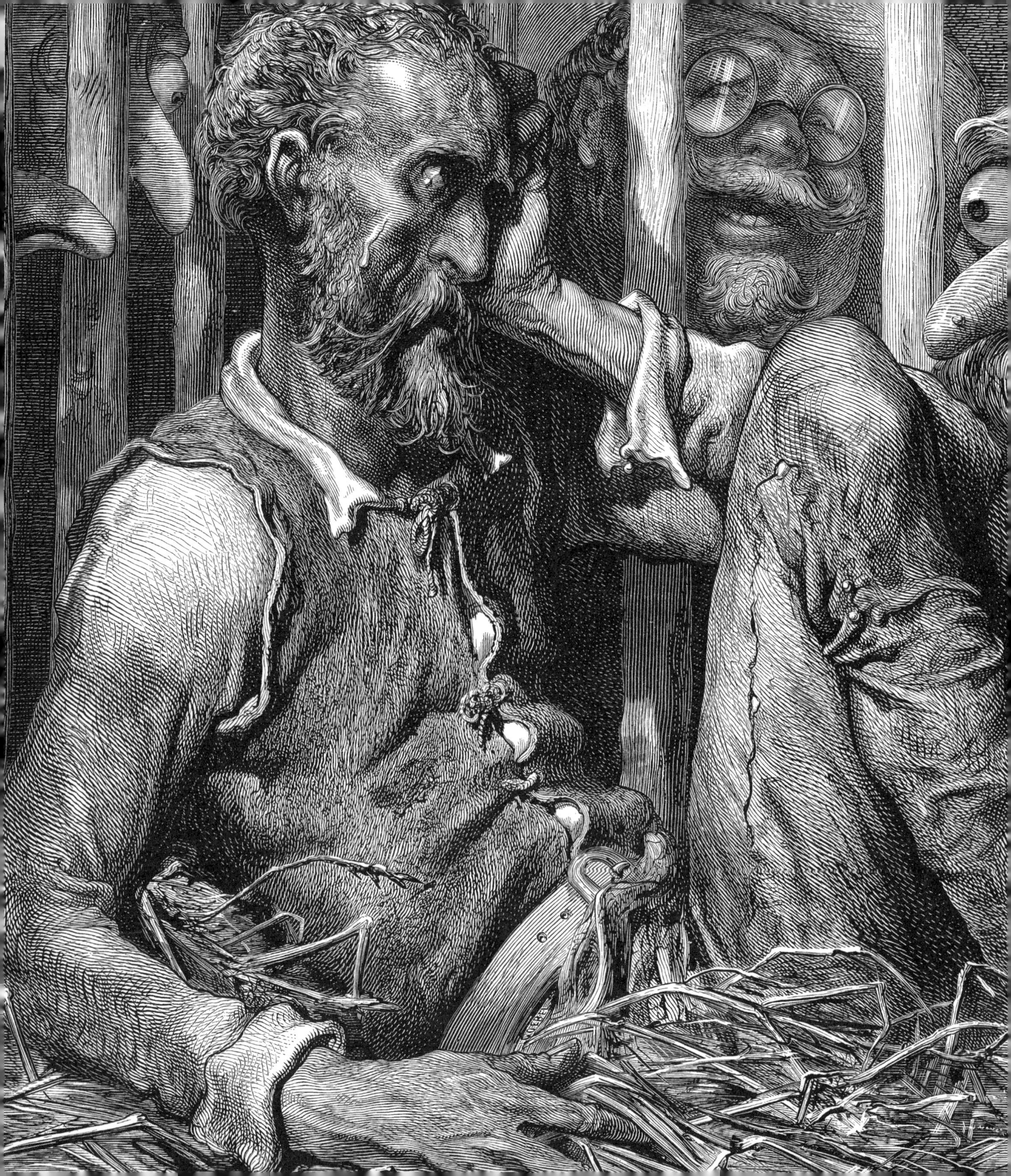

Contents

Gustave Doré: Unsung Creative Genius

Gustave Doré (1832–83) was an untrained prodigy who became the highest-paid illustrator in France at the age of 16. A prolific painter and sculptor, by the 1860s he was the most famous artist in the world – mainly thanks to his literary folios, which are now etched into our collective subconscious. As Doré's fame died out in the twentieth century, his influence increased in new artistic media, and nowadays most people are familiar with his art (Chewbacca in the *Star Wars* films and Puss in Boots in *Shrek 2* being just two examples) often without being aware of his name. Doré has become the world's most borrowed artist in hundreds of popular culture genres.

'Gustave Doré stands just now as the most startling art phenomenon in Europe; his genius at each turn changes, like colours in a kaleidoscope, into something new and unexpected.'
Saturday Review, 1869

He reached unprecedented levels of worldwide fame and then controversy, with a major backlash to his fame by art elitists. During his lifetime, publishers used Doré's name on title pages to sell books.

Now, the film industry, music industry, merchandising and more, use Doré's art without his name to sell goods.

Child Prodigy

Gustave was born in Strasbourg, 'with a pencil in his hand': his earliest known detailed drawings are from when he was five (see the sketch of *Ant and Moth* shown here, from the first letter illustrated by Doré in 1837). He began carving his lithographs on stone at the age of 12 and, when he was 15, his family visited Paris. While there, he saw drawings in a publisher's window and faked being ill so he could be left at the hotel. He then snuck off and barged into the office of publisher Charles Philipon (1800–61) to show him some of his drawings. Philipon looked at them and then at the youth before him, and could not believe that Gustave had done them, so he asked him to make new drawings right there, on the spot. The speed at which Gustave drew was legendary: Philipon refused to let the young boy leave. He sent some men to find Gustave's father and convinced him to leave his son in Paris, in his care. That is how Gustave Doré became the highest-paid illustrator in France and his family's breadwinner after his father died – see his illustration for the *Labours of Hercules*, opposite, from 1847. As a teenager, he had thousands of illustrations published in Philipon's *Journal pour rire* (*see* right), as well as in three lithographic albums, for which Gustave wrote stories and made drawings – and even carved them on stone himself.

'Boy Genius'

Although Philipon's contract with Gustave's father gave him exclusive rights to Doré's illustrations for three years, the young artist also exhibited original art at the Paris Salon

from the age of 16. At 18, he began exhibiting oil paintings –
mainly landscapes – and after the contract expired, Doré also did
hundreds of engravings for other Paris book publishers. In 1854,
his engravings for the works of François Rabelais (1494–1553),
such as for *Gargantua and Pantagruel* (*see* overleaf and pages
73–76), caught the attention of major French writers Alexandre
Dumas (1802–70) and Théophile Gautier (1811–72), then France's
leading art critic, who dubbed Doré the 'boy genius' – even though
he was actually 22 by then – and predicted that he would become
France's leading artist. Doré's first major international exposure
came in 1855, when British periodicals *Illustrated London News*
and *Illustrated Times* published dozens of his large illustrations
of the Crimean War. Doré exhibited several paintings at the 1855
Exposition Universelle in Paris, including the large *Battle of Alma*,
and followed up his 105 Rabelais engravings with 425 Balzac
engravings, which also proved very popular. In 1856, he illustrated
10 book titles, as well as producing hundreds of engravings for
several periodicals; by the time Doré was 24, he had produced
4,000 published engravings.

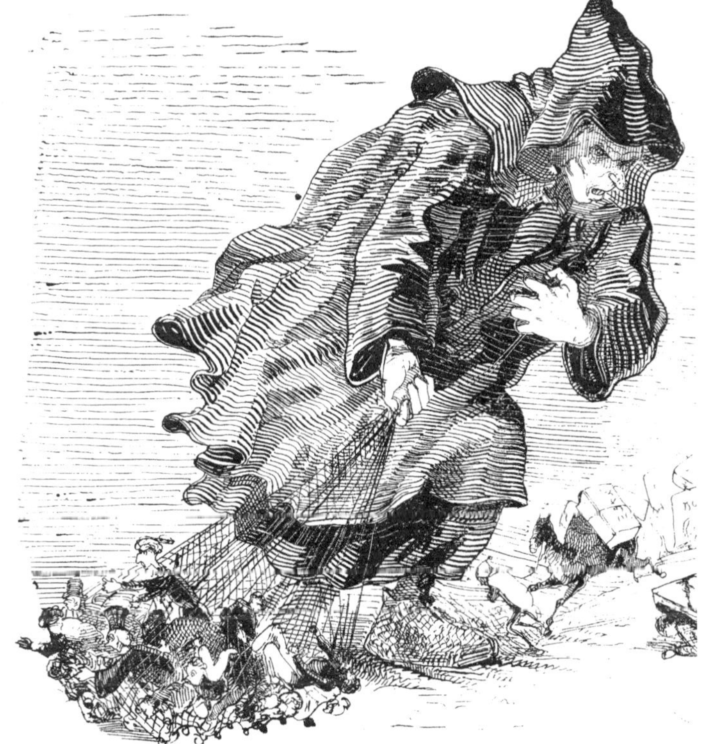

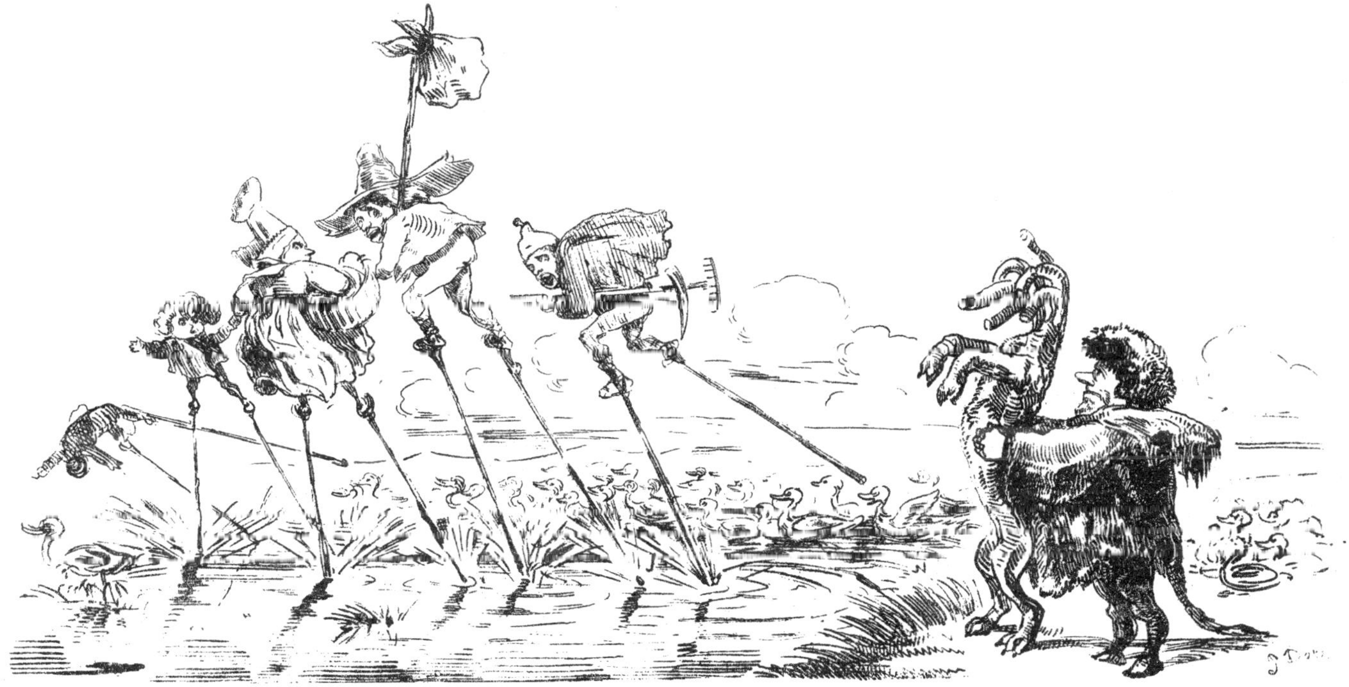

Battle of Inkerman

By 1856, Doré's artistic output had caught the attention of the Emperor Napoleon III (1808–73), and the French government commissioned him, paying him 10,000 francs, for a large oil painting meant to be displayed in a new museum in Versailles. Doré's *Battle of Inkerman* was exhibited, together with another nine of his paintings, in the 1857 Paris Salon, where it received an Honourable Mention. The Emperor even invited Doré to dine with him at the palace on more than one occasion: everything was looking up and the artist announced his intention to start work on a series of folios of the great classics of literature, each comprising hundreds of large engravings. But the project was a commercial risk: most books sold for 10 francs and Doré wanted to do large folios that would sell for 100 francs or more (classic book sizes include, from smallest to largest, 'duodecimo' or '12mo', 'octavo' or '8vo', 'quarto' or '4to' and 'folio' – most books are octavo). His main publisher by then was the prominent Louis Hachette (1800–64), who balked at Doré's audacious plan, asserting: 'You will be lucky to sell a hundred copies.' Since the artist replied that he would pay to print the expensive folio himself, Hachette agreed to put his name on the edition and advised him to only bind a small quantity at first, in order to lessen the blow of Doré's inevitable financial disaster.

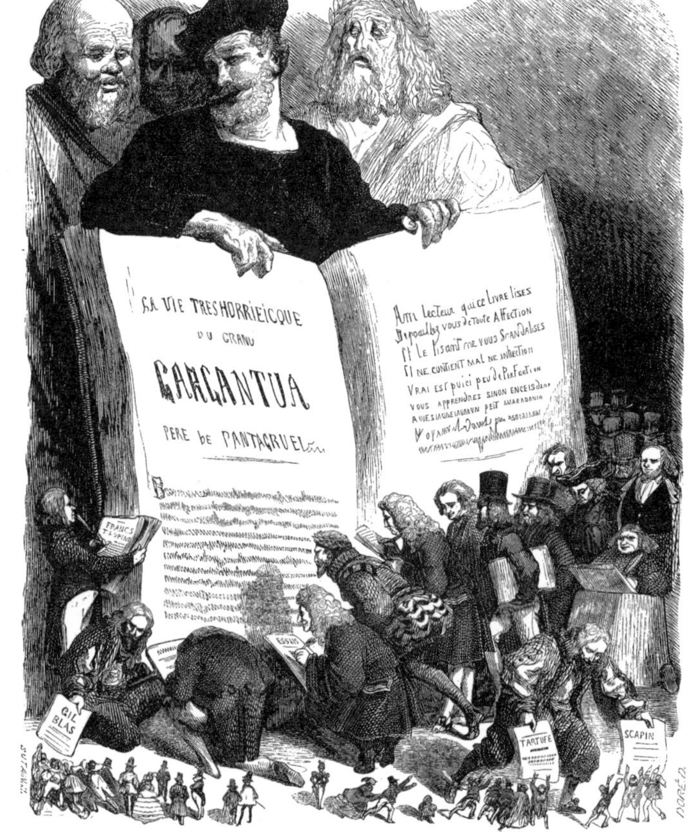

'I Am an Ass', the Success of *Inferno*

The year 1861 marked the beginning of Doré's literary folio series, with Dante's *Inferno*, but it was much more than just a book: he had learned the secret of what we would now call multimedia marketing and produced five different types of art. Besides the folio, Doré exhibited in the 1861 Paris Salon three drawings based on scenes from the *Inferno* and a large oil painting, which won another Honourable Mention, although French articles at the time asserted that Doré deserved a higher award. He also exhibited photographs – that new invention – of the three drawings. For the folio, Doré's engravers carved the images that the artist drew directly on to wood blocks, which were then made into electrotype mouldings, allowing an unlimited quantity of perfect print impressions. As the engravers sensed that this was something special, they exhibited 18 of those original wood blocks in the Paris Salon; all this produced an explosion of excitement and several dozen laudatory articles. Shortly after the folio went on sale, Doré received an urgent telegram from Louis Hachette, which read, 'Success! Come quickly! I am an ass!' Far from selling only 100 copies, there have been hundreds of editions of Dante's *Inferno* with Doré's engravings. About a month later, at the age of 29, Doré was awarded the French Legion of Honour.

Farinata's Tomb

Doré's *Inferno* engravings were the visual equivalent of what Edgar Allan Poe (1809–49) represented poetically for the horror genre. Eleanor Roosevelt (1884–1962) said that his folios were the 'terror of small children', referring to both the scary images and the weight of

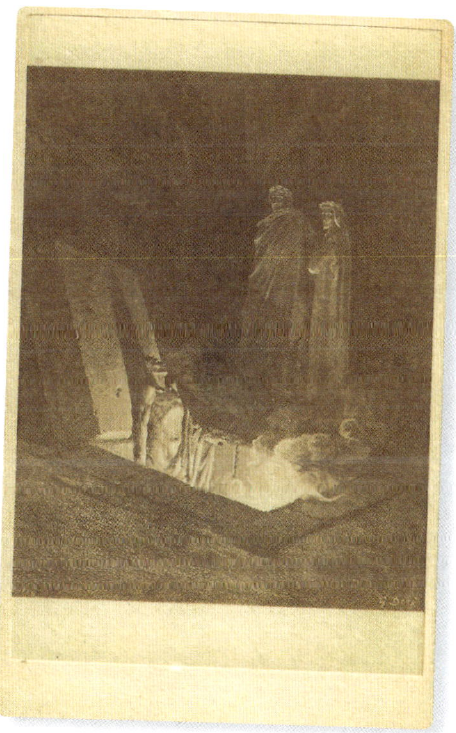

the volumes. Out of those 76 plates (otherwise written as '76-B', where 'B' indicates full-page, black-and-white plates), the one that quickly caught the attention of reviewers was *Farinata's Tomb* (*see* page 33, and the 'carte de visite', below), which shows the corpse coming up out of his flaming sepulchre to talk to Dante and Virgil. The dramatic chiaroscuro contrast of the darkness of Hell with the brightness of the flames is breathtaking and one of the first of Doré's engravings to become an iconic image for a historical or literary scene. It became a painted poster for one of the early *Dante's Inferno* films and was also reprinted or redrawn for many music album covers, posters, tattoos, T-shirts, political cartoons by Steve Bell (b. 1951) and even a black leather motorcycle jacket.

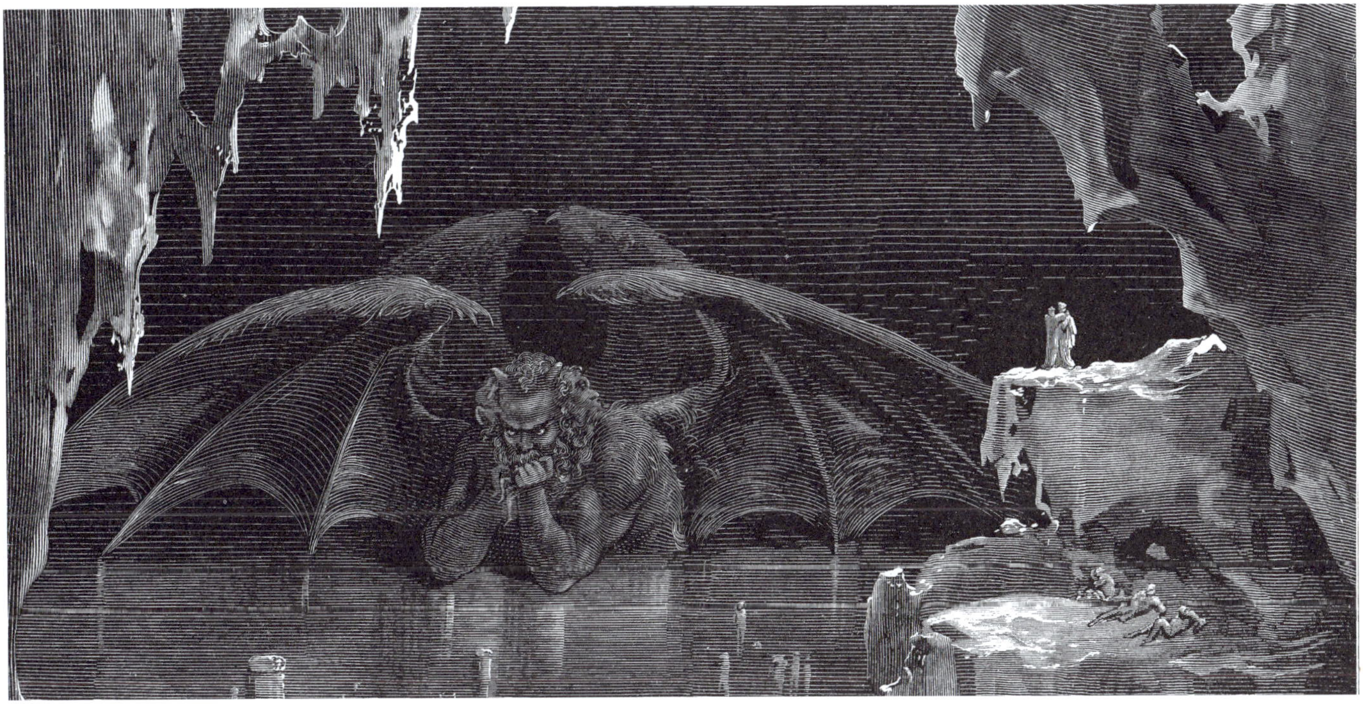

Hitler: A Film from Germany

In 1977, Germany was attempting to come to terms with the Second World War with the help of a seven-hour film by Hans-Jurgen Syberberg (b. 1935), co-produced by the British Broadcasting Corporation and released in the United States by Francis Ford Coppola (b. 1939). Dozens of Doré's engravings appear in the background, but one seven-minute scene in particular got all the attention and was reprinted on the covers of several books, posters and articles, as well as the DVD itself: a re-enactment of Doré's *Farinata's Tomb* – a perfect example of the power of his dramatic, mystical imagery. In the scene, Adolf Hitler (1889–1945), clad in a Roman toga, comes up out of a fiery grave to attempt to justify his atrocities; however, the tomb is not his, as it is clearly marked 'RW' and belongs to Richard Wagner (1813–83).

Fairy Tales

Doré made a point of following up his horror genre with children's fairy tales to show his incredible versatility. Just a few months after *The Inferno* by Dante Alighieri (1265–1321), the French reading public was treated to *Fairy Tales* (42-B) by Charles Perrault (1628–1703): illustrations 'fit for the children of a king', as one reviewer asserted. As these images have also permeated popular culture, from now on the art that this sphere has borrowed from Doré will be referred to as 'Doreana', which in the case of these tales became dispersed into individual editions of the nine stories. Three popular images were *Prince Charming Finding Sleeping Beauty* (*see* page 87), *Little Red Riding Hood in Bed with Wolf* (*see* below and page 85) and *Bluebeard Showing His Wife the Keys* (*see* page 86). The latter was selected to be on a French postage stamp for the anniversary of Doré's death, while Little Red Riding Hood was reprinted as the cover of many books, including titles on psychoanalysis. Now an iconic image of an innocent young girl facing a fiendish predator, in 1994 *Time* magazine reprinted it with the face of Mike Tyson (b. 1966) superimposed over the wolf. In the 1997 short black-and-white film *Little Red Riding Hood*, Christina Ricci (b. 1980) was selected to play the lead role because her face resembled the original Doré engraving.

Shrek

In 2014, a major Doré exhibition at the Musée d'Orsay in Paris drew over 300,000 attendees, before moving to the National Gallery of Canada. The main Doré image used for books, posters, articles and

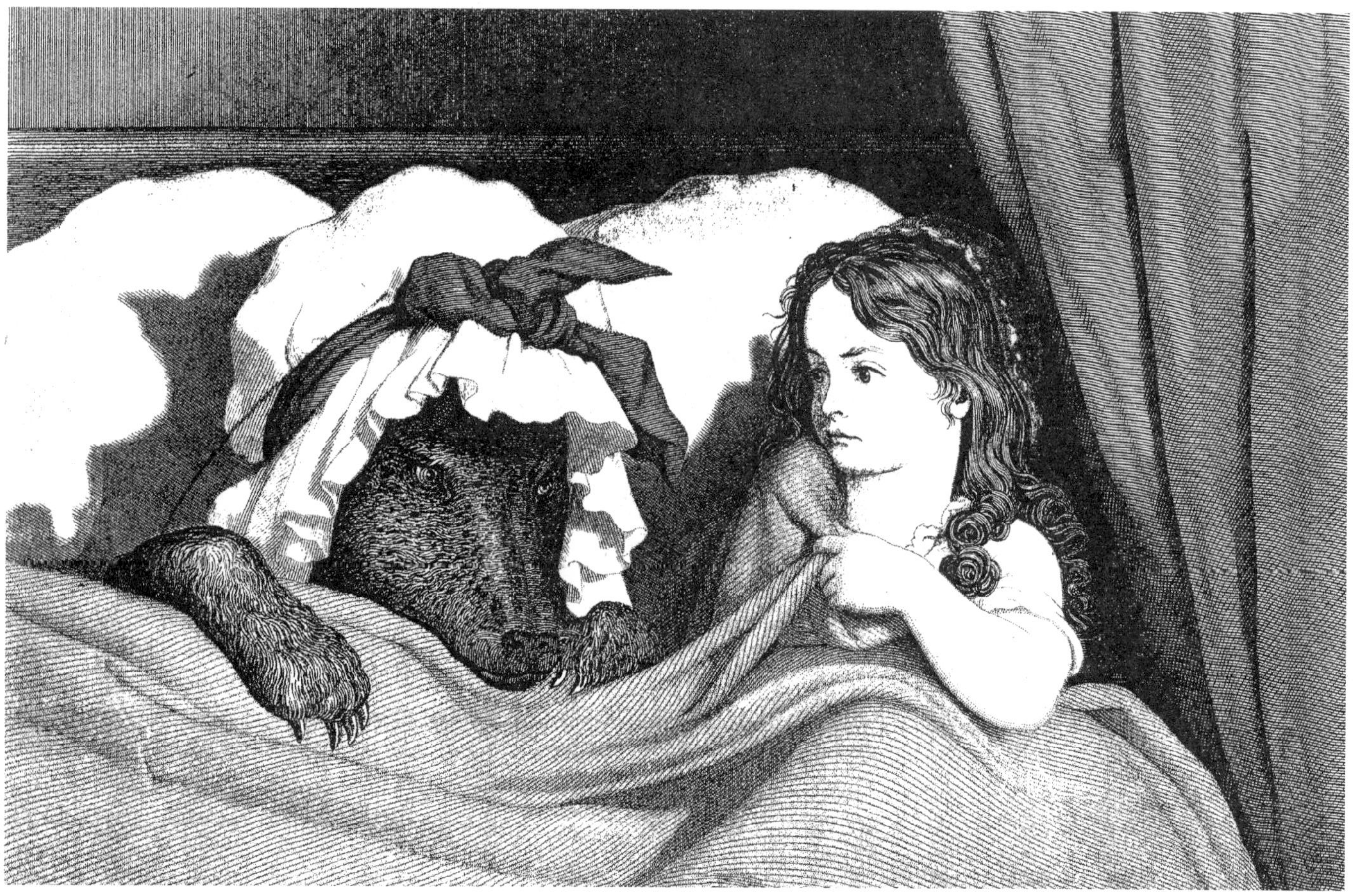

promotional material for the exhibition was *Puss in Boots* (*see* page 84). It has now become truly world-famous after it was borrowed for the *Shrek* movie series and the spin-off *Puss in Boots* films – hundreds of millions of people have been introduced to Doré's artwork without knowing his name. Many knowledgeable reviewers did acknowledge him as the artistic source, but few filmgoers were informed. There had been many Doreana 'Puss in Boots' long before the *Shrek* films: Doré changed the legendary feline creature, giving it a swashbuckling personality. He gave the Perrault characters much more character than earlier illustrators had done, which is why his drawings have become such iconic images.

Baron Munchausen

In the early 1860s, the latest Doré folios in new literary themes were appearing about every six months: next up was the light-hearted fantasy *The Adventures of Baron Munchausen* (*see* right). More modest in size than the works of Dante and Perrault (a quarto rather than a folio), it still contained several now-iconic scenes, reprinted all over the world in books and major films; the frontispiece, for example, depicted a bust of the colourful Baron (*see* page 88), which was made into an actual sculpture after the 1984 movie. Two of Doré's most famous scenes are the Baron riding his horse under the ocean, amid very large curious fish (*see* page 89), and a ship leaving the surface of the sea and sailing right on up to the Moon (*see* page 90), which was made into a beautiful green-and-yellow black-light poster. Perhaps the most curious Munchausen Doreana was a 1943 Nazi film made at great expense to entertain the German people in a desperate attempt to distract them from the inevitable approaching collapse of their country.

French Classics

Doré also illustrated dozens of titles by French authors – many with smaller engravings, but two with larger ones – which would be little known today without his imagery, including three stories by Ernest L'Epine (1826–93), such as *La Légende de Croque-mitaine* (20-B,157-b, where 'b' indicates a smaller vignette black-and-white

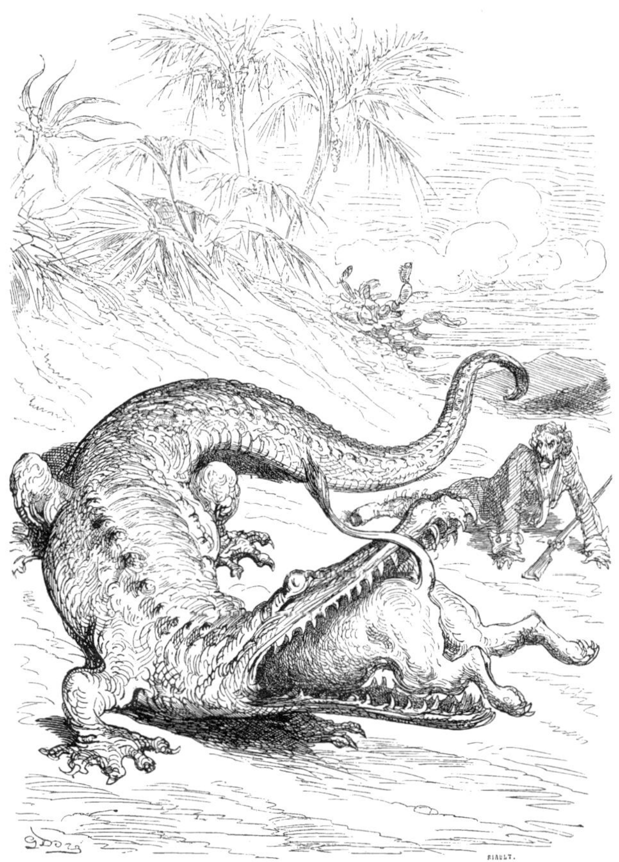

plate): an adventure story set in the time of Charlemagne (*c.* 742–814). The frontispiece, reprinted gilded on the front cover, was *Mitaine and Oghris* (*see* page 62); this historically significant image is considered one of the earliest precursors of the popular twentieth-century genre of the warrior woman, made popular by Frank Frazetta (1928–2010) and others. It shows an armour-clad girl (Mitaine) with her huge pet lion (Oghris); this book also contains many monsters and other creatures, including a crocodile bridge. *Spare Room at the Inn* (*see* page 63) depicts a hilarious scene, in which a knight peeks into the only available room: a tiny space with dozens of the largest spiders ever seen, several of them as big as cats – his expression is priceless.

A French classic that is little known today is *Atala* (30-B, 14-b) by François-René de Chateaubriand (1768–1848), who fled to the US after the 1789 French Revolution. There, he wrote an early 'noble

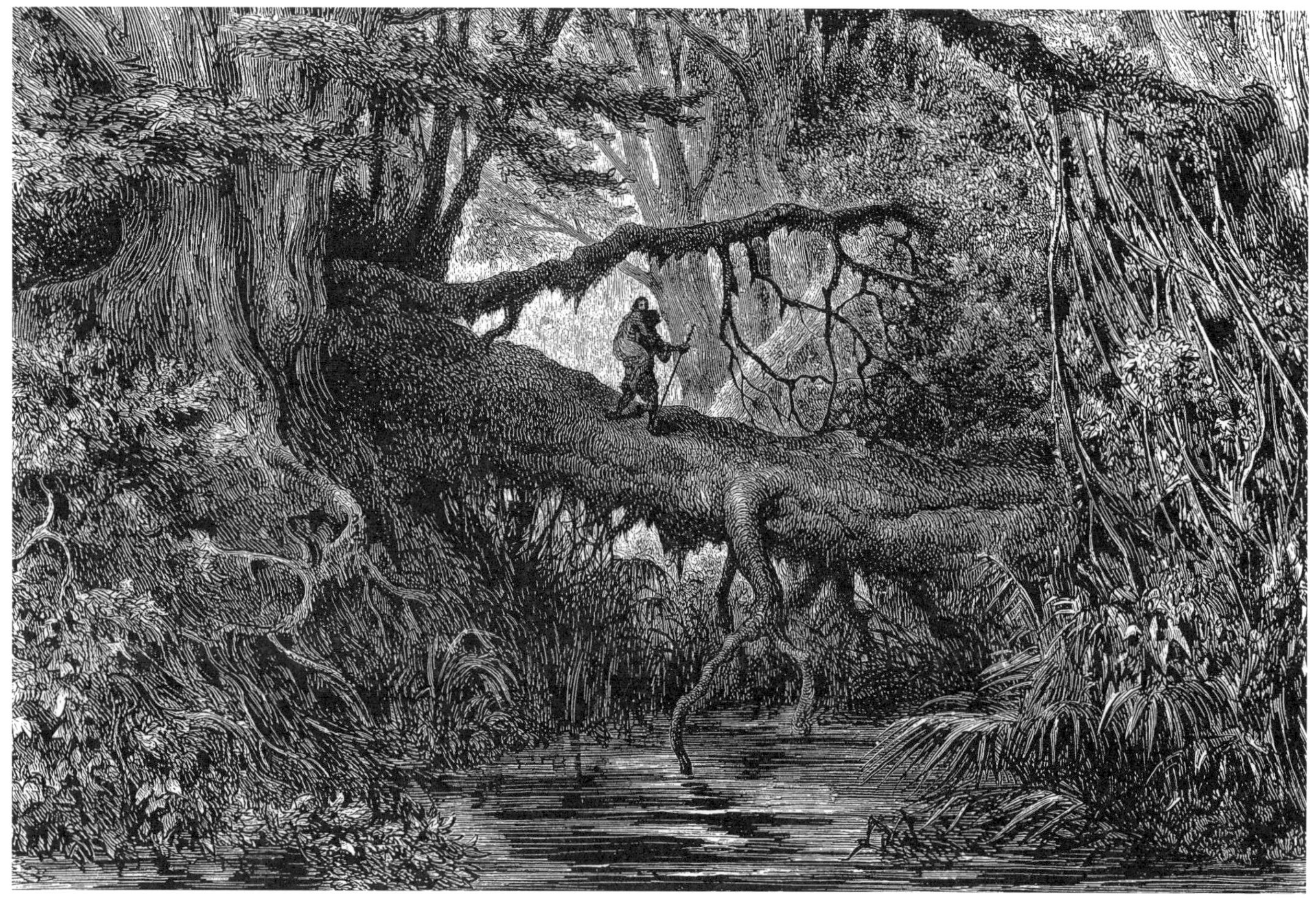

red man' story, predating James Fenimore Cooper (1789–1851). It is a romance about two Native Americans fleeing a warring tribe and perhaps Doré's greatest depiction of nature in a pure setting, including *Niagara Falls* (*see* page 67). It shows his mastery of images that are entirely white-on-black, like the campfire at *The Lean-to* (*see* page 66), and contains many beautiful scenes, one of which – although little regarded at the time – was to become world-famous in the twentieth century…

The Log Bridge

In 1863, no one could have imaged that a Doré scene from *Atala* (*see* above and page 65) could become a three-dimensional item in over a dozen major Hollywood movies. Although you might recognize it from the 1937 film *Snow White*, it became renowned from the epic 1933 *King Kong*. A boy named Ray Harryhausen (1920–2013) went to see the film and it changed his life: he was so enthralled that he arranged to see the director, Merian Cooper (1893–1973), and when he walked in, he noticed that the walls were covered with Doré engravings. Cooper had told his artists to create jungle scenes resembling the illustrations for Doré's Dante, Milton and Chateaubriand. Harryhausen went on to become a pioneer special-effects guru, who has expressed his love for Doré and told of the many ways in which he borrowed Doré's art in his own films. Recent directors have said, 'We all stand on his shoulders,' and later reference works about *King Kong* stress the high regard they had for Doré's imagery.

Don Quixote

By the end of 1863, Doré's folios were getting larger in size and
number of engravings, as well as more expensive: the two-volume
folio of *Don Quixote* (120-B, 257-b) by Miguel de Cervantes (1547–
1616) was selling for 160 francs. At the same time, he was doing
over 300 serialized travel engravings of Spain, which we will examine
later when we discuss the 1874 book edition. With *Don Quixote*,
reviewers were once again mesmerized by the scope of Doré's
creative genius. It was also the pivotal title that motivated major
British publishers to start issuing his folios in book editions and then-
popular parts issues. The earlier ones had been noticed approvingly
in London, but mainly as just a French phenomenon; however, less
than a year after the French folio, a major British publisher (Cassell,
Petter & Galpin) began a 30-month parts issue of *Don Quixote*,
and by the time that was complete, the world of art had changed
forever. Two Quixote engravings became famous immediately, while
another only more recently: the frontispiece – *Don Quixote in His
Study* (*see* page 91) – shows dozens of creatures coming to life
in the protagonist's imagination and has been reprinted, redrawn
and painted many times, including on the front cover of theatre
programmes in the 1960s and 1970s for *Man of La Mancha*, by
Dale Wasserman (1914–2008); the other renowned print was *Don
Quixote Tilting at Windmill* (*see* page 92), which was also reprinted in
many ways; and one of the most recent to become famous is *Knight
Approaching Lake* (*see* page 94), whose many gruesome monsters
can be seen in films. See also the vignette of the flying horse from
folklore that features in *Don Quixote*, 'El Clavileno', shown above.

Le Salon des Refusés

The period from early 1864 to late 1865 appeared to be a quiet
one for Doré, but the stage was being set for a titanic struggle for
control of the art world. It had begun with the 1863 Paris Salon,
when the jury infuriated a large number artists by rejecting most of
what had been submitted for the exhibition. A major organization of
hundreds of French artists (famous and infamous) organized a revolt
against the establishment and selected two amongst their members

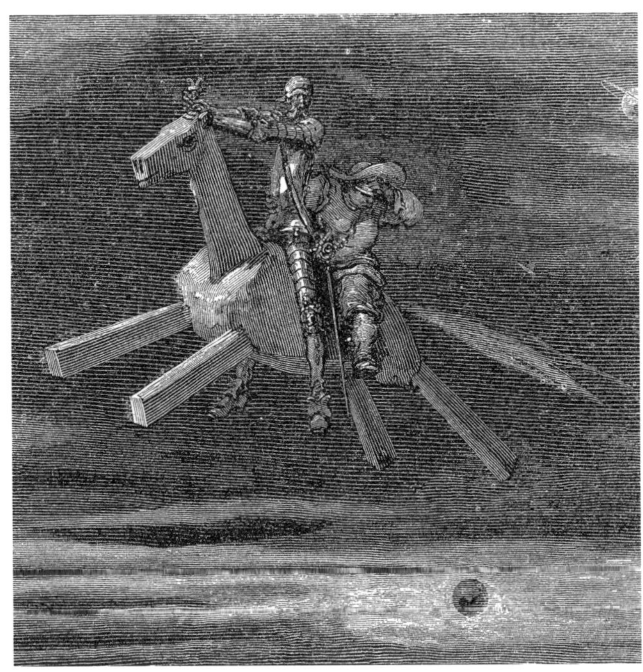

to present a petition directly to Napoleon III to appeal for leniency.
That petition led to the establishment of Le Salon des Refusés and
the birth of Impressionism, and those two artists were Gustave Doré
and Édouard Manet (1832–83), who were born a few days apart
and would die a few days apart. They represented opposite ends
of the spectrum: all of Manet's paintings were being rejected and
denounced at the time, whereas almost all of Doré's pieces were
accepted and praised by reviewers. However, he was annoyed that
he was not getting higher awards, so in 1863 they banded together in
a revolt against the establishment, which would lead to the death of
the Salon in the 1880s. Although some people now assert that Doré
was an Impressionist, he was his own school – a sort of precursor of
Impressionism.

The Bible: The Still Before the Storm

Word was getting around that something major was about to happen
and, in early 1862, the largest religious publisher in the world – Alfred
Mame (1811–93) of Tours – contracted with Doré to illustrate the
Bible (a chromolithograph re-engraving of the *Deluge* is shown above,

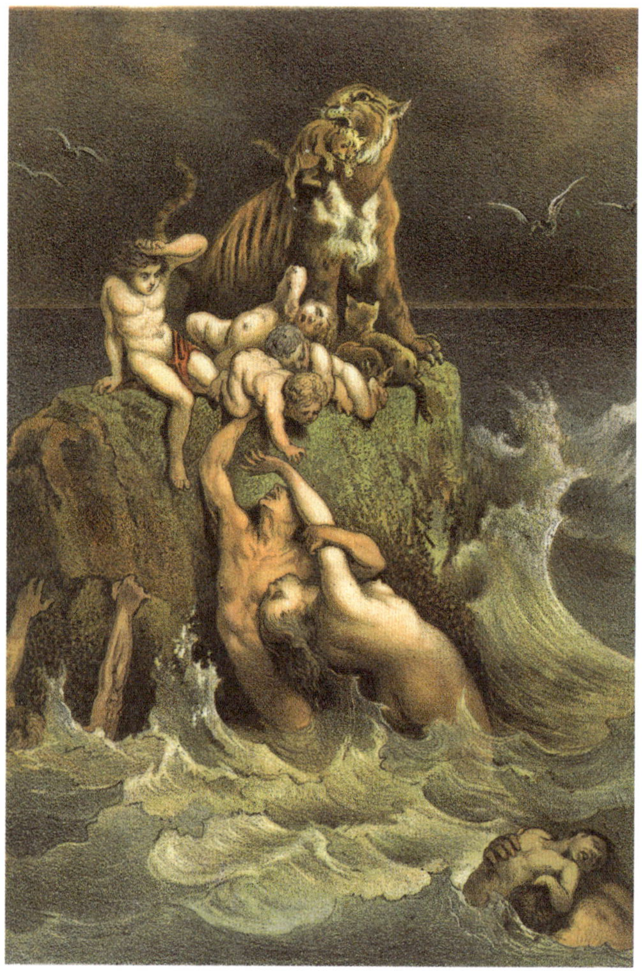

and *Death on a Pale Horse*, opposite). Many of those drawings were seen by reviewers in exhibitions and in Doré's studio, and two of the wood blocks were even exhibited at the 1863 British Royal Academy by the engraver William James Linton (1812–97). Also, another of Doré's paintings – *Tobias and the Angel*, exhibited in the 1865 Salon – was purchased by the French government so, on the surface, everything seemed normal and very positive. However, things were about to change for him in several ways: reviewers had begun to praise Doré to such a degree that, as we shall see later, it was to alienate some very powerful people, producing a backlash right at the time of his greatest triumphs. A good example of this praise is British art critic Philip Gilbert Hamerton (1834–94), writing in the October 1863 *Fine Arts Quarterly Review*:

'Doré is a great and marvelous genius, a poet such as a nation produces once in a thousand years. He is the most imaginative, profoundest, and productive poet that has ever sprung from the French race.'

A year later, Hamerton increased his praise of Doré in nearly a hundred pages in the same journal (October 1864), saying:

'Doré passes the utmost limits I had supposed possible … his ideas are numberless and brilliant … an intellectual revelation … Doré's Bible will be a monument, the culminating work of his life…'

1 December 1865

The day the Doré Bible was published was very similar to the day The Beatles landed in New York and took the world by storm. On 1 December 1865 that very expensive illustrated Bible (228-B) went on sale – in a two-volume (2V) folio – for 200 francs, and 10 days later every copy had been sold; *The New York Times* counted the number of days it took to reach the US 'by late steamer' (17, in case anyone is interested). Among the first people to examine the copies were the engravers of the American Bank Note Company, who marvelled at the effects that Doré created on wood blocks, with the detail of expensive steel engravings (all of Doré's engravings in this book are wood engravings unless otherwise stated).

The 60-month British Doré Bible parts edition began with 30,000 subscribers just in the London area and the novelist Amelia Edwards (1831–92) said that you could find his folios 'in every English-speaking home where anyone can spell the word "art"'. Hundreds of French articles and thousands of English ones were written about it, and a dozen companies in the US claimed to be the 'US agent' for all of Doré's folios. To say that they were the most popular illustrations ever made would be an understatement: they were published in 25 countries in the nineteenth century – even the Pope kept a copy of it on a table in his office and perused it daily.

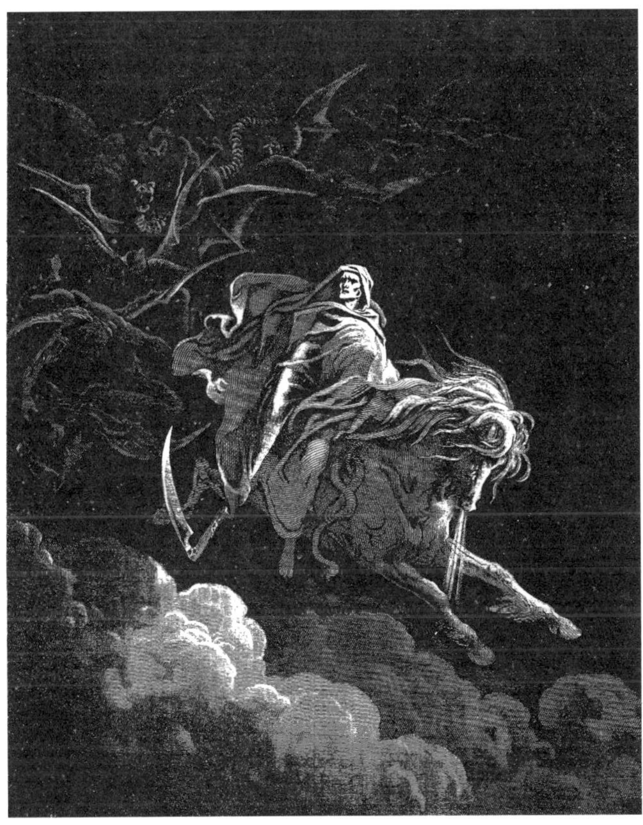

The Backlash

But then something bizarre happened. Right after Doré was described as the 'greatest artist in the world', he also became known as the 'worst artist in the world'. This sudden change took on different forms in France and England, but the cause was basically the same: Doré had become a threat to the art establishment. To the French Salon jury, it was unthinkable for an untrained artist to become the most famous in the world and, although early on they had seen him as just a curious oddity, the situation had turned serious. After Doré's 1861 burst of Dante fame, an article appeared in the Russian periodical *Osnova*, praising him and Eugène Delacroix (1798–1863) as two great cutting-edge artists free to express artistic imagination, while Russian artists were chained down by their own intransigent art establishment. However, that statement was only partly correct: when Doré was 29, in 1861, the average Salon judge was 68, and they were clinging

to traditions. After he became so famous, those crotchety old jurors determined they were not going to let him dominate the fine arts the way he had dominated the field of illustration. So the story was widely circulated that 'Doré was rejected by the French art establishment', but there was only a sliver of truth to that, as he was greatly respected by most French artists, writers, composers and art critics, who agreed that he had been mistreated by the jurors.

John Ruskin

In England, the issue was that the Frenchman Doré was getting all the glory, as in the late 1860s he became much more popular there than any British illustrator. The Brothers Dalziel, for example, waited 17 years to publish *The Dalziel Bible Gallery* because the Doré version dominated religious art. In 1868, the Doré Gallery was opened in London to showcase and sell his art, particularly large religious paintings, and remained open for 24 years before touring the US to record audiences. Doré then angered elitists further by illustrating the Poet Laureate Alfred Tennyson (1809–92), who had read those articles by Hamerton and insisted on getting Doré to illustrate *The Idylls of the King*. All this was too much for men like John Ruskin (1819–1900) and Frederic George Stephens (1827–1907), art editor for the *Athenaeum*: their response to the over-praising of Doré was to over-villainize him. Although in 1861 Stephens had mildly praised Doré's *Inferno* engravings, after the artist became too famous, he 're-examined' them with the 'revolt of our senses against egregious error … we protest the outrageous laudation of Doré … "raised book illustration to a higher art" … sheer nonsense'. They blamed the British public for Doré's popularity, and John Ruskin said that people would be better off going to see the Devil than the artist's paintings. In France and England, Doré's fame had become a serious threat to the influence of the art establishment.

Bible Influences

In fine arts, you only need to appeal to a small group of wealthy and influential people, whereas in illustration, you try to appeal to a large portion of the public. Hamerton later wrote that Doré's popularity was

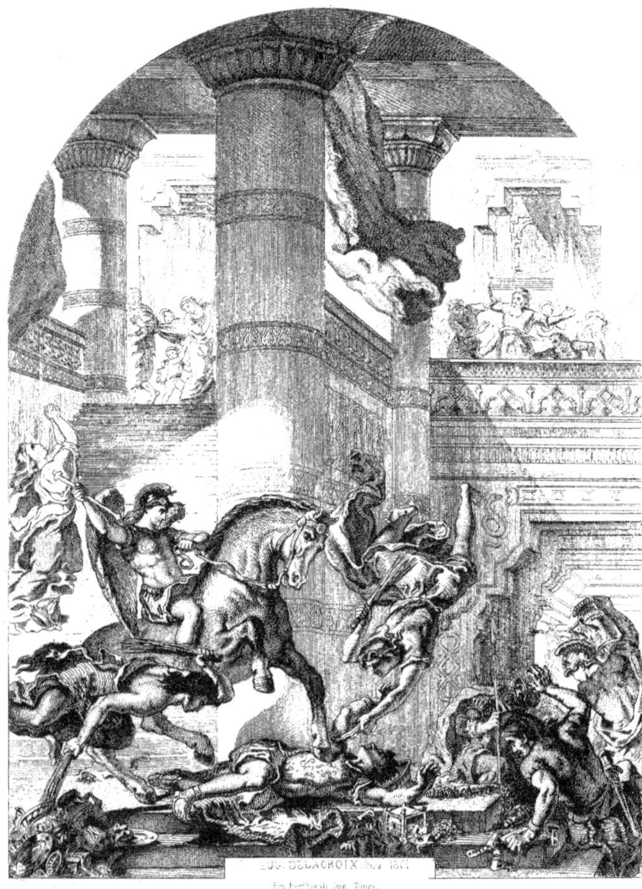

enough in itself to make him rejected by many art elitists, who saw the general public as unsophisticated peasants. But the 'peasants' who loved the Doré Bible were scattered across dozens of countries and included the Emperor of France, the Queen of England, the Pope, Mark Twain (1835–1910) and Leo Tolstoy (1828–1910). Doré's Bible was praised for its originality but, having produced nearly 400 engravings, drawings and paintings of biblical scenes, some did show definite similarities to previous artists' work. By far the biggest influence was Delacroix, and two good examples are his 1861 murals *Jacob Wrestling with the Angel* and *The Expulsion of Heliodorus from the Temple* (1865 etching of the painting shown above). But Doré borrowed from several contemporary French painters and also from the Old Masters – in particular Peter Paul Rubens (1577–1640), such

as *Samson Fighting the Lion*. However, only a tiny percentage of all of Doré's Bible scenes reflect borrowing, and it could be argued that he improved on some earlier art.

Illustration Before Doré and Influences

For centuries, illustration had been dominated by Dutch copperplate prints, but the early 1800s witnessed the advent of British steel engravings in two memorable multi-volume folio sets: the *Boydell Shakespeare* and the *Macklin Bible*. Thomas Bewick (1753–1828) also reintroduced wood engravings with *British Birds* and *Aesop's Fables*. There was also of course the work of British artist William Blake (1757–1827), who created illustrations for Dante's *Divine Comedy* over three decades before Doré – although Doré's images look very different from those of Blake, Blake was a forerunner in the use of mystical themes, which Doré was to portray so well. There are also similarities to Doré in the dramatic imagery of Henry Fuseli's (1741–1825) *Milton Gallery*. But a British artist most often noted in comparison with Doré was John Martin (1789–1854) and his famous large panoramic engravings of the Bible and Milton, which are evident when comparing the similarities in the two artists' portrayal of Elijah's chariot to Heaven (*see* page 46). The major development in Doré's engravings was the improvement in the lower-cost wood engravings, which achieved the same quality as the higher-cost steel ones.

Bible Doreana

The Doré Bible was quickly borrowed in new media. The US was not part of any international copyright law until 1891, so publishers there went wild when borrowing his work. Over 700 US publishers issued thousands of editions in the late nineteenth century, including the ubiquitous quarto family Bible, sold by subscription. After complaints from ministers that circuses were not good family entertainment, the Van Amburgh Circus Company painted Doré Bible art on to all their wagons and cages. Alas, none of those survived – not even photos of them – so all we have are just the newspaper articles written about them. Biblical Doreana took on many forms: hundreds of US steel engravings, hundreds of Dutch chromolithographs and, in 1867, all

Doré Bible engravings were made into hand-painted Magic Lantern glass slides. Missionaries like David Livingstone (1813–73) used them in the jungle: they draped a large sheet over a low-hanging branch in a clearing and used an actual fire – an oil lamp – inside their metal Magic Lantern projector to show an image 7.6 cm (3 in) in diameter on to it. Villages emptied out to see such 'magic'. The scope of recent Bible Doreana is too vast to include here: hundreds of music album covers, movie scenes – Harryhausen changed *Samson Destroying Temple* (*see* page 45) into a creature from outer space destroying the Parthenon – posters, postcards, tattoos on celebrities like David Beckham (b. 1975), T-shirts (such as Led Zeppelin's *Stairway to Heaven*), decorative plates, jigsaw puzzles, colouring books, comic books (the cover of Marvel's *Deadpool* No. 22, based on a recent film), and endless covers of books and periodicals – even *American Atheist*.

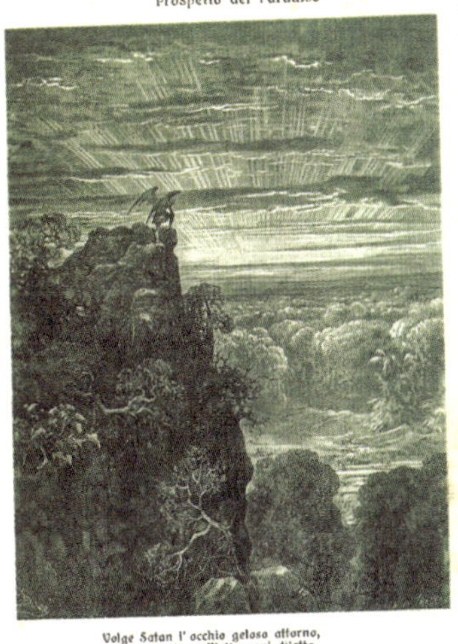

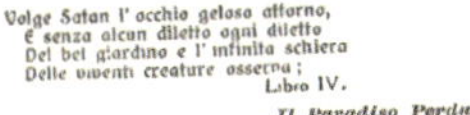

Falling to Earth (showing Delacroix's influence; *see* page 53) and *Satan Overlooking Paradise* (*see* page 54, and the 1900 blue-tint Italian postcards shown here) – a major influence on the jungle scenes in *King Kong*. Amazingly, Milton Doreana began even before the folio was published, as British metalwork firm Elkington commissioned artist Leonard Morel-Ladeuil (1820–88) to make a 61 x 81.3 cm (24 x 32 in) *Milton Shield*, with scenes similar to those created by Doré. A 20.3 cm (8 in) centre circle of Adam and Eve with an angel, in particular, is a mirror image of Doré's engraving, because Morel-Ladeuil saw the artist's drawing before it was engraved – and prints are mirror images of wood blocks. The *Milton Shield* won a Gold Medal for metalwork at the 1867 Paris Exposition Universelle and was then purchased by the British Museum, who reproduced it using electroplating, both as the full shield and the centre panel by itself. One of the electroplated reprints is in the US White House.

Milton: *Paradise Lost*

Before the Bible, all of Doré's folios had French publishers, whereas after it, half of them had foreign publishers. The first foreign commission was by Cassell for Milton's *Paradise Lost* (50-B): half of the engravings featured angelic conflict and many of the rest, featuring the Garden of Eden, were later combined with his Bible scenes. Doré's Milton was published in a dozen countries, including Russia, but curiously not in France. Among the many iconic images of angelic conflict – which are now featured on many music album covers, posters, tattoos and more – two of the most famous are *Satan*

Tennyson: *Idylls of the King*

Cassell published a dozen Doré folios from 1865 to 1868. The only real British competitor was the publisher Moxon, who printed four individual Tennyson tales: *Elaine, Vivien, Guinevere* and *Enid*, which were then combined (37-B) – shown overleaf is an 1867 photogravure of the original art for *Lancelot and Guinevere in the meadow*. They were Doré's first steel engravings (by British engravers). But Moxon's manager, J. Bertrand Payne (1833–98), really went overboard and, besides the steel engraving editions, they also offered large-page India-paper proofs and sepia photos of the original drawings,

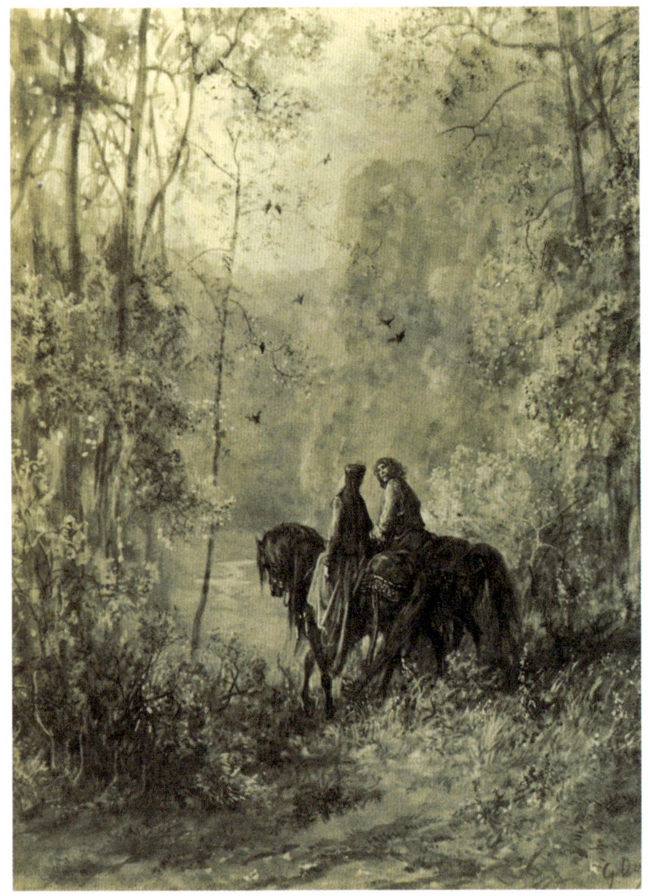

La Fontaine: *Fables*

Jean de La Fontaine (1621–95) wrote the French version of the *Fables* by Aesop (620–564 BC), and the Doré folio engravings (84-B, 248-b) show a delightful serenity. Even though they are not as dramatic as his Dante and Bible, they served to increase the range of his artistic output. The full scope of these 332 scenes clearly shows Doré's love of animals, and some of the more famous ones are *Wolf Turned Shepherd* (*see* page 98) and *Council of Rats* (*see* page 97). The latter shows several close-up depictions of the rodents, which might remind you of the 1970s movies *Willard* and *Ben*. Doré's *Fables* engravings were still very popular and, in the 1890s, 30 of the scenes were made into chromolithographic trade cards by the Kolarsine medicinal company (shown below). These were widely published and became some of the smallest Doreana ever made. There were many brass and silver high-relief buttons – some 1.3 cm (½ in) in diameter – but by far the tiniest one was the early experimental micro-dot glass slide made by Pumphrey Brothers of Birmingham, *c.* 1870.

plus an elephant (extra-large) folio of *Elaine* with three-colour chromolithographs. Doré did dozens of scenes of mystical medieval castles in several folios, but by far the most memorable one was *Elaine's Body on a Barge* (*see* page 68). Here, we should point out a major mistake: at the point where her body reaches Camelot and they are reading her letter, Doré forgot she had died and depicted her seated in a chair, as though she had fainted (*Elaine's Body on a Chair*; *see* page 69). It is one instance where his rate of production finally caught up with him, but the editor should have caught that. In a private letter, Tennyson commented on the images and asserted, 'One I hated.' But after the project was completed, Tennyson visited Doré in Paris and had a very cordial time. Needless to say, the Doré Tennyson folios were very popular, and they were reprinted in France by Hachette.

CASSELL'S ILLUSTRATED CATALOGUE.

"There both, I thought, the eagle and myself,
Did burn."

THE DORÉ DANTE.

Dante's Purgatory and Paradise. Illustrated by GUSTAVE DORÉ. The English Translation by the Rev. H. F. CARY, M.A. Crown Folio, bound in cloth, $20.00; morocco gilt, $35.00; elegantly bound in full morocco, $60.00.

"On the whole, however, the illustrations to the 'Purgatorio' are the most satisfactory, because they deal with more definite subjects, and exhibit a greater variety. The gloomier scenes recall the designs in the first of these volumes, where the 'Inferno' was treated, but towards the latter end the scenes grow brighter with the coming glories of the 'Paradiso,' and the last one, in which we see Dante drinking of the sacred stream which bounds the region of Purgatory, is a most exquisite landscape, grave with solemn beauty, and peopled with stately and gracious shapes. It would be impossible for us to go *seriatim* through all these beautiful illustrations. Suffice it to say that they are worthy to accompany the immortal cantos of Dante, and that the volume is produced with a solid handsomeness as regards printing, paper, and binding, which does the highest credit to the enterprise of Messrs. Cassell Petter & Galpin."—*Daily News.*

Cassell Petter & Galpin, London, Paris & New York.

Dante: *Purgatory* and *Paradise*

In 1868, Doré finally got around to finishing Dante's *Divine Comedy*, with *Purgatory* and *Paradise* (GO-B). It did not take long for the two parts to be joined and this new edition produced some of Doré's most iconic images. They are so mystical that many people believe Doré existed in a different dimension which transcended time and space (*Glorified Souls* in the *Paradiso, see* page 39, looks remarkably like a flying saucer) Two of the most famous images are *The Eagle* (*see* page 36) and *The Empyrean* (*see* page 40), also known as *The Celestial Rose*. The former has been reprinted in many ways, as shown in the album by Led Zeppelin's Jimmy Page (b. 1944). Charles Dickens (1812–70) wrote that while most illustrators showed people standing in a room talking, Doré was showing him things he had never seen before, like the depths of outer space. In 1868, reviewers could not grasp *The Empyrean*, whereas now people are colourizing it, using dozens of monochrome tint and multi-colour variations. How many science-fiction movies have space scenes with a ball of light opening in the distance? Dante and Beatrice see Heaven open like that, followed by rings of light that turn into rings of angels – Doré was so far ahead of his time.

There is a great revival of interest in Dante in popular culture, and Doré's iconic images are at the centre of it: the French artist Moebius (Jean Giraud, 1938–2012) made all of Doré's *Paradiso* prints into watercolour paintings (published by Nuages in 1999). The 'Dante Xperience', which toured Europe and is very popular in Russia, combines Dante's text with the *Dante Symphony* by Franz Liszt (1811–86) and, while that is being performed, a 6 x 9 m (20 x 30 ft) screen behind is showing all 136 colourized images of Doré Dante. In the 1860s, Franz Liszt and Camille Saint-Saëns (1835–1921) performed that symphony on two pianos in Doré's home. In the US, Sandow Birk (b. 1962) has readapted Doré Dante in drawings and paintings for books and films set in urban America.

The Franco-Prussian War

By 1870, Doré's folios were world-famous; his gallery in London was very popular and buyers of his paintings included Queen Victoria (1819–

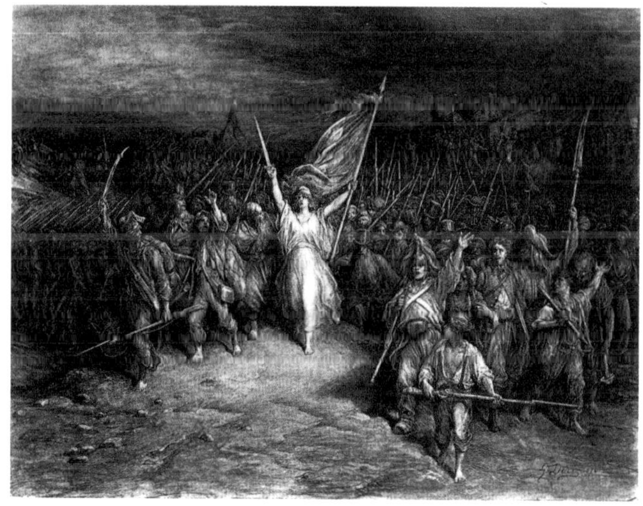

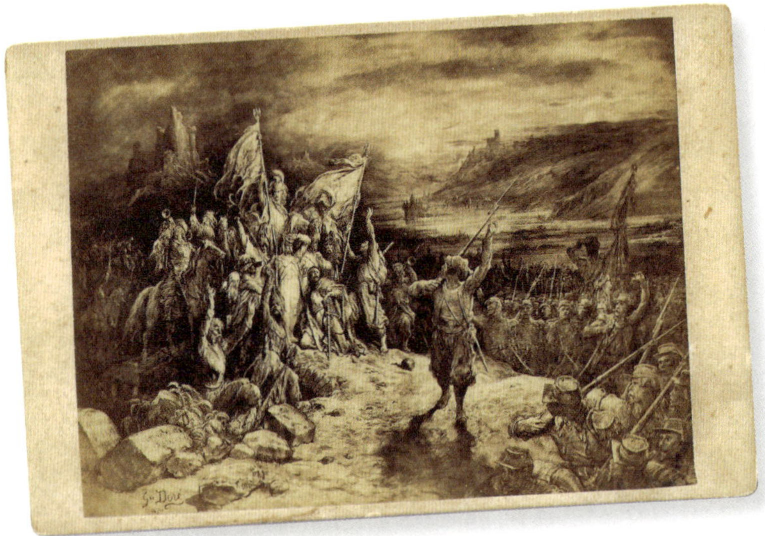

1901), but troubles in Spain led to disaster in France, when they declared war on Germany. Fifteen years earlier, Doré did many engravings of war and peace, which consisted of celebrations in Paris, and in 1870, he did new drawings and paintings. The most famous was *La Marseillaise* (*see* page 19), showing a ragged group of soldiers led by an allegorical female with a sword and a flag. It was reprinted many times in books and postcards all over Europe until the First World War, after which conflict lost its lustre. In 1870, that lustre lasted only a few weeks: after those rumours from Alsace were confirmed, Dante's *Inferno* was brought to Paris, first by the Germans and then by the Commune – a war won far away is very different from a conflict lost right at home. Two paintings reflected the before and after of the war: *To the Rhine* (an 1870s sepia cabinet card version is shown here) shows French troops marching off to a certain, glorious victory, with the souls of past French war heroes rising up out of the ground to cheer them on. *The Enigma*, on the other hand, shows death and destruction all around – Doré saw it first hand and showed it up close and personal.

London, a Pilgrimage

The war ended in January 1871, life gradually returned to normal, and Doré finished up a completely new artistic endeavour: social commentary. In his least popular folio – published in England, in 1872, *London, a Pilgrimage* (*Under London Bridge,* shown opposite)

– he showed too much: although it was acceptable to display the glories of the city, the wealthy did not want to be reminded of the squalor of the East End, where children were dying, like in *Found in the Street* (*see* page 110). Doré even showed the zoo from the monkeys' perspective, complete with spectators gawking at them. This folio was not really appreciated until much later, when films of Dickens' works – such as the 2005 *Oliver Twist* by Roman Polanski (b. 1933) – used it for background imagery.

There are two specific examples of London engravings that only became famous because of later developments. In 1890, Vincent van Gogh (1853–90) painted *Prisoners Exercising (after Doré)*, which featured on the cover of *Art News* when in April 1958, they published a major article on 'Art under Communism'. When he painted it, van Gogh was virtually unknown, whereas Doré was world-famous, and he was decent enough to list the latter's name right in the title. Like *The Log Bridge* (*see* page 65) from *Atala*, this scene was used in many major films, such as the 1971 *A Clockwork Orange*. Doré concluded the 1872 folio with *The New Zealander* (*see* page 111), another visionary image, imagining the destruction of London, 'with the tourist New Zealander upon the broken parapets, contemplating something matching [Poe's] "The glory that was Greece, / The grandeur that was Rome"'. That engraving has been reprinted on many book covers; no one back then could have imagined that, 70 years later, it would look eerily similar to the bombing of London.

Rabelais (New and Improved Version)

Doré actually illustrated very few French classics in his series of folios. In 1854, he made 105 small engravings for a thin octavo edition of Rabelais but, thinking that perhaps he had not really done it justice, in 1873, he did 719 engravings for a huge two-volume folio of Rabelais's *Gargantua and Pantagruel*. Unfortunately, the octavo version had just been published in England, so it was over a century before the folio illustrations were published in an English edition. A sweeping saga of humour, knighthood, adventure and fantasy, that brilliant satire had

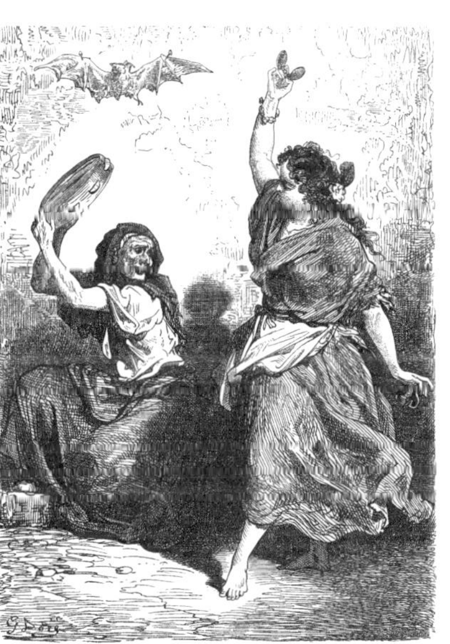

originally poked fun at the king so cleverly that he never realized it. There are so many great scenes to choose from, such as *Pantagruel with 4,600 Cows* (*see* page 74) and *Pantagruel and the Sea Monster* (*see* page 75) – but the most significant engraving must be *The Divine Bottle* (*see* page 76) at the end of volume two. That was the earliest depiction of what would become Doré's most famous work of sculpture *The Doré Vase* (*see* page 121).

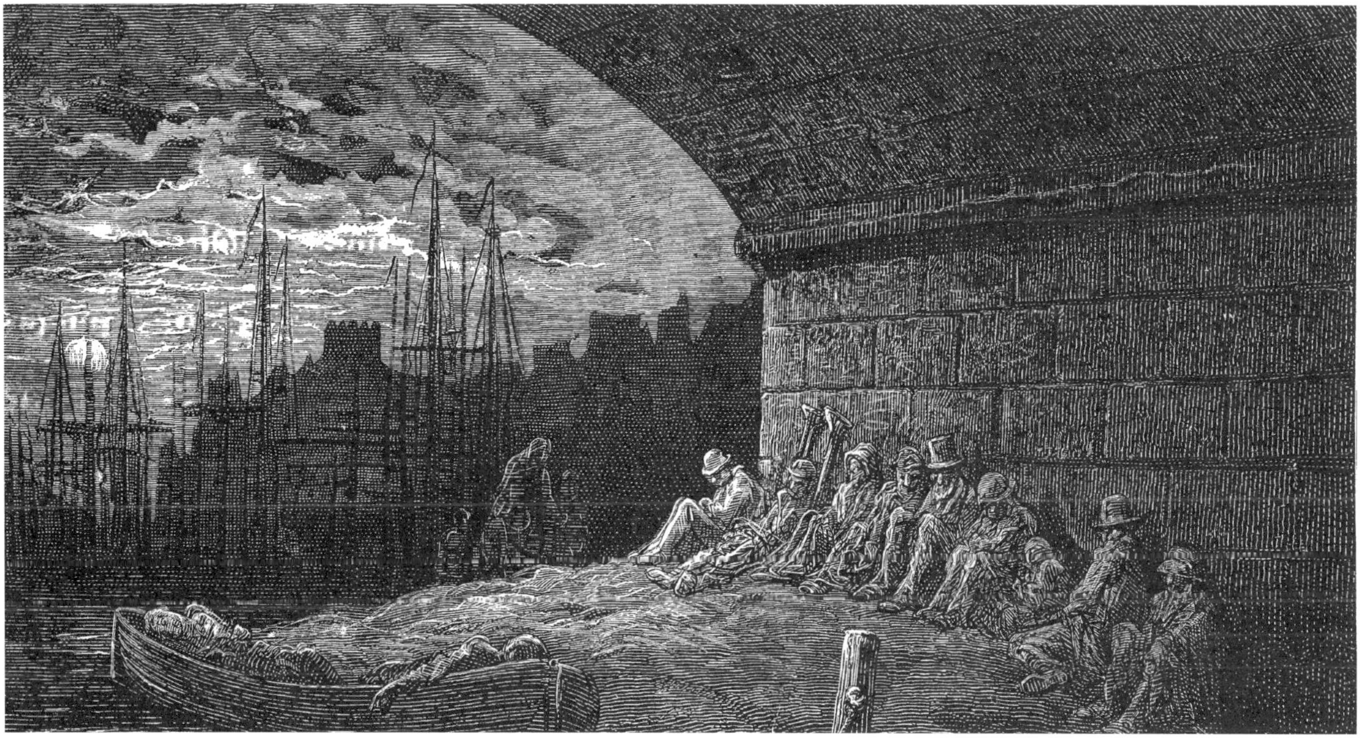

Spain

From 1861 to 1873, Doré serialized his travels in Spain with Baron Charles Davillier (1823–83) in *Tour du Monde*. Though there is no narrative, it depicts the Spanish people in such a colourful way that it seems to be full of stories. These were finally collected and published in the 1874 folio *Spain* (164-B, 160-b). Added to the work he did for *Don Quixote*, Doré did over 700 engravings related to Spain and he seemed particularly fascinated with gypsies. All of this was a major influence on the 1875 opera *Carmen* by Georges Bizet (1838–75), who died thinking it a failure and before all the critics who condemned it began to praise it. One of the main *Carmen* posters showed a gypsy dancing girl holding a tambourine overhead, in the same position as Doré's *Gypsy Girl Dancing the Vito* (*see* page 113). This engraving can be found on twentieth-century programmes for *Carmen*, but the Doré folio depicts much more, such as very detailed Spanish architecture, as well as the lives of the people in the cities and the countryside – some of the dramatic images show a coach falling off the edge of a cliff (*see* page 112) and (unfortunately) bullfighting.

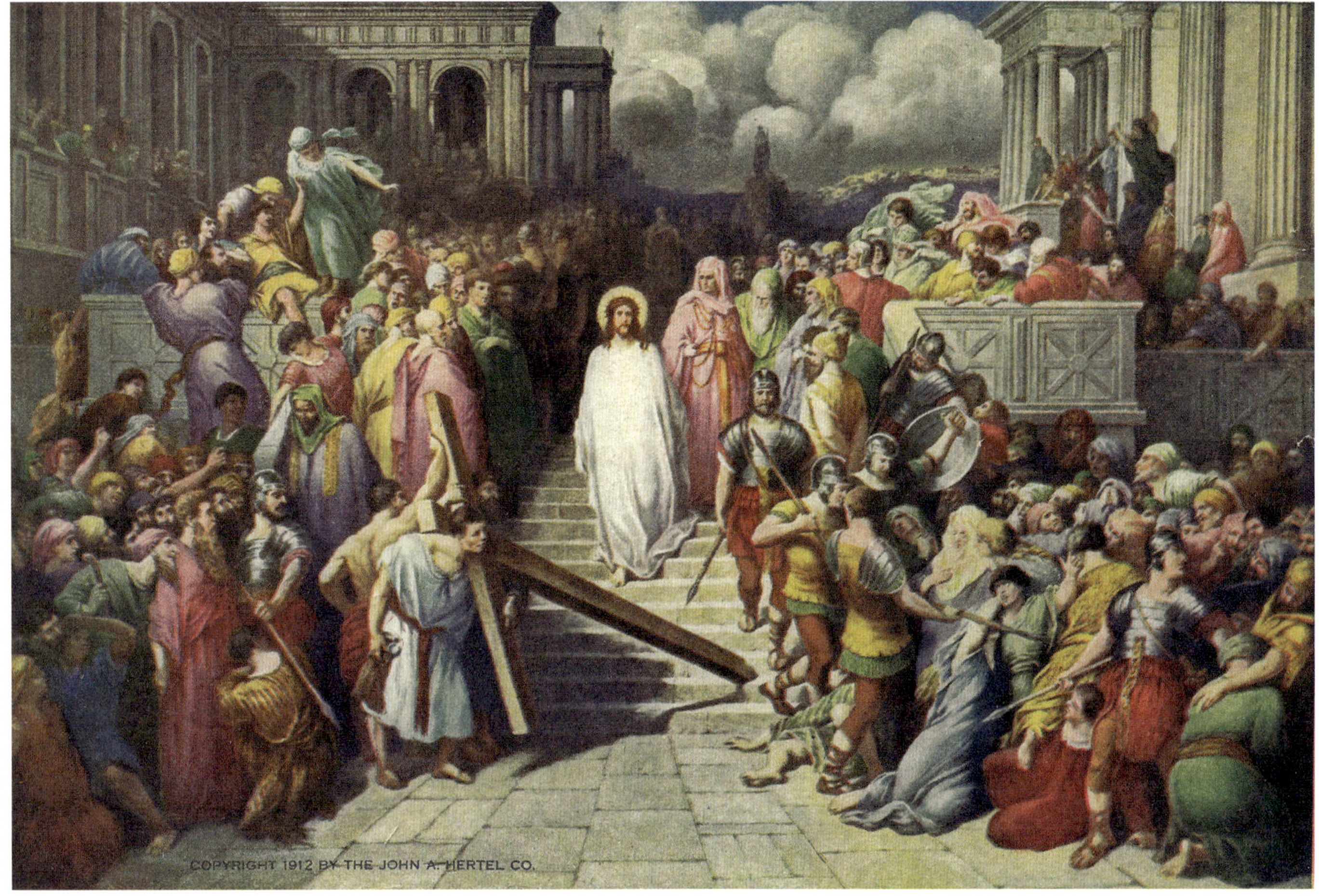

Religious Paintings

Although Doré was still producing major folios every couple of years, he was concentrating more and more on his paintings – over 500 of Doré's oil paintings, plus hundreds of watercolours and mixed media sketches, have now been catalogued. When he contracted for the Doré Gallery with James Liddle Fairless (*c.* 1829–91) and George Lord Beeforth (*c.* 1823–1904), his first large religious painting was *Triumph of Christianity over Paganism*, which depicted dozens of angels fighting pagan gods and was reminiscent of Rubens. Each year, Doré would send new works of art to London, where the ones that got most of the attention were large religious pieces, but also many landscapes and genre paintings. The major ones were on permanent display, but dozens of paintings were sold from the gallery. There were also several instances where wealthy patrons were so enamoured of those major paintings that they had Doré produce another version, usually a little smaller. Eventually, the two main works of art in the gallery were the paintings *Christ Leaving the Praetorium* (1872, a chromolithograph of the painting is shown above) and *Christ's Entry into Jerusalem* (1876) – both 6 x 9 m (20 x 30 ft) and showing hundreds of characters. The Doré Gallery also offered steel engravings of the major paintings – usually 56 x 81.3 cm (22 x 32 in) for larger ones – which took between three and five years to carve and were often more expensive than the folios. Catalogues came out almost annually, but they were not illustrated until 1896, when the Doré Gallery was touring the US and over a million people viewed it at the Art Institute of Chicago. So they added photos of the 25 steel engravings (some of those now very rare) to the new catalogue, with 10 x 15.2 cm (4 x 6 in) images. A major criticism of his religious paintings was that they were just enlarged illustrations, to which his many fans replied, 'So what?'

Rime of the Ancient Mariner

Doré saw the enormous profits that his publishers made from his folios – even without taking into account what was happening in America – and decided to become his own publisher, which turned out not to be a great idea. Before Doré came along, *The Rime of the Ancient Mariner* (1798) by Samuel Taylor Coleridge (1772–1834) had only been released in a handful of editions in its first 77 years,

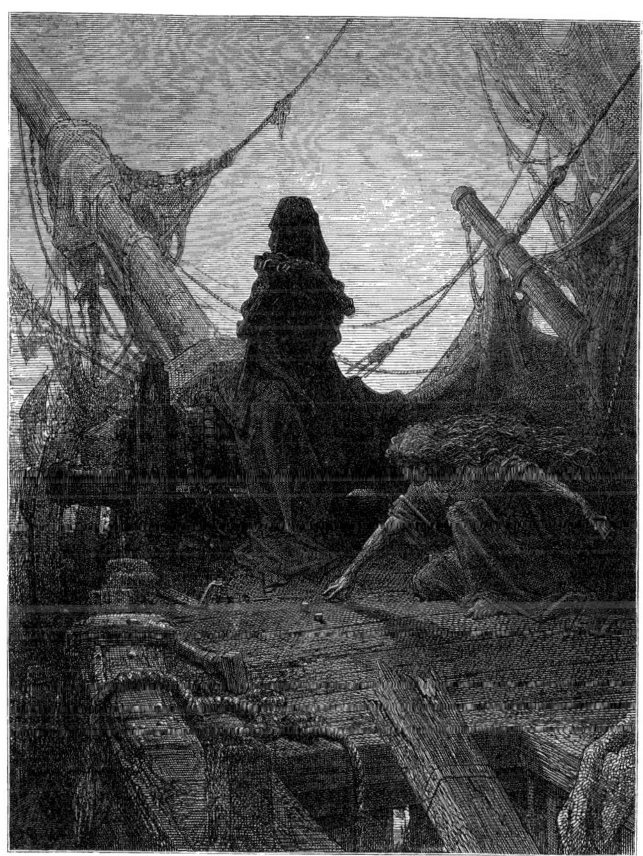

considered too bizarre a story, so it took the artist all his imaginative powers to bring it to life and help it along its way to its status as a literary classic. The official publisher was the Doré Gallery and he retained all rights, but he did not understand marketing and it sold poorly in England. He sold rights to other countries; in the US, Harper Brothers bought them and gave up unauthorized reprinting of Doré's engravings. They knew about publishing and marketing, and they issued a new large folio volume of the Mariner every year for a dozen years. There were also French, German, Italian and Russian folio editions. Doré had increased the image size from just under 20.3 x 25.4 cm (8 x 10 in) to 23 x 30.5 cm (9 x 12 in), so they were full images, which are now considered the ultimate seafaring adventure illustrations, borrowed for other titles such as *Moby Dick* and *Frankenstein*. Many of the scenes – such as *The Ice Ship* (*see* page 100), *Mariner on the Rigging* and *Death on the Ghost Ship* (*see* left and page 102) – are popular, and have been reprinted in black-light posters, on music album covers and in colourized films of the Mariner, one narrated by Orson Welles (1915–85). The engraving patterns are most fascinating in *Sailors Feeding Albatross* (*see* page 101).

The Crusades

Just when you thought Doré had covered every literary genre, he issued a straight historical folio: using the text of Joseph Michaud (1767–1839), *The Crusades* (100-B) was published in 1877 (*Astonishment of the Crusaders at the Wealth of the East,* shown overleaf). Of course, Doré could not resist adding many mystical elements to the historical images; he treated the Crusades much like his early Franco-Prussian War artwork before the conflict, as I think we can assume that no angels flew overhead as the Crusaders travelled to the Holy Land. Although these have become the definitive depictions of those events, by the time they came out, each new work was praised but barely noticed, since much more attention was focused on his paintings. There were many gruesome scenes in this work, with decapitated heads strewn about, and some of the most popular ones were *Richard the Lion-Heart and Saladin* (*see* page 115), *Louis IX's Fleet Led by Angels, Celestial Light* (*see* page 117) and the pitiful *The Children's Crusade* (*see* page 116). Doré included

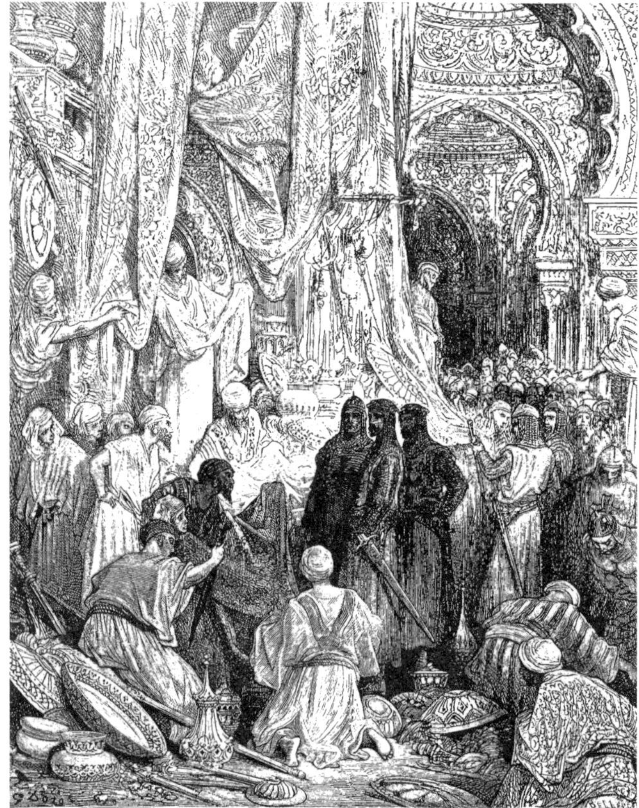

reprinted in the UK or the US, where such an obscure title was not considered to be commercially viable. Today, the work is most famous for all the connections to the blockbuster *Harry Potter* movie series, with its Hogwarts Castle, hippogriffs and countless other creatures. It even features Chewbacca – in Ariosto, he is a giant monster who eats men, but the face and the hair of the familiar Wookiee from *Star Wars* are unmistakable (vignette shown below). Only in recent years have people seen the full beauty of thousands of Doré's folio engravings on the internet and in the low-cost 20-volume archival series by Dover Press – and when examining the full scope of his output, it's overwhelming to think that just one person could produce all this.

many personal touches, such as the troubadours singing the glories of the Crusades, the anguish of waiting for news from the front and elderly veterans recalling their adventures. It was also very striking just how much detail he put into each engraving, with the assistance of his school of engravers.

Orlando Furioso

This was the last Doré folio published in France, and it was another sweeping saga of knightly adventure and fantasy. *Orlando Furioso* by Ludovico Ariosto (1474–1533) would not be such a well-known Italian classic if not for these 618 Doré engravings (82-B, 536-b). This masterpiece, which covers the known world, the sky and even the Moon (Astolfo travelled to the Moon in Elijah's chariot), also contains many of Doré's most beautiful romantic scenes, with lovers and cupids galore, as well as his most dramatic. The folio was not

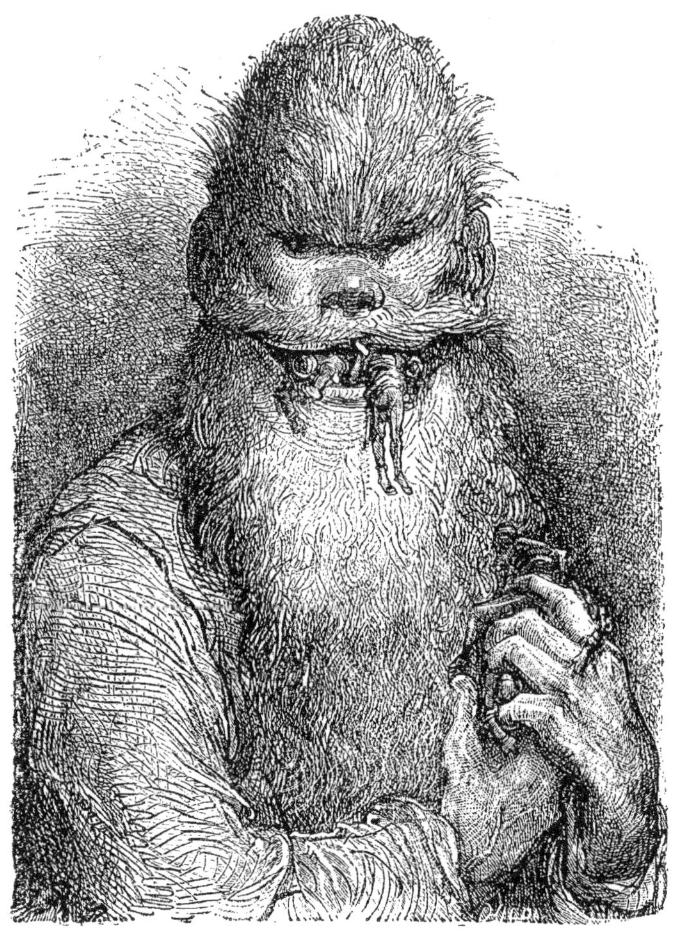

Sculpture

The large folio of *Chefs-d'Oeuvre d'Art of the Paris Universal Exhibition 1878* introduces Doré with this clever comparison to Alexander the Great (356–323 BC): 'The year 1877 found Doré, after a little weeping for new worlds to conquer, bethinking him that the domain of sculpture was still left to his prowess…'. In the last six years of his life, Doré created about 30 major works of sculpture, in addition to dozens of paintings and over a thousand book illustrations. He also took up etching during this time, his most famous being *The Neophyte* (a young monk in the midst of dozens of very old monks) and several versions of *The Head of Christ*. In sculpture, Doré proved his amazing creativity once again. One unique work was his 1880 *Human Pyramid* (now in the Ringling Museum in Florida), showing a circus act of 10 men and boys in the midst of climbing up on each other to stand 10 high. But his most famous work, which was only seen after he died, was his monument in three parts to his good friend Alexandre Dumas, which still stands in the Place Malesherbes in Paris: *The Three Musketeers*. The most artistically mesmerizing is the statue of d'Artagnan; the nobility in the face of the seated swashbuckling figure, with his sword across his lap, is breathtaking and the image has been reproduced on many postcards (as seen here).

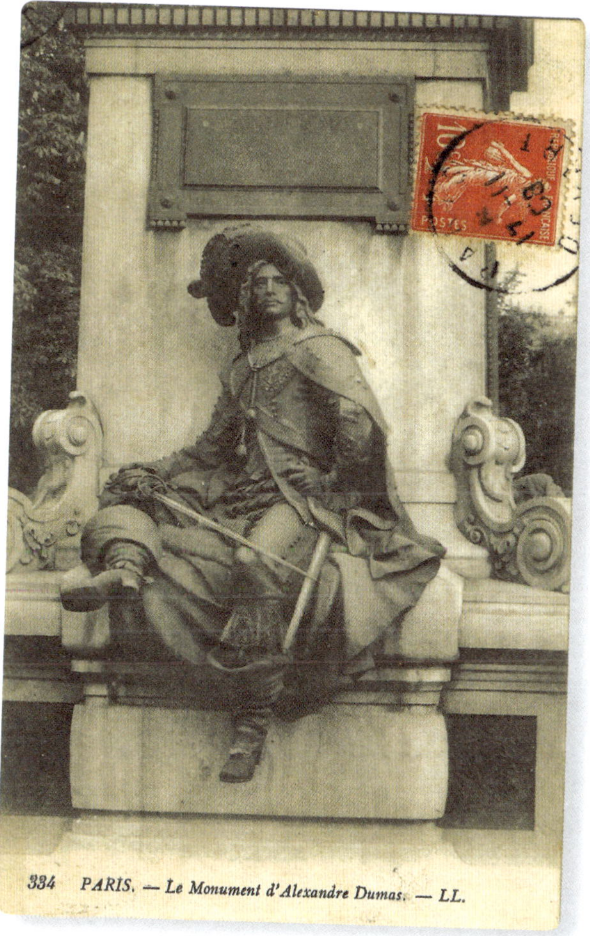

334   PARIS. — *Le Monument d'Alexandre Dumas.* — LL.

The Doré Vase

One of Doré's sculptures drew more attention than all his others put together: at the 1878 Paris Exposition Universelle, he unveiled *La Vigne*, a 4.3 m (14 ft) Italian wine bottle with a hundred mystical creatures playing on the vines (*see* page 121). A titanic struggle erupted when it was unveiled, between overwhelming praise for its originality and brilliance, and intransigent jurors fearing that he would dominate yet another field of art. The Doré vase was the overwhelming favourite to win the Grand Prize, but it did not win anything and was not even listed in the eight-volume official catalogue of over 2,000 pages: the Salon jurors sabotaged it, effectively defining it out of existence. They asserted that it was not really sculpture, placing it in the category of 'decorative arts', which consisted mainly of furniture. The director of the expo saw the injustice and put it in a place of honour, near the main entrance, but in the catalogue, decorative arts were listed by manufacturer, and – since Doré was not one – it was not even listed. Over 100 articles in a dozen countries were written about the Doré vase at the expo, and since then over 600 have been written, nearly 100 of which were illustrated. The outrage was so great that in 1879, they made him an Officer of the Legion of Honour. In 1882, the vase was cast in bronze and exhibited at the Salon, but it still received no medal. Above, you can see it behind a bust of Queen Victoria in a rare photo of the French Exhibition in 1890 at Earl's Court Exhibition Centre in London.

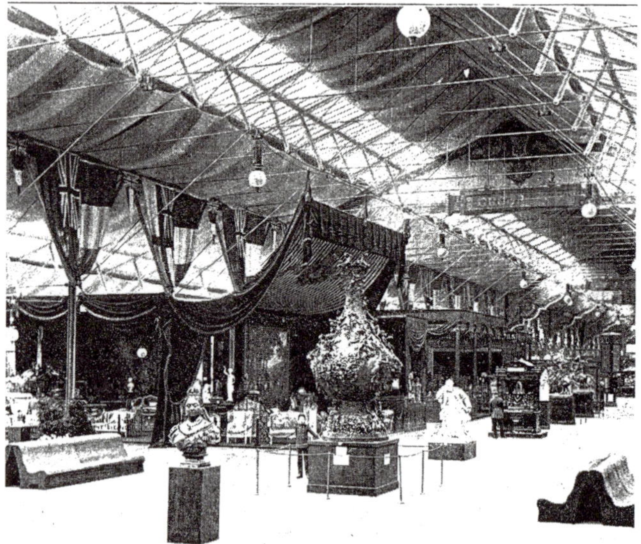

other artists had been treated. He had just begun a set of a thousand engravings for the works of William Shakespeare (1564–1616), but all that was found were a couple of dozen scenes from *Macbeth* and *Hamlet*. If only he had lived a few more years, he might have finally gained the respect he so desperately craved from the official French art establishment, like the initially despised Impressionists, who became world-famous. On a personal note, Doré never married; he had been emotionally dependent on his mother all his life and after she died in 1881, he began deteriorating rapidly. Doré did have romances with several of the most famous women in the world at the time, including the actress Sarah Bernhardt (1844–1923) and the opera singer Adelina Patti (1843–1919, shown below). He wanted to marry the latter, but

M.H. de Young

Even worse was to come: Doré died before paying the bill to Thiebaut Brothers for that bronze casting, so they became its owners and showed it at major art exhibitions in Antwerp (1885), Barcelona (1888), London (1890) and Chicago (1893), but found no buyer due to the high price. It got universal praise in Chicago, where the California delegate to the Columbian Exposition was M.H. de Young (1849–1925) – publisher of the *San Francisco Chronicle*, who dreamed of the Doré vase becoming the symbol of the California wine industry. He convinced most of the Chicago exhibitors to bring their goods to the San Francisco Midwinter Exposition of 1894 just three months later, so the Doré vase headed west and, after that show ended, de Young purchased it from Thiebaut. It was placed right in front of the M.H. de Young museum that opened in Golden Gate Park in 1895, and – except for the time it spent inside over several decades – that is where it remained for the next 24 years.

Doré's Death

In 1883 Doré died at the age of 51 from stroke, brought on by overwork, and with him, the Salon jury system also died – a coincidence, but probably partly because of the outrage at how he and

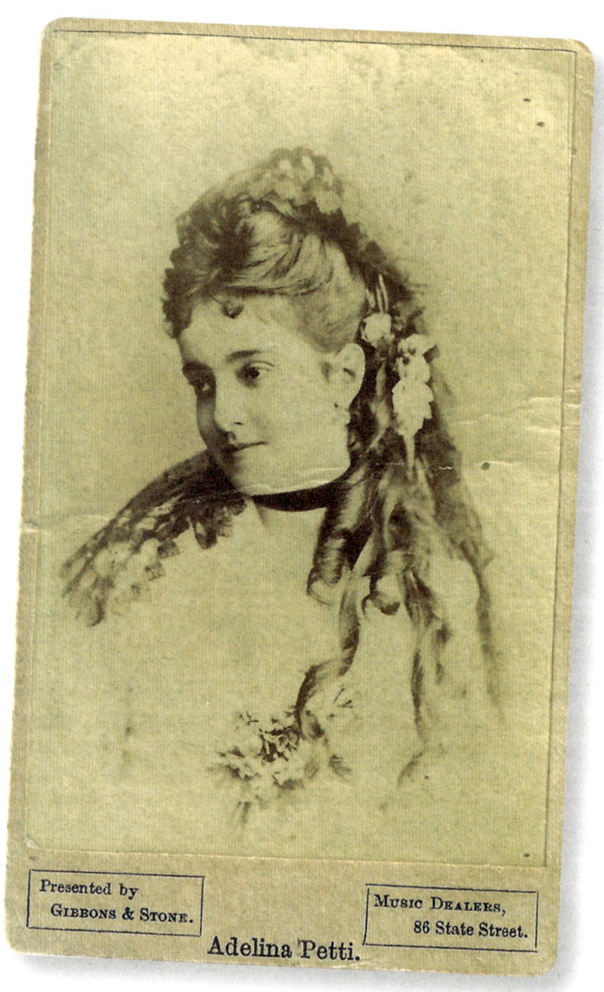

she had so many suitors and wanted to marry into nobility; she came to regret that decision and, in 1893, she wrote an anonymous book about her great romance with Doré.

Poe's *The Raven*

Like the Dumas monument, Doré's last set of illustrations was published posthumously. Ironically, it was also his first commission from the US, as Harper Brothers had been pleased with their Mariner and asked him to create a matching large folio volume (23 x 30.5 cm/9 x 12 in) for the great American poem *The Raven* (26-B) by Edgar Allan Poe. So, Doré died right after finishing illustrations for a poem about death.

The illustrations were sent to the American engravers and published at the end of 1883, but attracted little notice outside the US; although there was a British edition, it is very rare. However, in the twentieth century, they came to be regarded as the greatest Poe illustrations ever made, and they are prominently featured in the Poe Museum. At the

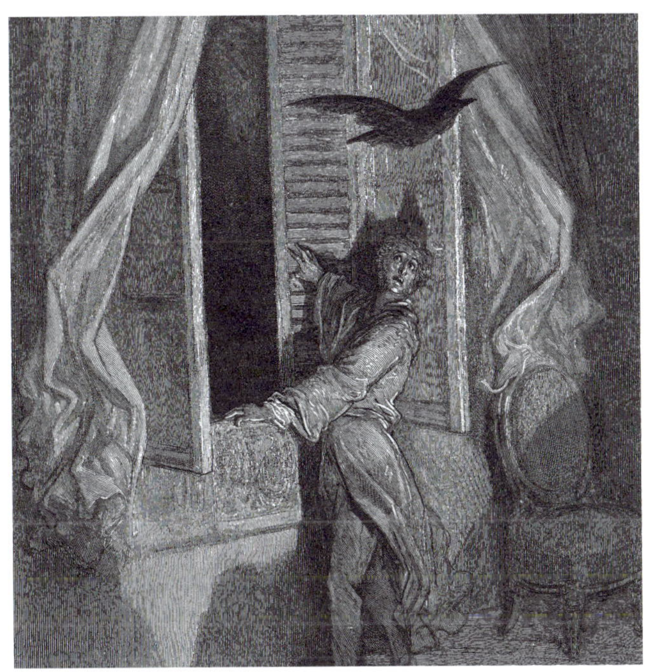

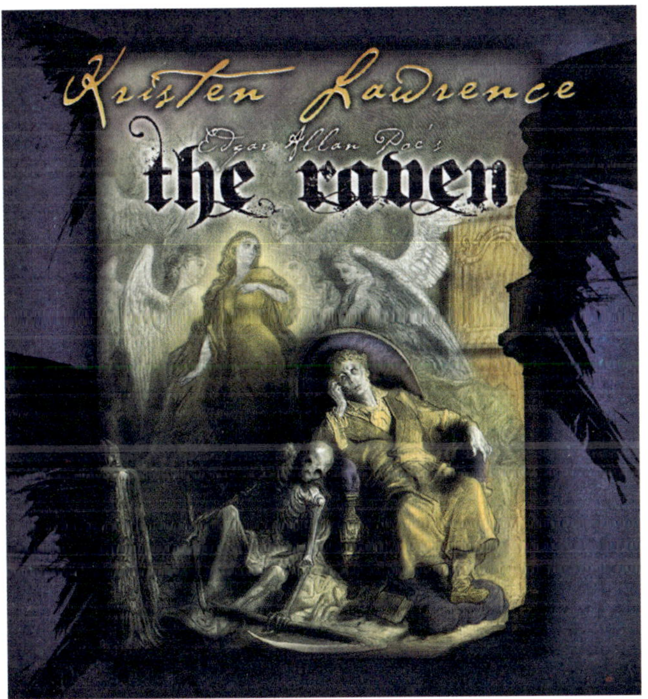

time, the most famous of the scenes was *Sorrow for the Lost Lenore* (*see* page 118, and left as used on the CD cover of Kristen Lawrence's *Edgar Allan Poe's 'The Raven'* of 2012), but nowadays, by far the most renowned and significant is the allegorical *Death on the Globe* (*see* page 119), which during the Second World War became a symbol of worldwide fighting. During the Vietnam War, it was used as an anti-war poster, featuring the head of Lyndon Baines Johnson (1908–73) – the US president at the time – superimposed on the face of the skeleton. In 1951, Doré's Raven engravings were colourized for an educational film, offered as a video in 1978.

Doreana

'Doré seems fated to being eternally revived for the popular culture of succeeding generations.'
Prof. W.H. Herendeen, 1982, *Victorian Studies*

The story of Doré's art does not end with his death, which in many ways was just the end of the beginning. His art was then reused for wave after wave of new artistic media: thousands of his images

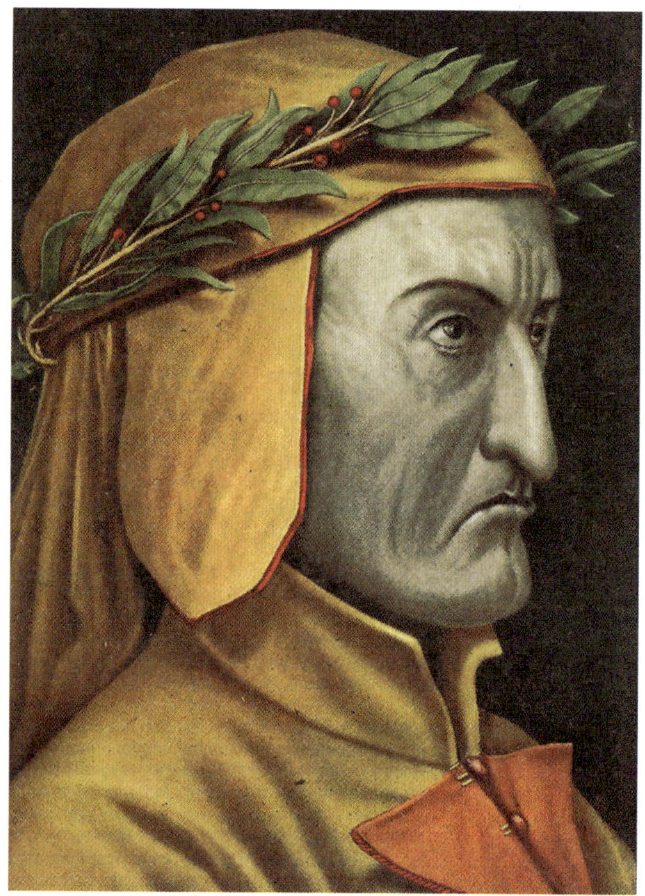

the most borrowed artist for film scenes and, around that same time, there was widespread borrowing of Doré Bible images for calendars and Sunday school materials. After the Second World War, a whole new set of the artist's images was borrowed: Holocaust survivors compared the death camps to his Dante images, and the 1961 documentary about Hitler – *The Black Fox*, narrated by Marlene Dietrich (1901–92) – is filled with Doré images. Then came the hippie movement, with many posters based on Doré's artwork: his Bible engraving of Jephthah and her friends singing and dancing became girls at a rock concert, borrowed by the Grateful Dead and The Doors – an article from the 1990s was about heavy metal music's love affair with Doré's artwork. Classical music also borrows heavily from Doré's art, but all of those past examples pale in comparison to the effect of the internet and online marketplaces that enable the creation of independent products and the placing of almost any artistic image on to anything, thus making it possible to dress from

were redrawn and hand-painted on Magic Lantern slides; then came the picture-postcard craze, with many sets of Doré prints reprinted, redrawn or colourized on to postcards all over the world – perhaps the most amazing and bizarre is a set of eight beautiful chromolithograph postcards of Dante's *Inferno* published in Japan (estimated to have been produced shortly after 1900, they are the earliest known Doré images in that country – Doré's portrait of Dante from the frontispiece is shown above). For the 400th anniversary of *Don Quixote*, a Spanish publisher had artist Salvador Tusell (1800–1900) convert all 377 Doré prints into watercolour paintings, published in a heavy two-volume folio as chromolithographs. Within the film industry, Doré's images were used for many early productions like *Life and Passion of the Christ* (1903) and *L'Inferno* (1911). In 1930, an article in a film trade journal asserted that he was

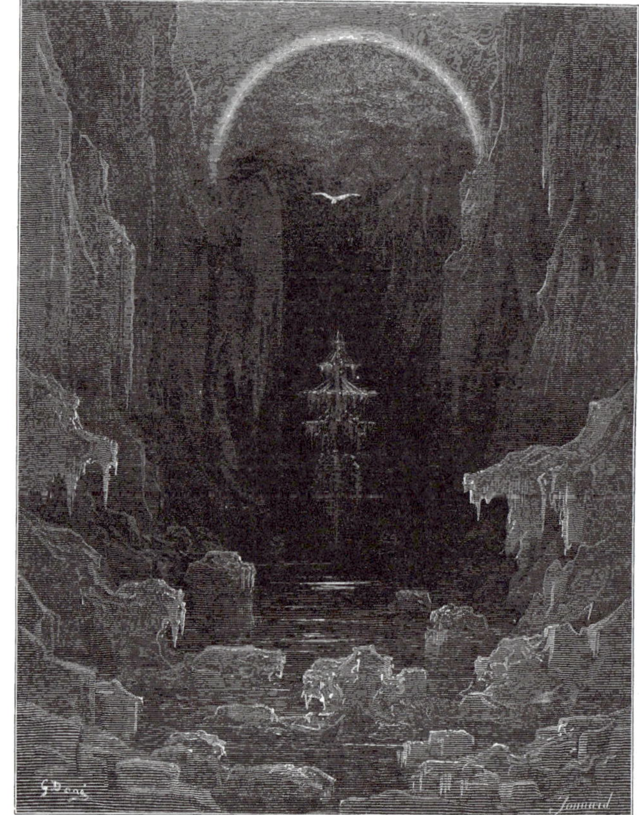

head to toe in Doré clothing – not to mention all the available tattoos. In recent years, there has been a major revival of interest in Doré's art in France: in his engravings, fine arts and Doreana.

Davy Jones' Pipe Organ

Doré's art is all around you, if you just know where to look for it. Here is one example: in the 2006 Hollywood film *Pirates of the Caribbean: Dead Man's Chest*, one of the many creepy characters is Davy Jones, a recently deceased man who has octopus tentacles all over his face. About an hour into the film, he waxes nostalgic and retires to his chambers to play his pipe organ, which has an orange mural of a nautical scene up on the front board. If you look closely, you will see that it is a montage of scenes from Doré's *Rime of the Ancient Mariner* (*see The Ice Ship*, left). This qualifies as multiple categories of Doreana: it is not just a scene in a major film, but also an artifact – a physical item that exists apart from the movie and can be viewed in the American Film Institute Showcase, a museum in Los Angeles. It was created by Academy Award-winning art director Rick Heinrichs (b. 1954), who wrote, 'We also designed a painting above the organ keys which has a weirdly sweet and romantic feel to it.' Doré's Mariner is so iconic that it was also borrowed for a *Puck Magazine* cartoon of Tammany Hall, for Wagner's *The Flying Dutchman*, for *Frankenstein* by Bernie Wrightson (1948–2017) and for a Steve Bell cartoon of President George W. Bush (b. 1946) – and that is just a little taste of the broad scope of Doreana.

Who Needs a Label?

Doré defies labelling. It was often stated that he was his own school, but there are really three different Dorés: the prolific painter and sculptor,

with original works of art in museums and private collections; the most prolific illustrator of all time, with over 10,000 published engravings, available to the general public through his original folios, in much cheaper reprints or on the internet; and then there is Doreana, the borrowing of Doré's art in hundreds of popular culture genres, which keeps on expanding with colourizing, redrawing and other adaptations. Doré seems to transcend all genres and categories. Exhibition books have tried to label him, referring to his art as romanticist, realist, mystical, visionary, impressionist, surrealist or gothic fantasy. When asked what he illustrated, Doré replied, 'Everything!' He tried to illustrate everything in the real world, plus a lot of things in many imaginary worlds.

He did have flaws: some said he was colour-blind, and he did have difficulties with colour. Many of his paintings appear monochromatic and one writer commented that Doré thought in black and white, but today, people can use their creativity to colourize his engravings in many different ways. The borrowing of Doré's art seems unlimited now, but what will the next generation create?

Don't Call Me 'Paul'

Doré achieved worldwide fame so quickly that many errors about him got published, which are now difficult to correct. An internet search of 'Paul' Gustave Doré turns up over 100,000 uses, but the artist's full official name was Louis-Auguste Gustave Doré – he had never been called 'Paul' or 'Christophe', which was his father's name. How all the errors started is too long a story to cover here, but the comprehensive 1931 Doré bibliography by Henri Leblanc actually showed a photograph of his birth certificate. The famous novel *Moby Dick* begins with the sentence: 'Call me Ishmael.' Let us end with: 'Don't call me Paul.'

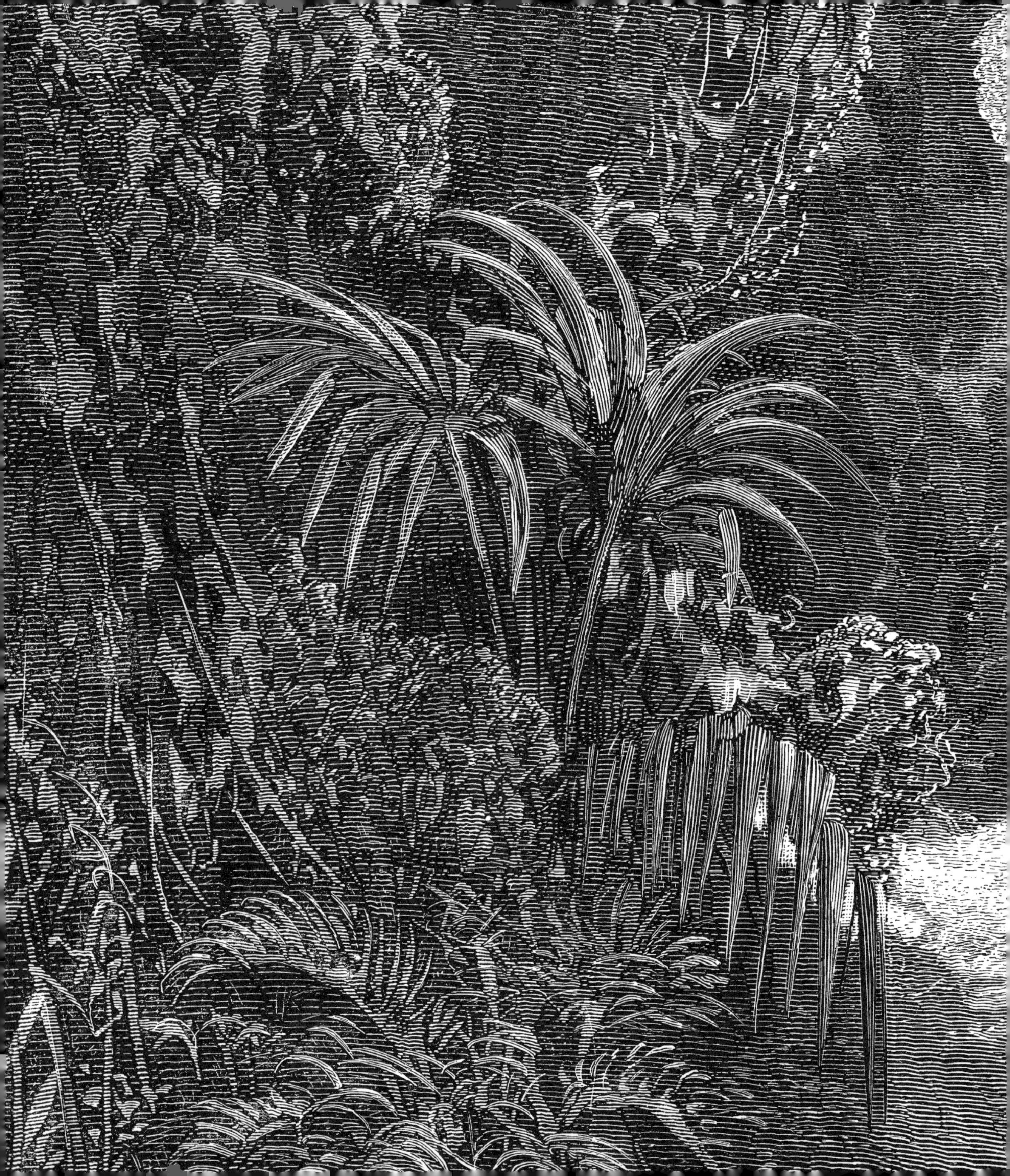

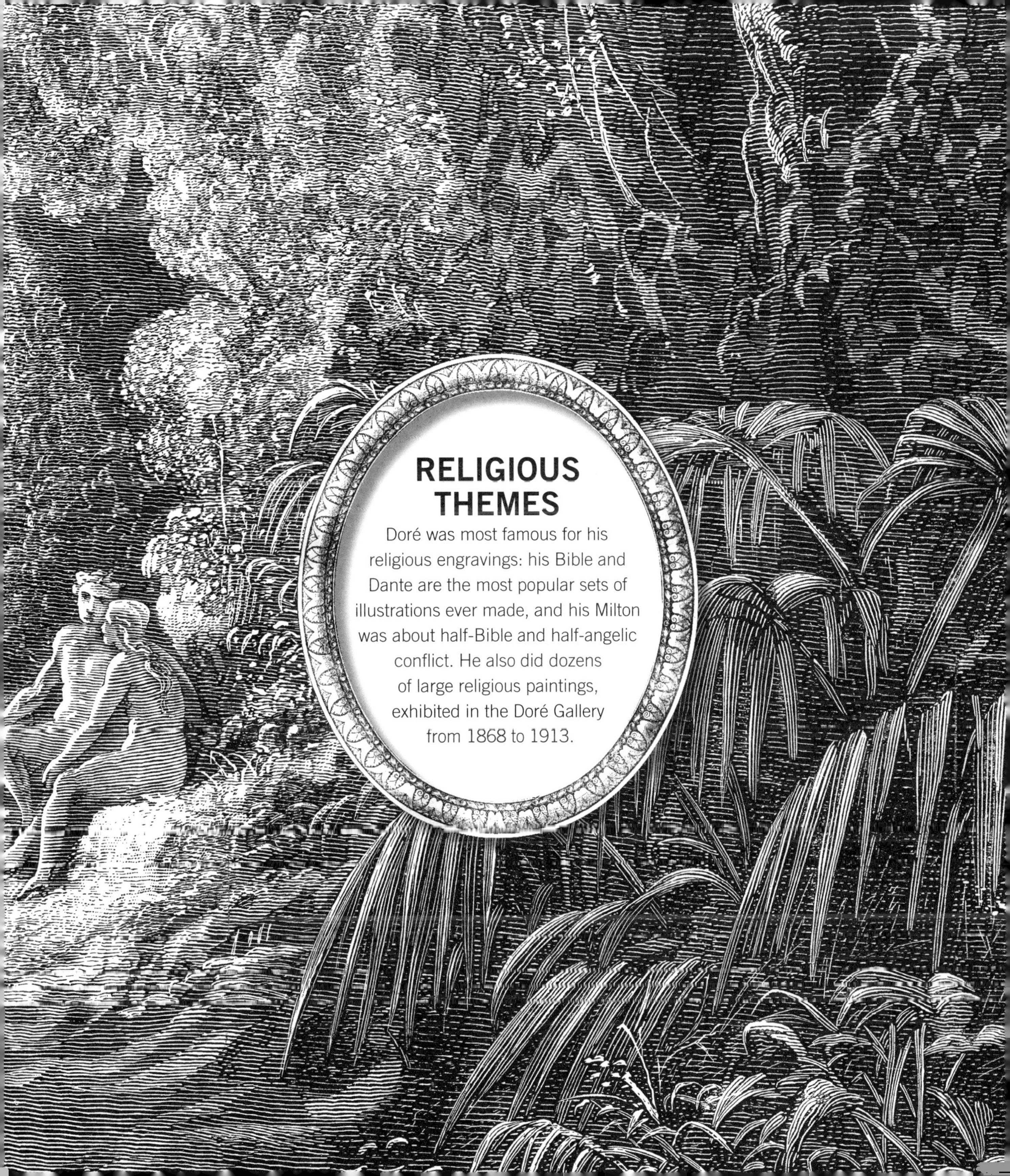

RELIGIOUS THEMES

Doré was most famous for his religious engravings: his Bible and Dante are the most popular sets of illustrations ever made, and his Milton was about half-Bible and half-angelic conflict. He also did dozens of large religious paintings, exhibited in the Doré Gallery from 1868 to 1913.

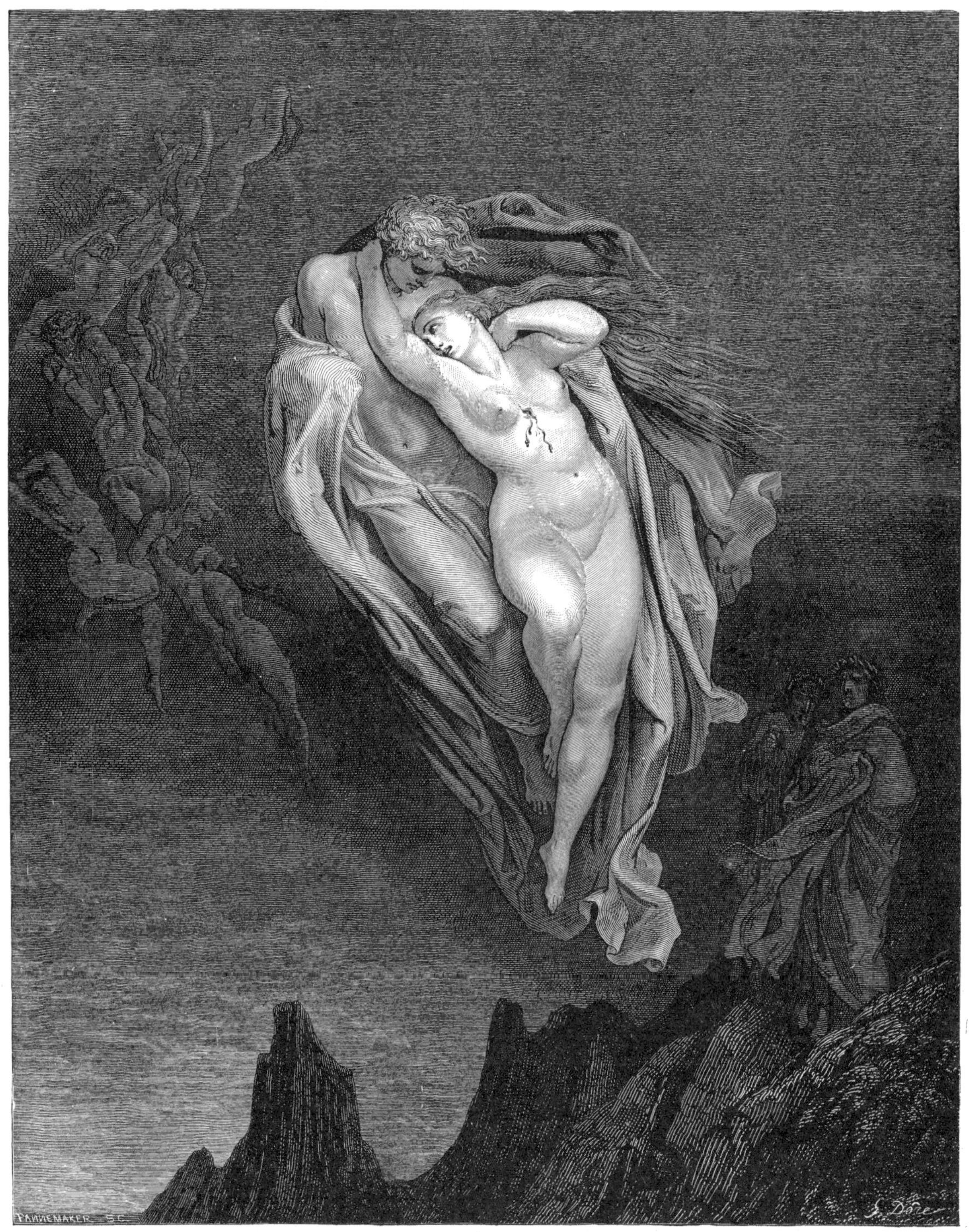

Paolo and Francesca, 1861

Plate 15, *Divine Comedy: Inferno*: Canto V, Dante Alighieri

• Engraver: A.F. Pannemaker (1822–1900)

The spirits of the doomed lovers – a stab wound visible in Francesca's chest – are buffeted in the windy skies among the lustful of the Second Circle of Hell. Doré made this into a large painting for the 1863 Paris Salon, later exhibited in the London Doré Gallery, and then made it into a steel engraving.

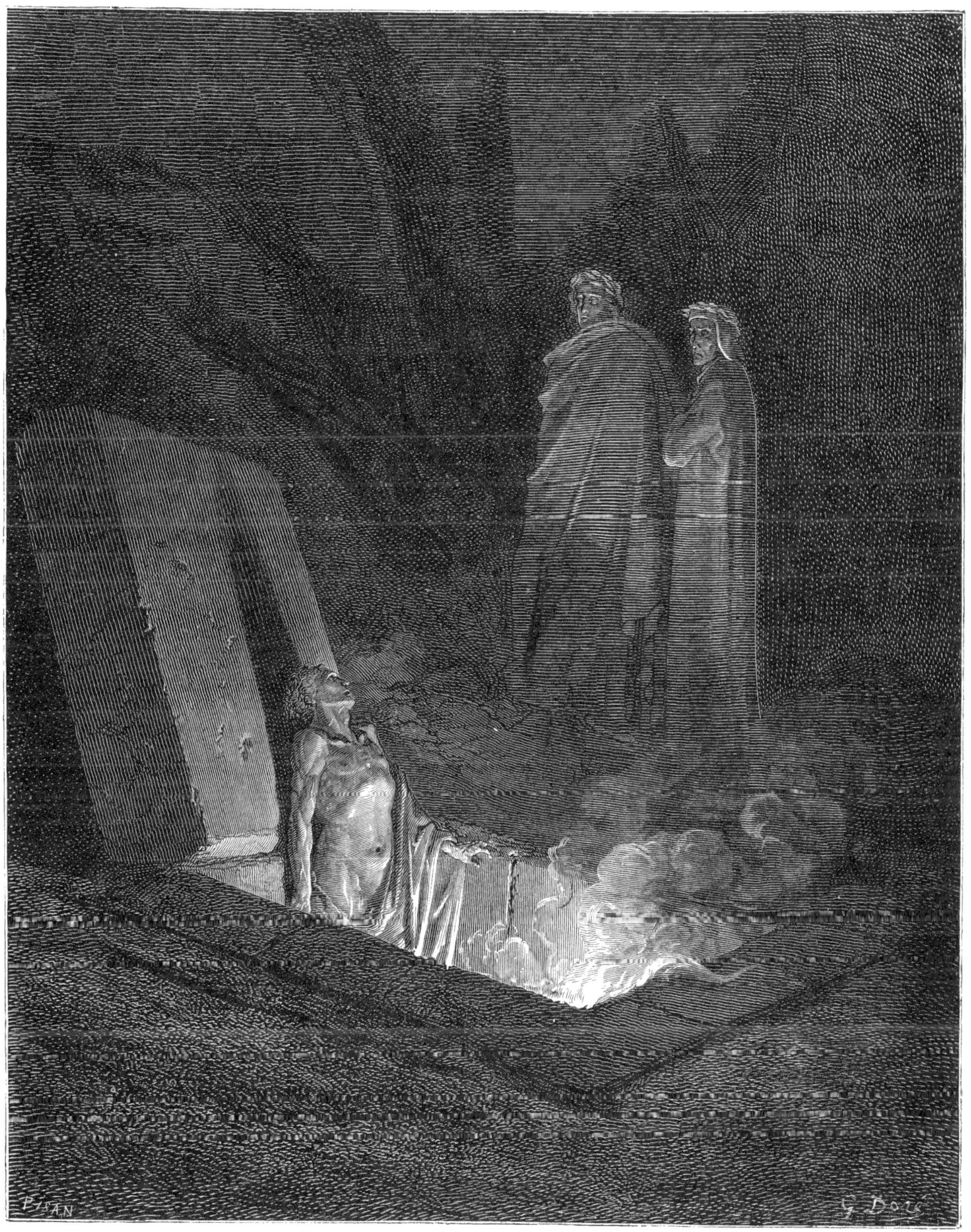

Farinata's Tomb, 1861

Plate 30, *Divine Comedy: Inferno*: Canto X, Dante Alighieri
• Engraver: Heliodore Pisan (1822–1900)

The scornful Farinata rises out of his fiery tomb to confront Dante and Virgil: 'Who were thine ancestors?' Acknowledged in 1861 as Doré's most powerful *Inferno* scene, this was borrowed in many ways (e.g. the 1924 *Dante's Inferno* film poster and the 1978 *Hitler: a Film from Germany*).

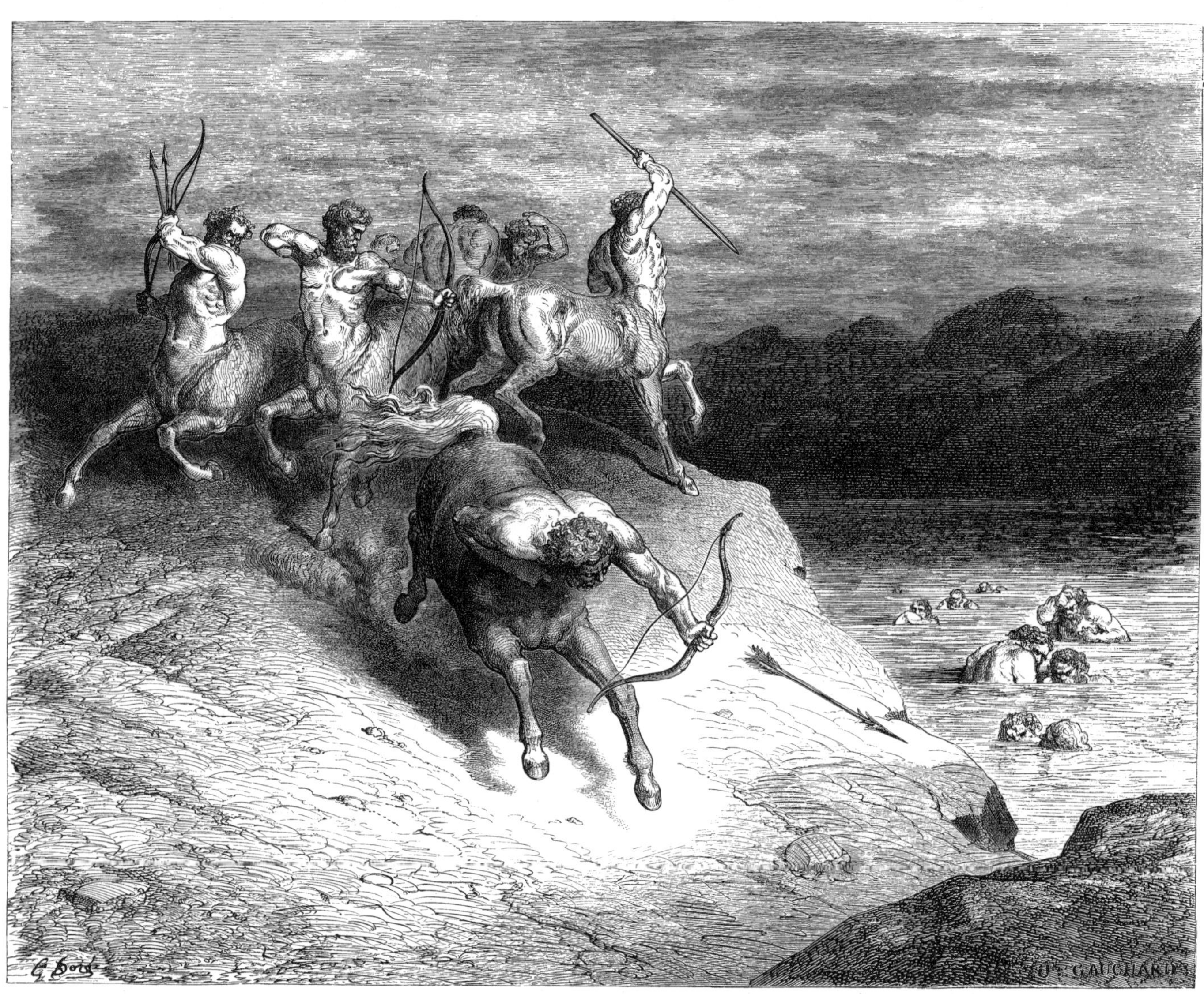

Chiron, 1861

Plate 34, *Divine Comedy: Inferno*: Canto XII, Dante Alighieri
• Engraver: F.J. Gauchard (1825–72)

Centaurs with bows and arrows attack fleeing tormented souls. Doré was often mentioned as Hollywood's biggest source for images of creatures, and the films borrowing his centaur engravings include Ray Harryhausen's *Jason and the Argonauts* (1963).

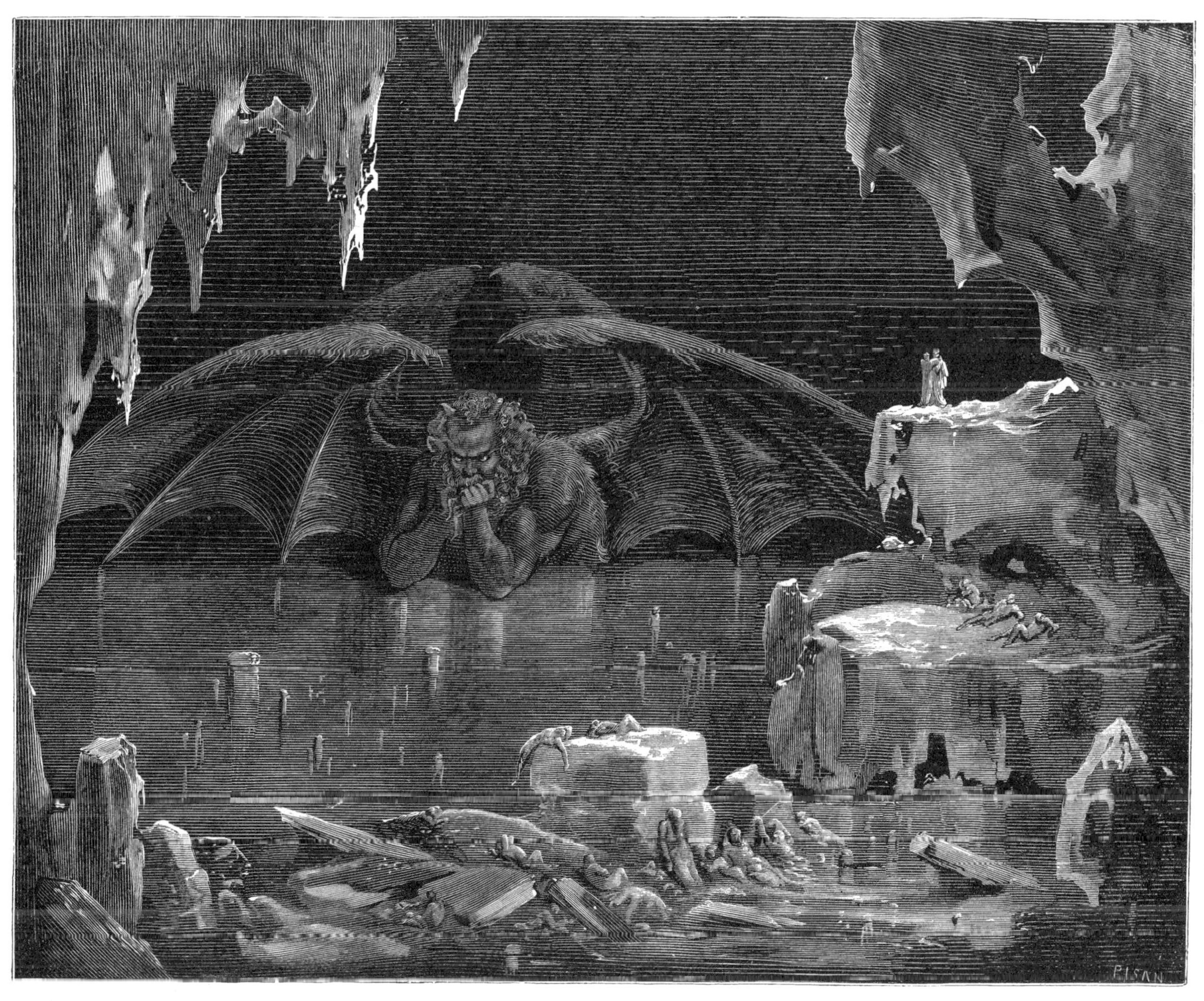

Lucifer, 1861

Plate 73, *Divine Comedy: Inferno*: Canto XXXIV, Dante Alighieri
• Engraver: Heliodore Pisan (1822–1900)

Tiny Dante and Virgil in the middle ground view an enormous Satan with batwings, trapped in ice, as he devours doomed souls. Writers have often remarked how similar Doré's Lucifer and demon batwings are to those on the 1939 *Batman* comic-book character.

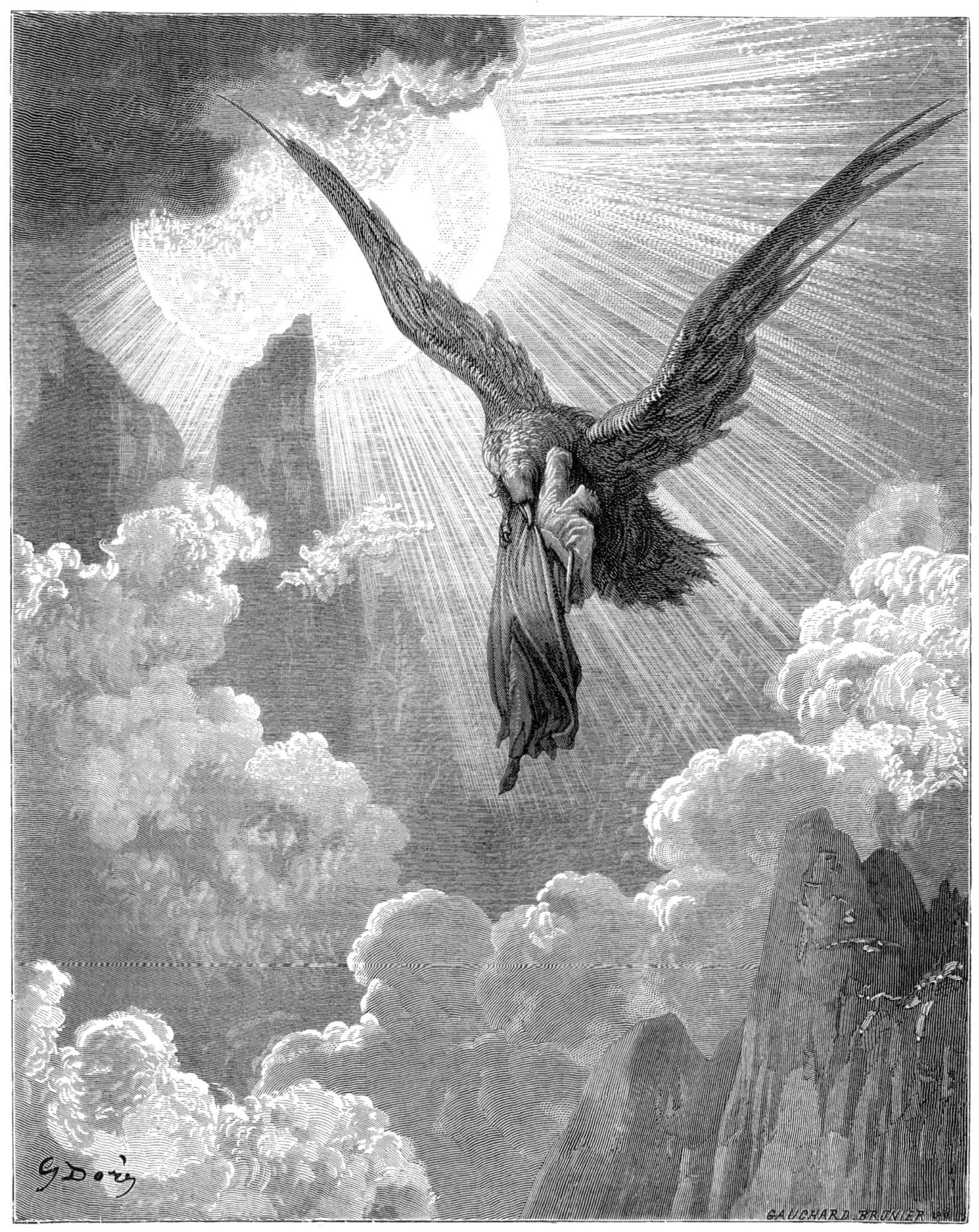

The Eagle, 1868

Plate 15, *Divine Comedy: Purgatorio*: Canto IX, Dante Alighieri

• Engraver: F.J. Gauchard (1825–72)

Dante begins his ascent from the Inferno into the heavens, lifted by a giant eagle:

'He snatched me upwards towards the sun.'

This powerful symbolic image is very popular, borrowed for many book covers, posters, postage stamps and covers of music albums, like *Lucifer Rising,* the 2012 LP by Jimmy Page of Led Zeppelin.

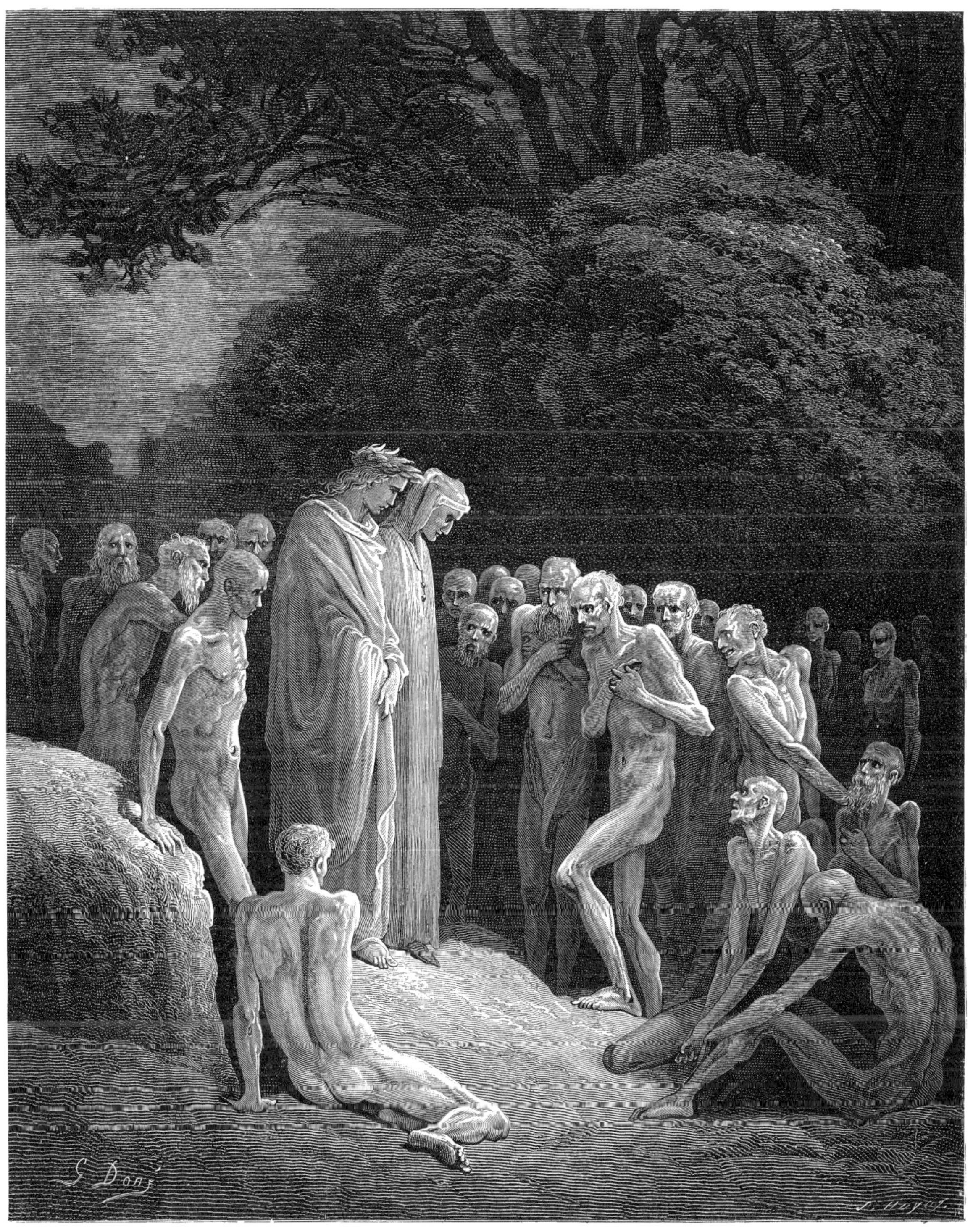

The Gluttons, 1868

Plate 30, *Divine Comedy: Purgatorio*: Canto XXIV, Dante Alighieri

• Engraver: Jules Huyot (1841-1922)

Gaunt 'doubly dead' souls approach Dante and Virgil, amazed that they are alive. At the end of the Second World War, many Doré Dante engravings of emaciated souls or piles of bodies seemed prophetic of the Holocaust. Even the survivors said that these engravings reminded them of the concentration camps.

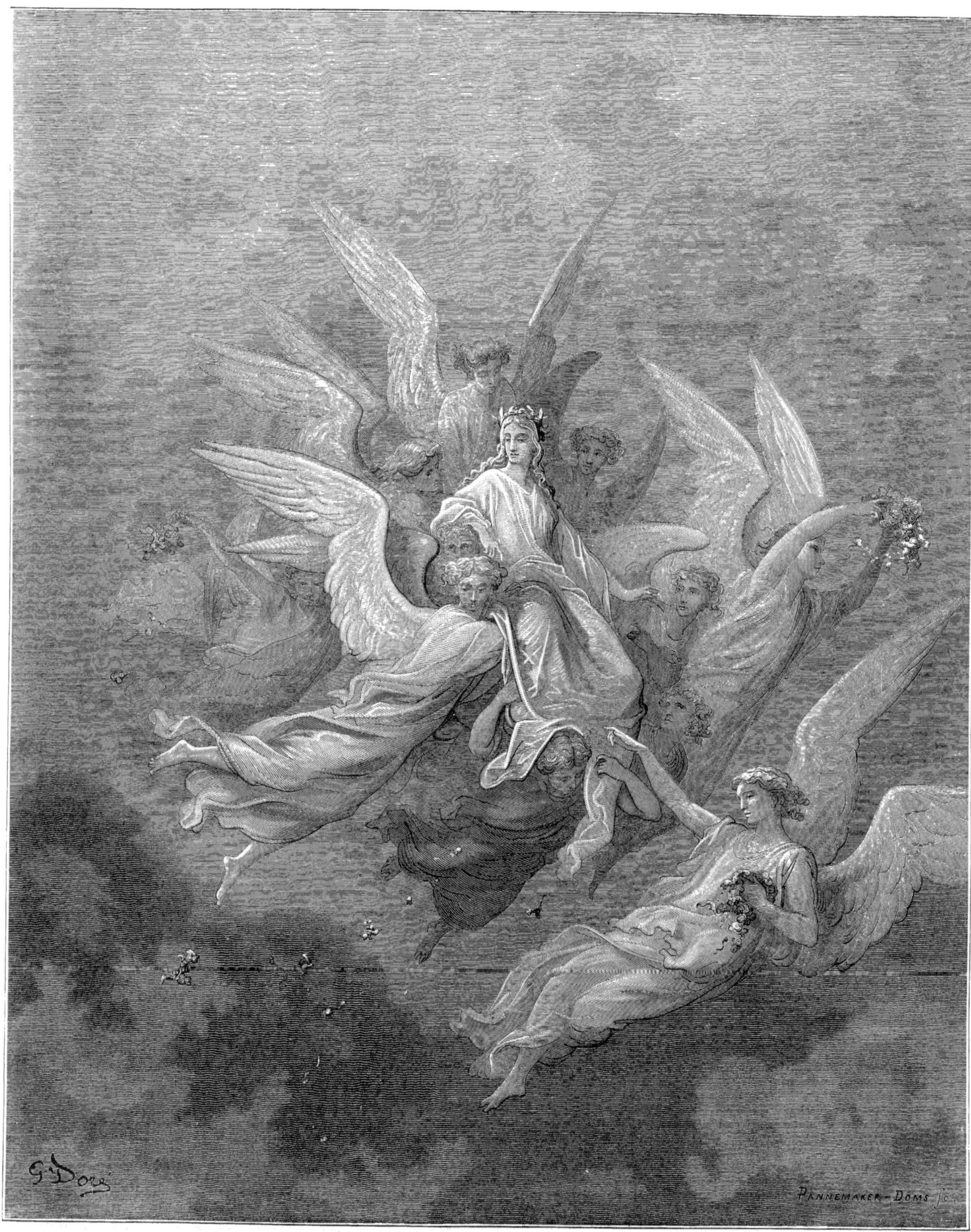

Beatrice, 1868

Plate 39, *Divine Comedy: Purgatorio*: Canto XXX, Dante Alighieri
• Engraver: A.F. Pannemaker (1822–1900)

A host of heavenly angels carry Beatrice to meet Dante, since she will replace Virgil as his guide to the Paradiso. Doré would later 'borrow' his own dreamy engraving for the 1883 scene of angels carrying Lenore to heaven in Poe's *The Raven*.

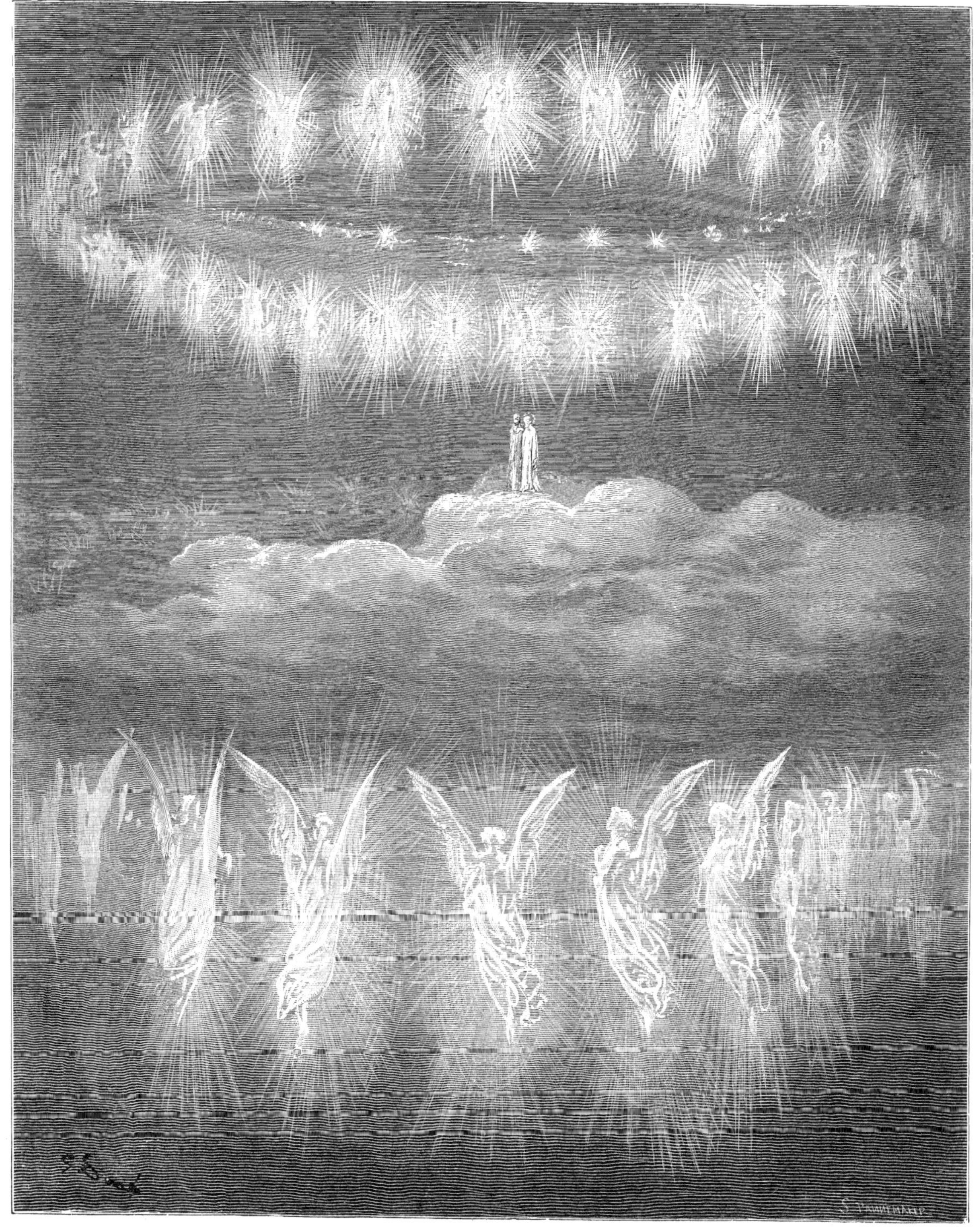

Glorified Souls, 1868

Plate 4, *Divine Comedy: Paradiso*: Canto XII, Dante Alighieri
• Engraver: Stéphane Pannemaker (1847–1930)

Typical of dozens of Doré's angel engravings, except that this particular image is amazingly visionary. Many people have noted that it bears an uncanny resemblance to a flying saucer, with rows of lights around the sides of the circle.

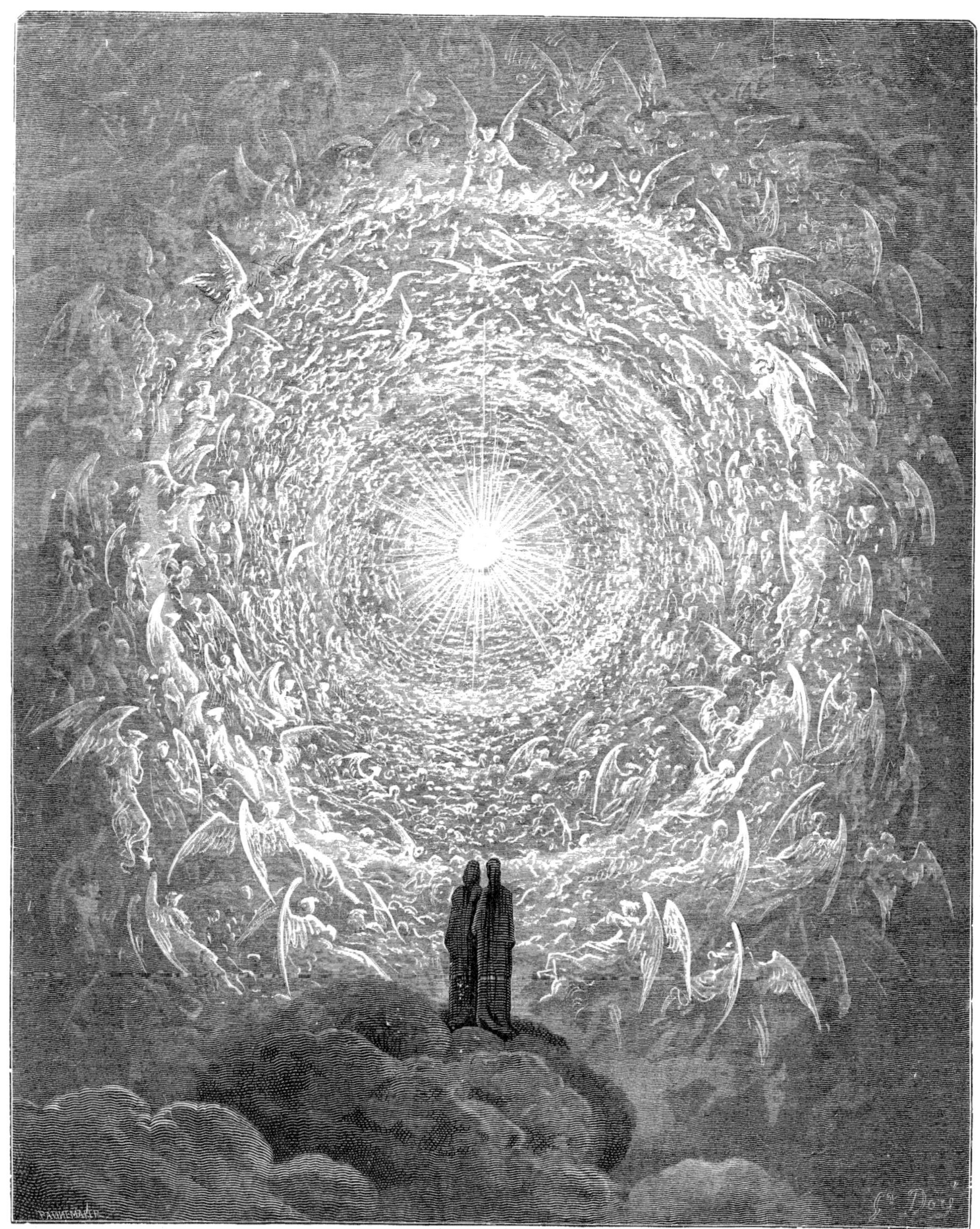

The Empyrean, 1868

Plate 17, *Divine Comedy: Paradiso*: Canto XXXI, Dante Alighieri
• Engraver: A.F. Pannemaker (1822–1900)

Dante and Beatrice see Heaven open as a distant ball of light which, as it gets closer, turns into rings of angels. This engraving, also known as the *Celestial Rose*, was mocked in 1868 for being too dreamy, but is now often cited as Doré's greatest artistic image, depicting the mystical confluence of the physical and spiritual, like a kaleidoscope.

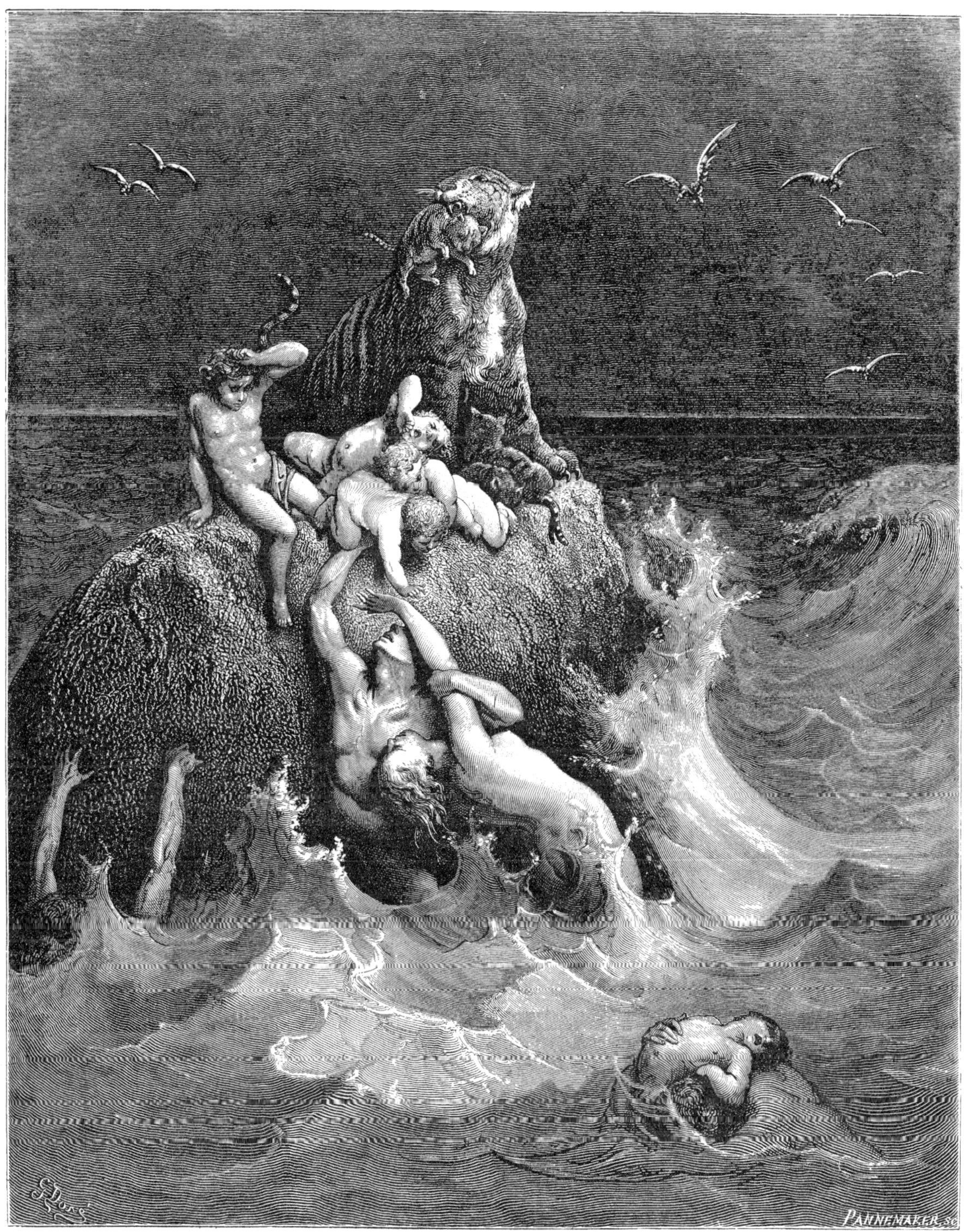

The Deluge, 1865

Plate 7, Volume 1, *La Sainte Bible*: Genesis 7:23, First French Edition
• Engraver: A.F. Pannemaker (1822–1900)

As the last few humans struggle to cling to a rock, a tiger ignores them, trying to save her cubs. Doré made his dramatic, symbolic imagery into a 5.5 x 9-m (18 x 30-ft) 1863 Salon painting. The scene also exists as a beautiful Dutch chromolithograph and as several paintings made by twentieth-century artists.

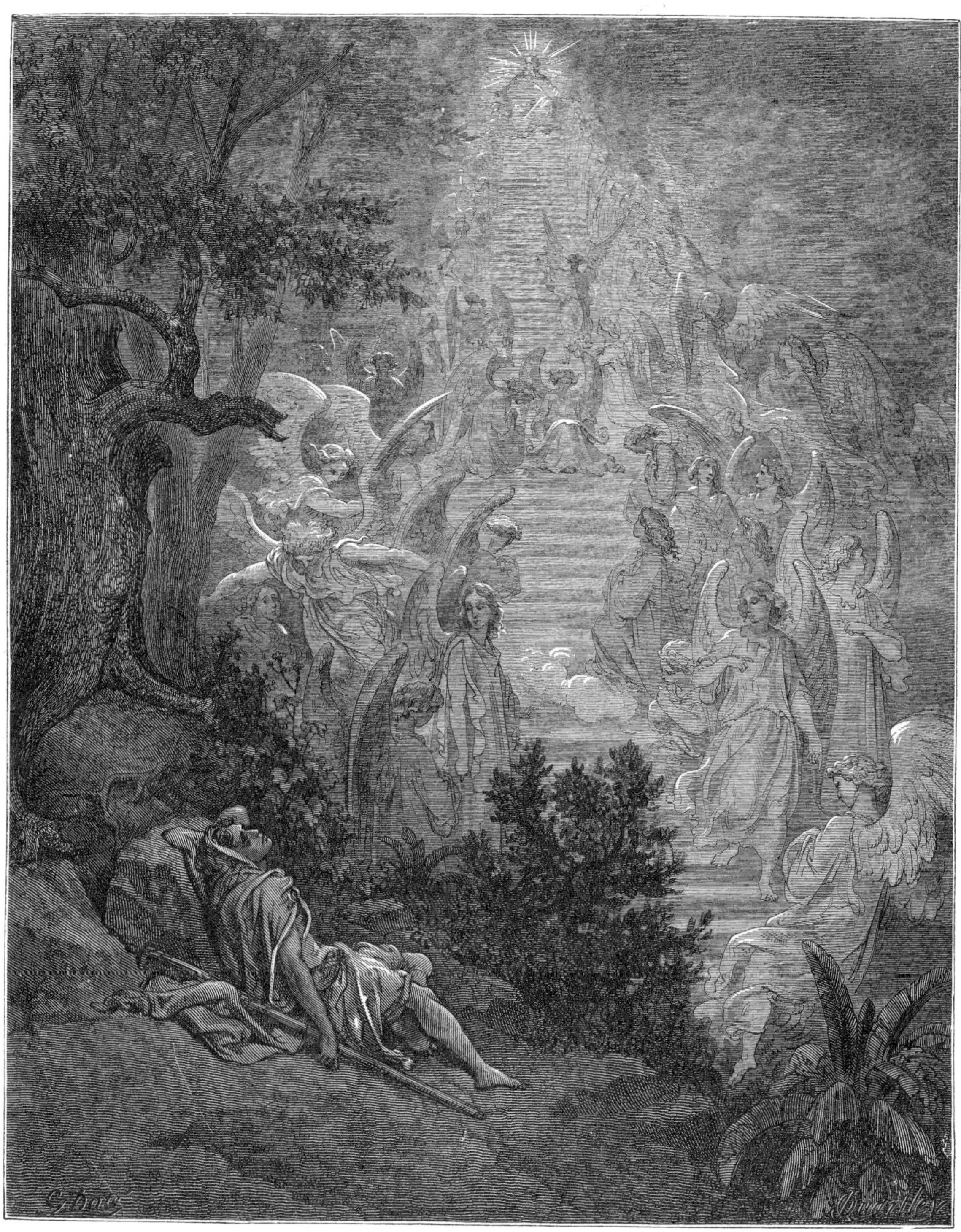

Jacob's Dream, 1865

Plate 20, Volume 1, *La Sainte Bible*: Genesis 28:12, First French Edition

• Engraver: John A. Quartley (*c.* 1821–88)

As Jacob flees from his brother's wrath, he dreams of an angelic stairway to heaven. There is a T-shirt with this image for Led Zeppelin's *Stairway to Heaven*. Doré depicted a different view of this scene in the 1859 Cassell's *Illustrated Family Bible*.

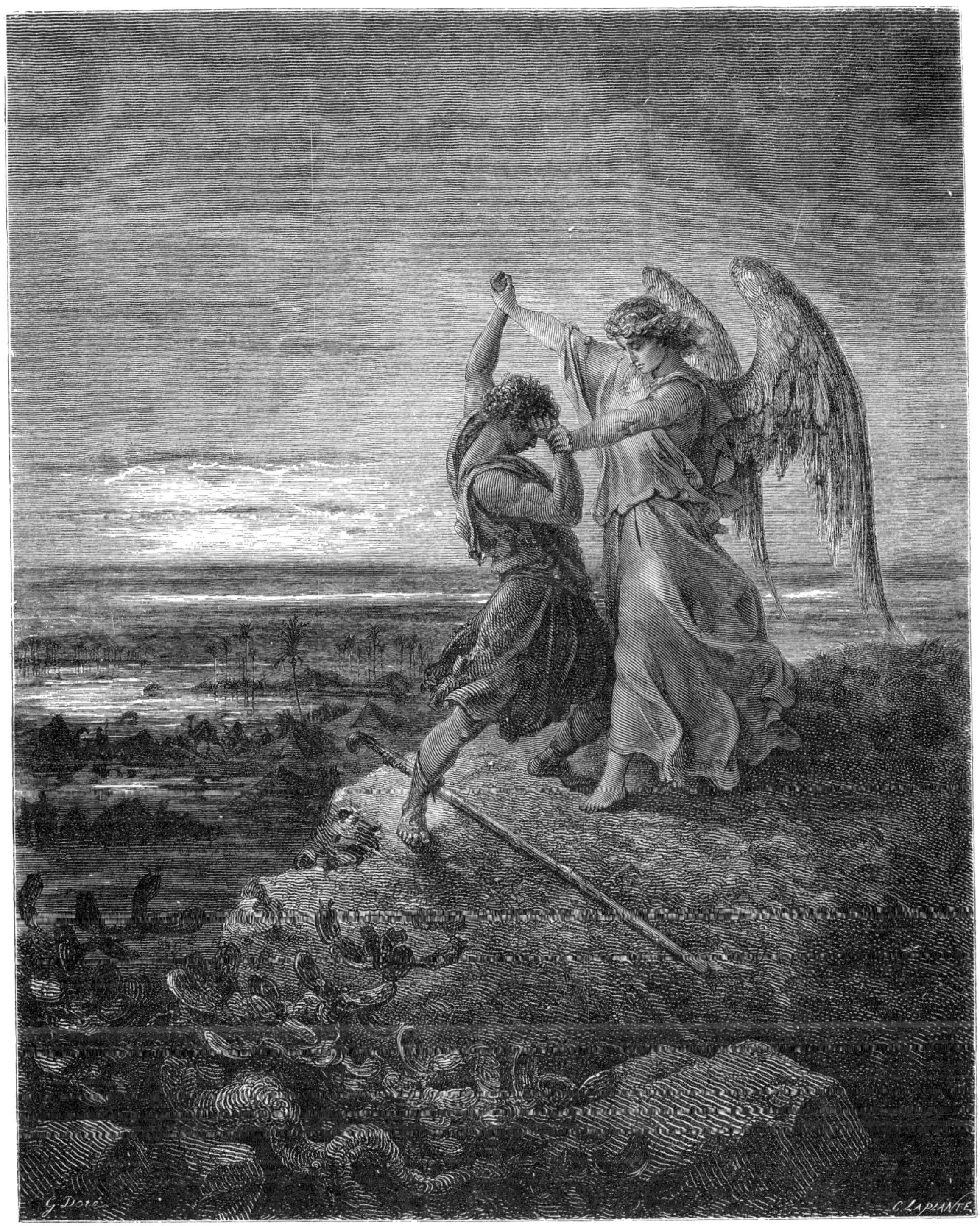

Jacob Wrestling Angel, 1865

Plate 23, Volume 1, *La Sainte Bible*: Genesis 32:24, First French Edition
• Engraver: Charles Laplante (1837–1903)

Perhaps the most popular artistic depiction ever made of the human Jacob straining against superhuman strength. Doré was certainly influenced by Delacroix's mural, but he isolated the action. This scene can be found on many book covers and it was made into a fused-bronze high-relief plate by Merri Roderick (1948–2018) in 1985.

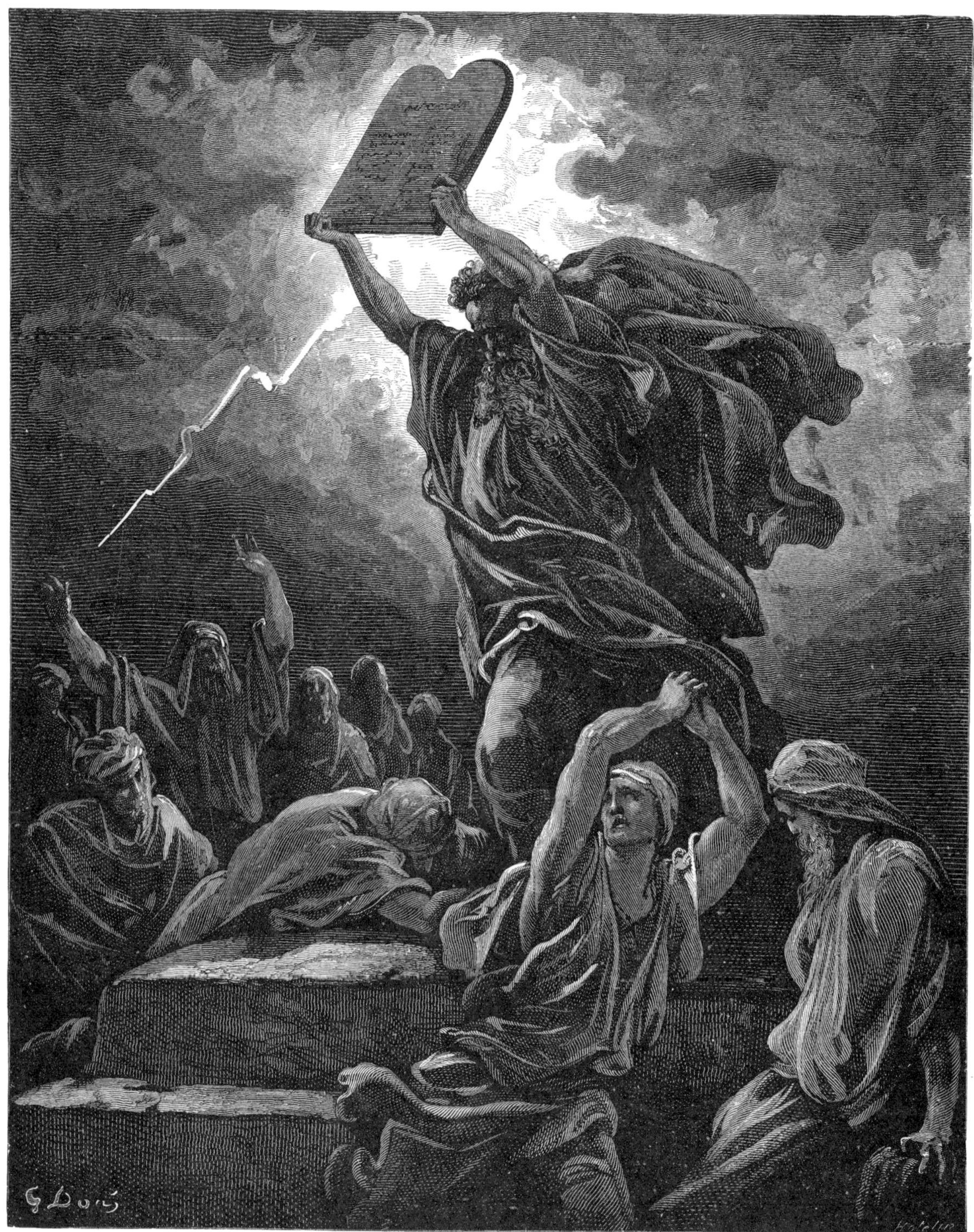

Moses Breaking Tablets, 1865

Plate 39, Volume 1, *La Sainte Bible*: Exodus 32:19, First French Edition
• Engraver: L.E. Hotelin (1821–94)

Lightning strikes as Moses breaks the Tablets of the Law before the idolatrous Israelites, in what is probably the most famous Doré Bible scene. In the 1860s, he was criticized for theatricality, but it was later borrowed for *The Ten Commandments* movie poster, showing Charlton Heston re-enacting the scene.

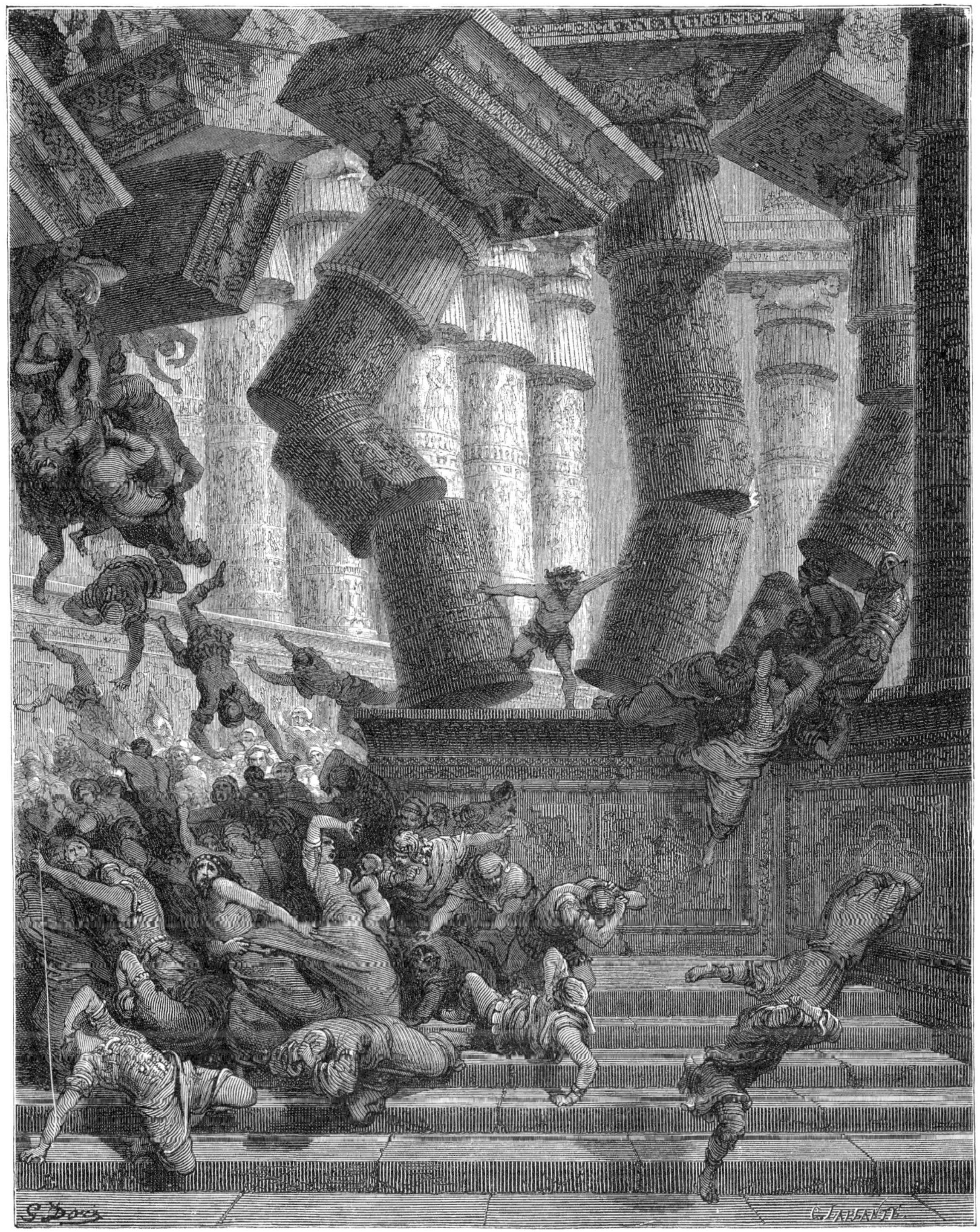

Samson Destroying Temple, 1865

Plate 62, Volume 1, *La Sainte Bible*: Judges 16:30, First French Edition
• Engraver: Charles Laplante (1837–1903)

A wildly dramatic scene of terror, as Samson, with superhuman strength, pushes the pillars apart, killing thousands, including himself. This Doré image was also widely borrowed: Ray Harryhausen took it and changed it to a creature from outer space destroying the Parthenon, in the 1957 film *20 Million Miles to Earth*.

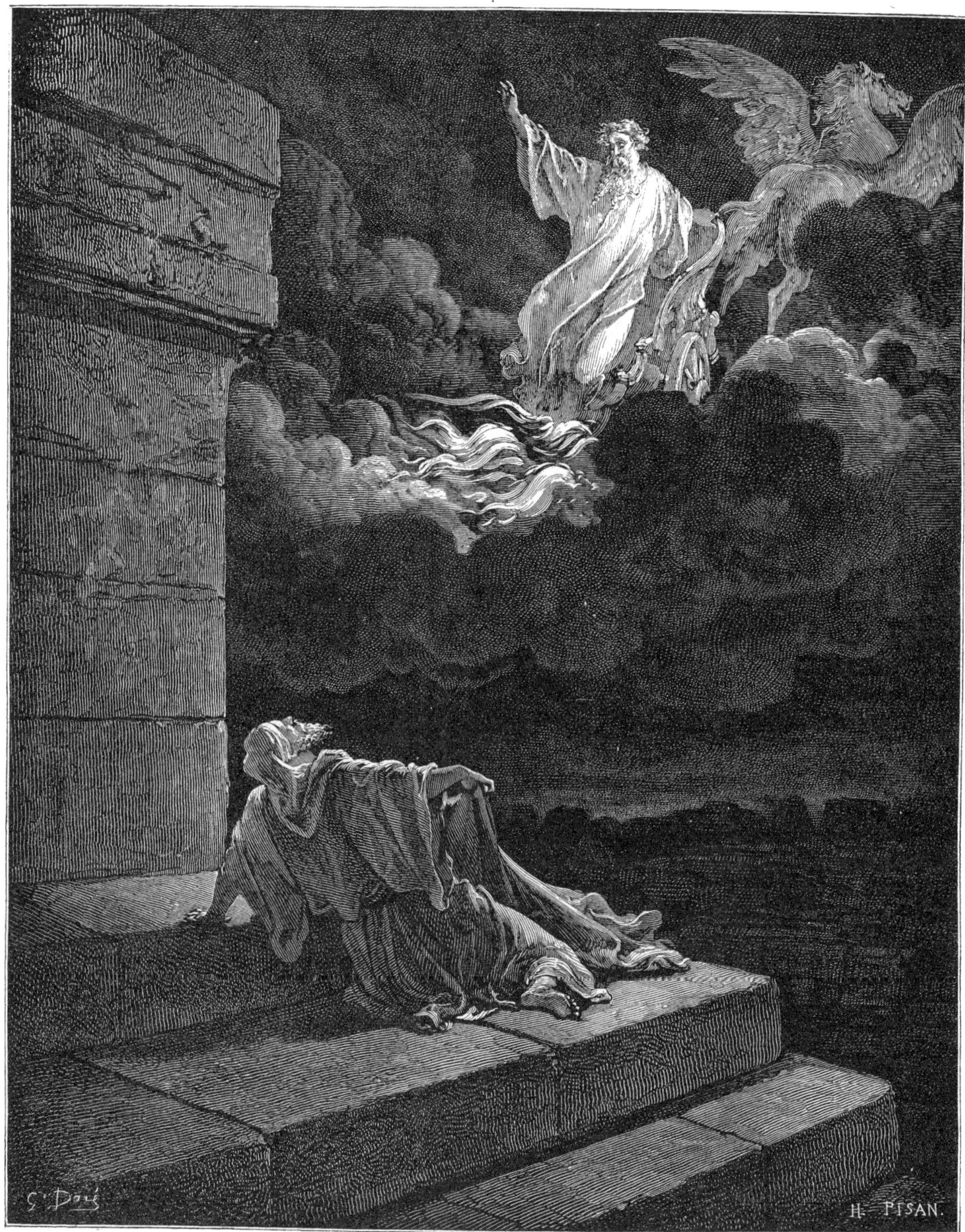

Elijah to Heaven in Chariot, 1865

Plate 94, Volume 1, *La Sainte Bible*: II Kings 2:11, First French Edition

• Engraver: Heliodore Pisan (1822–1900)

Elisha watches in awe as a fiery chariot with winged horses takes Elijah to Heaven. This image has also been made into paintings by many artists, plus a black-light poster in the 1960s and a Merri Roderick fused-bronze plate in 1985.

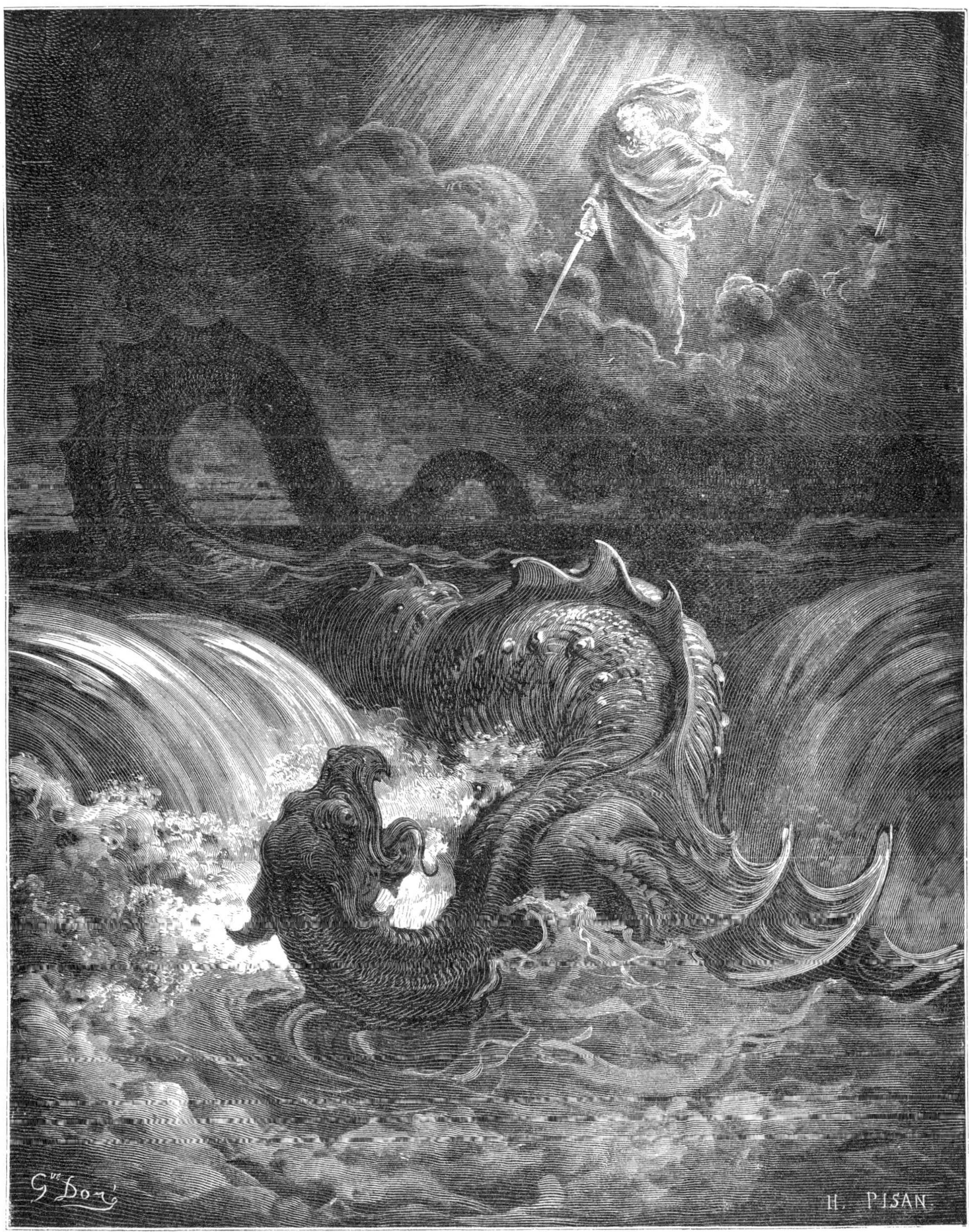

Judgement on Leviathan, 1865

Plate 5, Volume 2, *La Sainte Bible*: Isaiah 27:1, First French Edition
• Engraver: Heliodore Pisan (1822–1900)

This is an iconic image of God in the sky, slaying the dragon in the sea, which has become a widely borrowed scene in many popular culture genres. Theological differences caused Protestant and Jewish publishers to replace God the Father with an angel.

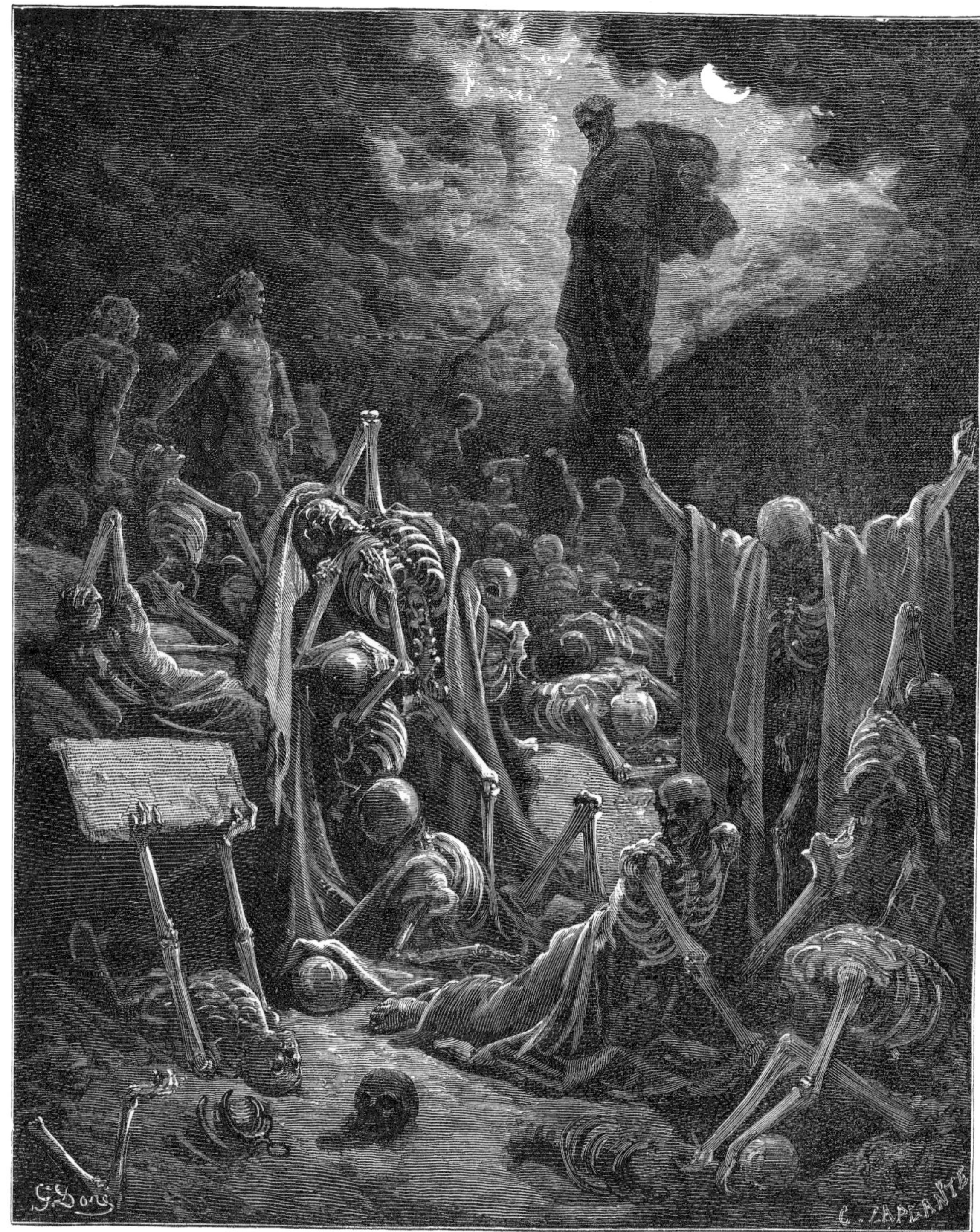

Valley of Dry Bones, 1865

Plate 11, Volume 2, *La Sainte Bible*: Ezekiel 37:3, First French Edition

• Engraver: Charles Laplante (1837–1903)

'Can these bones live again?' Graves open and skeletons come to life: a prophetic depiction of the revival of the nation of Israel and another widely borrowed Doré image in movie scenes, posters, tattoos and music album covers.

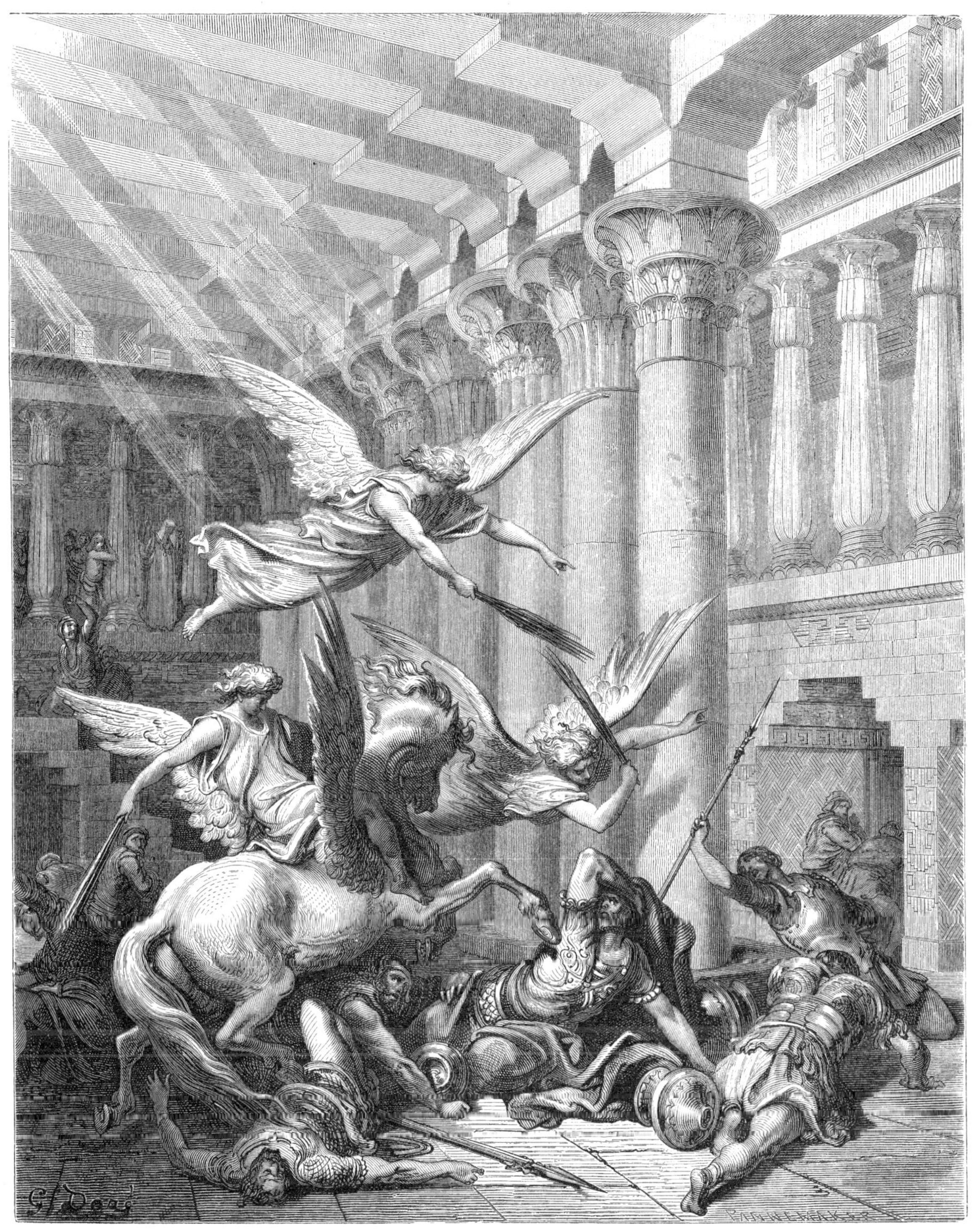

Heliodorus Cast Down, 1865

Plate 25, Volume 2, *La Sainte Bible*: II Maccabees 3:25, First French Edition
• Engraver: A.F. Pannemaker (1822–1900)

Roman General Heliodorus, attempting to plunder the temple in Jerusalem, is driven out by angels. Many artists depicted this scene; Doré was influenced by the 1861 Delacroix mural (*see* page 16) and did 21 scenes based on the Catholic Apocryphal books.

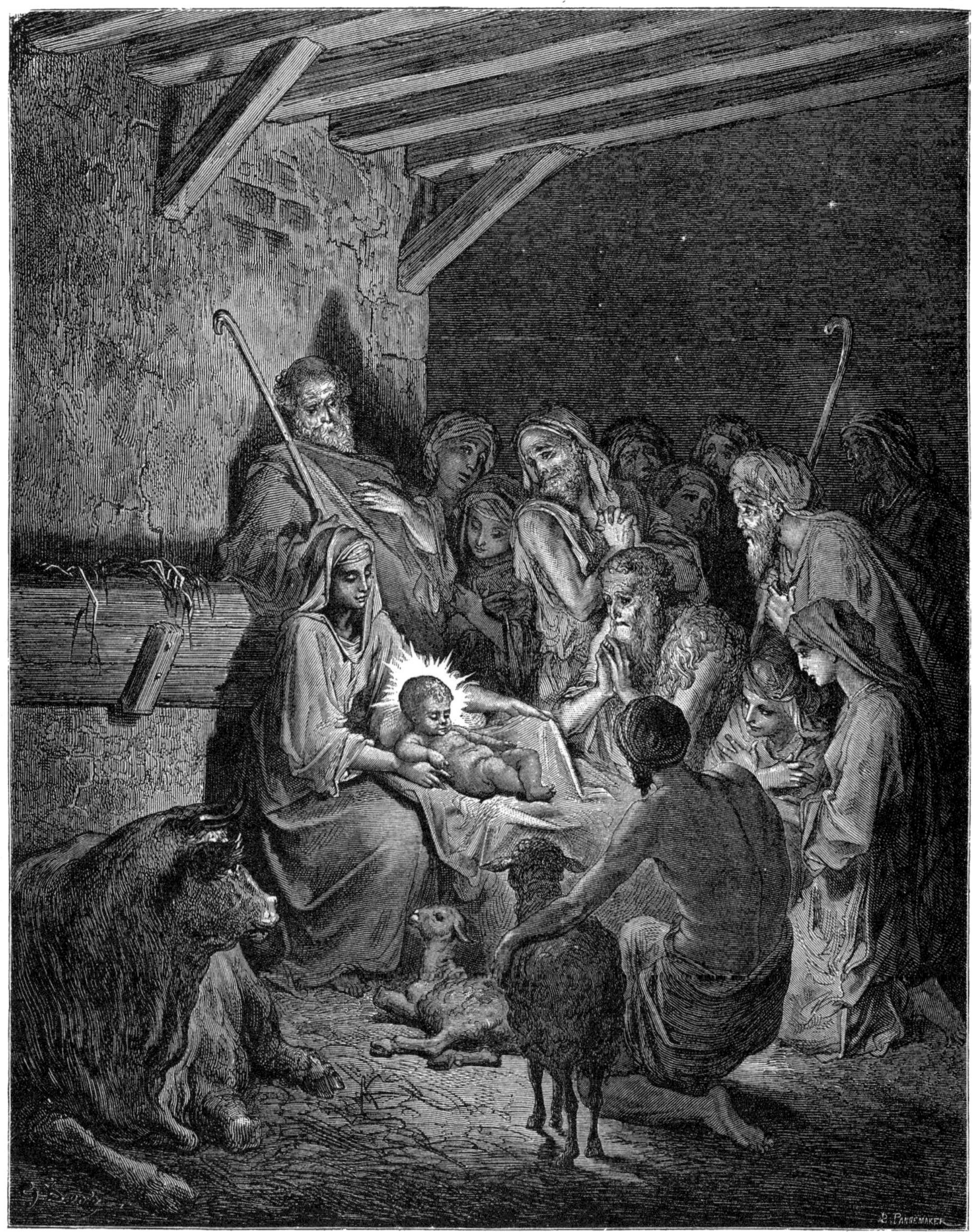

The Nativity, 1866

Plate 35, Volume 2, *La Sainte Bible*: Luke 2:16, Second French Edition

• Engraver: Stéphane Pannemaker (1847–1930)

Idyllic scene of shepherds visiting the Holy Family. This 1866 second edition corrected an error in the 1865 first edition, where Doré showed a burning oil lamp right next to the baby Jesus. This very popular scene was the first Doré engraving carved by Stéphane Pannemaker (son of A.F. Pannemaker) at the age of 19.

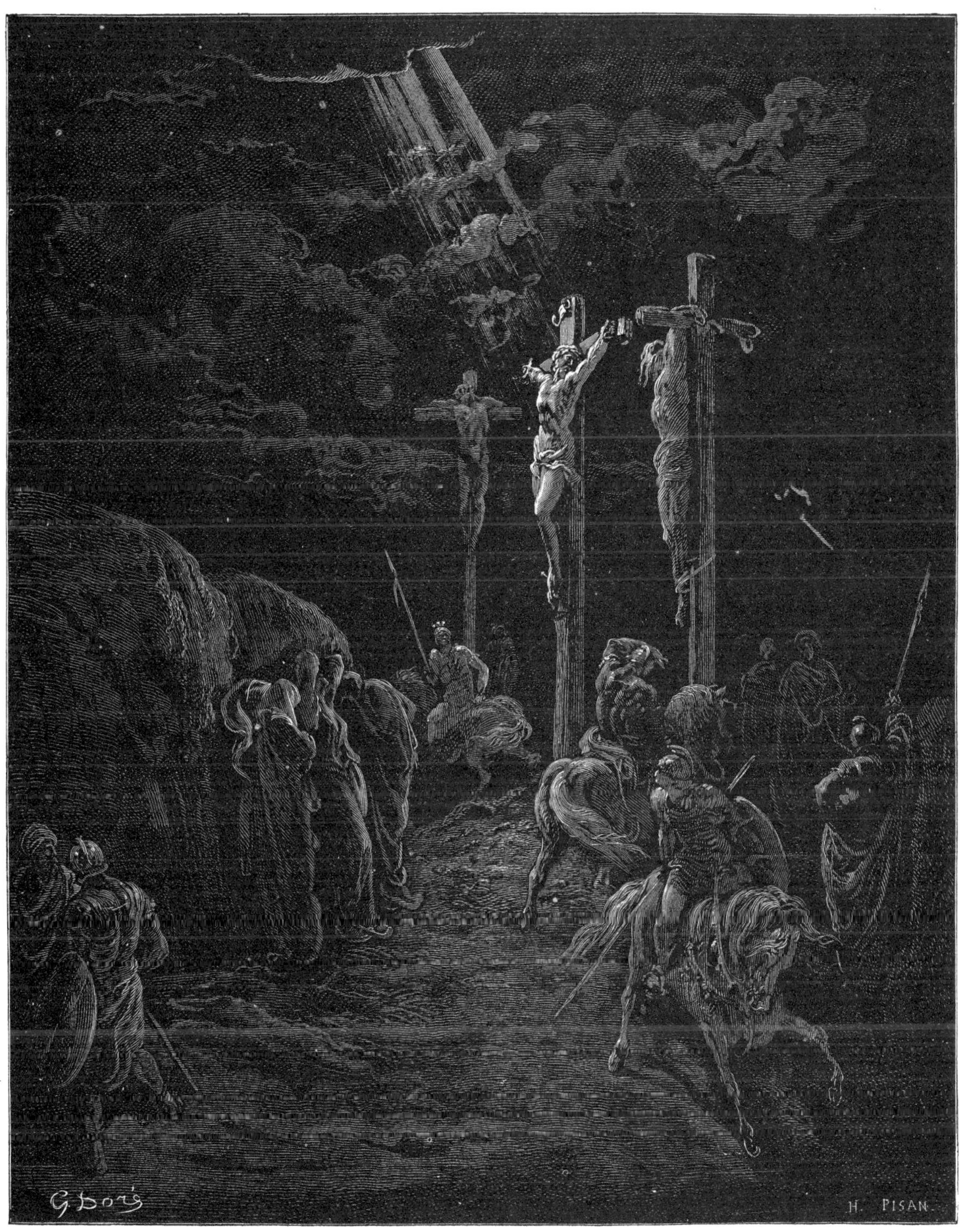

The Crucifixion, 1865

Plate 86, Volume 2, *La Sainte Bible*: Luke 23:34, First French Edition
• Engraver: Heliodore Pisan (1822–1900)

Mystical scene of light rays from Heaven shining through a tiny slit in the blackening clouds and directly on to the crucified Christ. This Doré image can be seen on the cover of many music albums (e.g. gospel music, classical music and rock music).

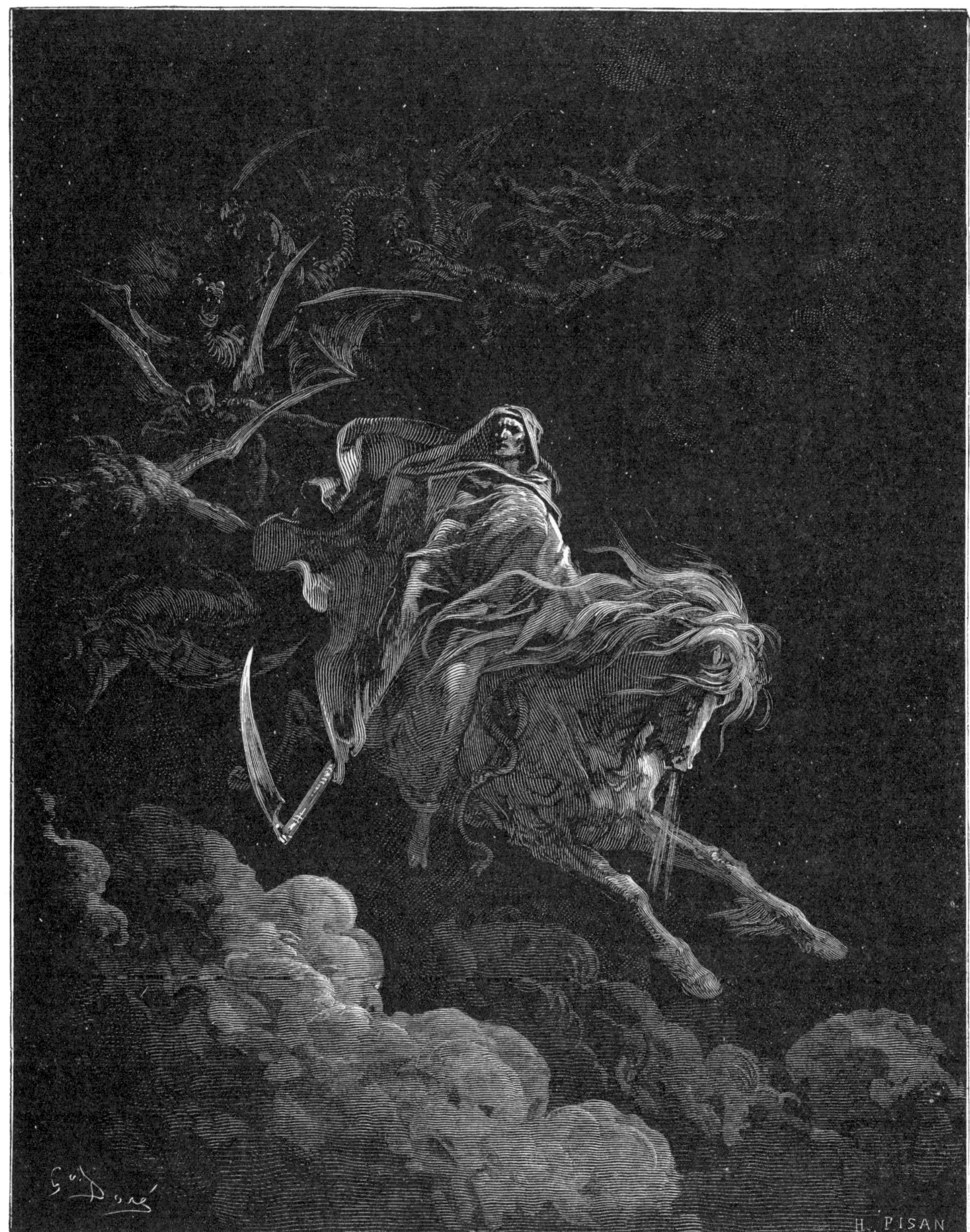

Death on a Pale Horse, 1865

Plate 106, Volume 2, *La Sainte Bible*: Revelation 6:8, First French Edition

• Engraver: Heliodore Pisan (1822–1900)

Many artists have portrayed the Four Horsemen of the Apocalypse: Anarchy (or War), Famine, Conquest and Death. Doré depicts an evil skeleton on a wild horse with a scythe, trailed by demons, which has been borrowed for dozens of album covers and posters – even the cover of the 2015 comic book *Deadpool* No. 22.

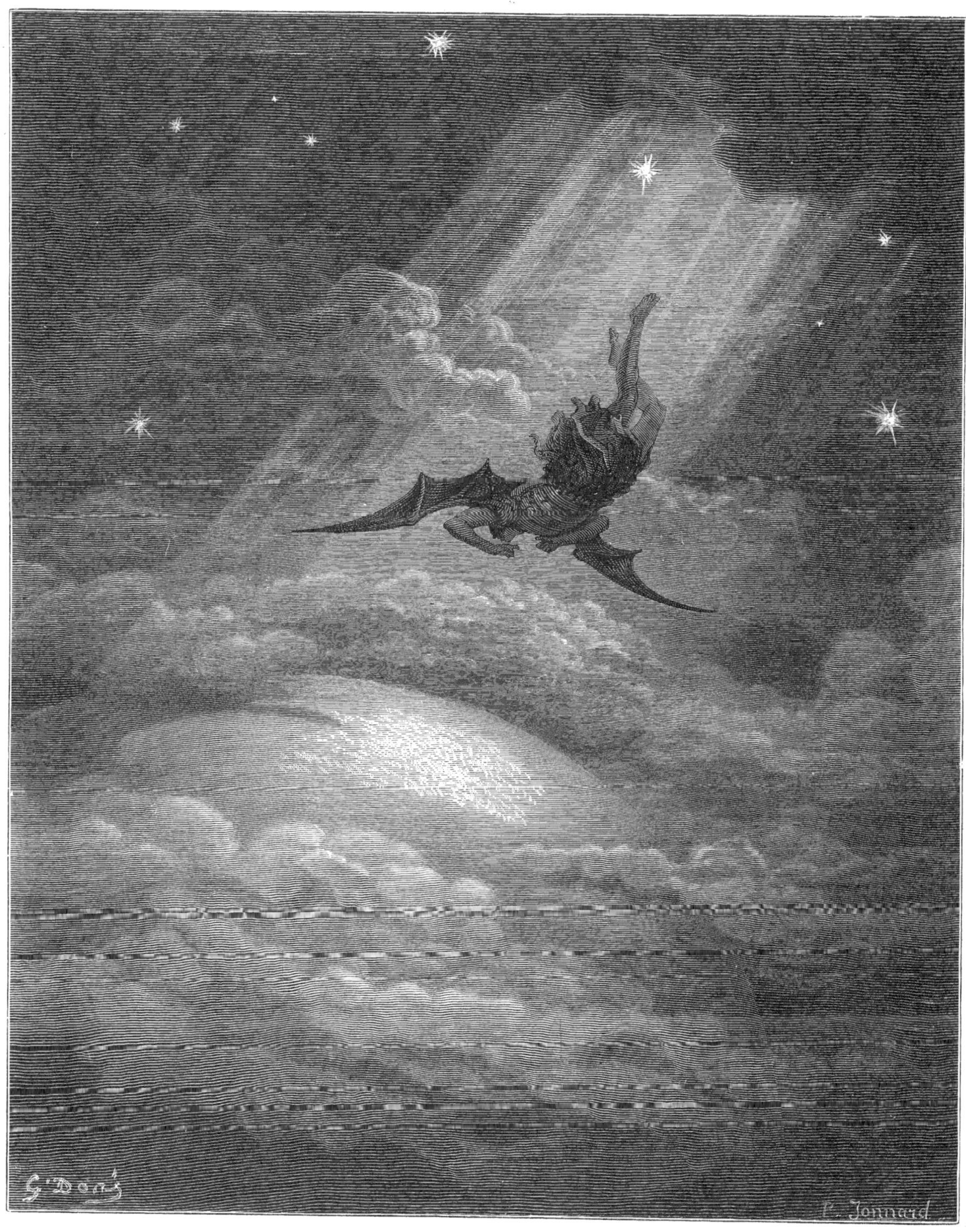

Satan Falling to Earth, 1866
Plate 12, *Paradise Lost*, John Milton
• Engraver: Paul Jonnard (1840–1902)

'I saw Satan as lightning fall from heaven.' (Luke 10:18) Doré did so many outer-space images that people believe he existed in a different dimension or century. This image, influenced by Delacroix's lithograph for *Faust*, has been borrowed in many popular culture genres – even on a poster for Satan worshippers.

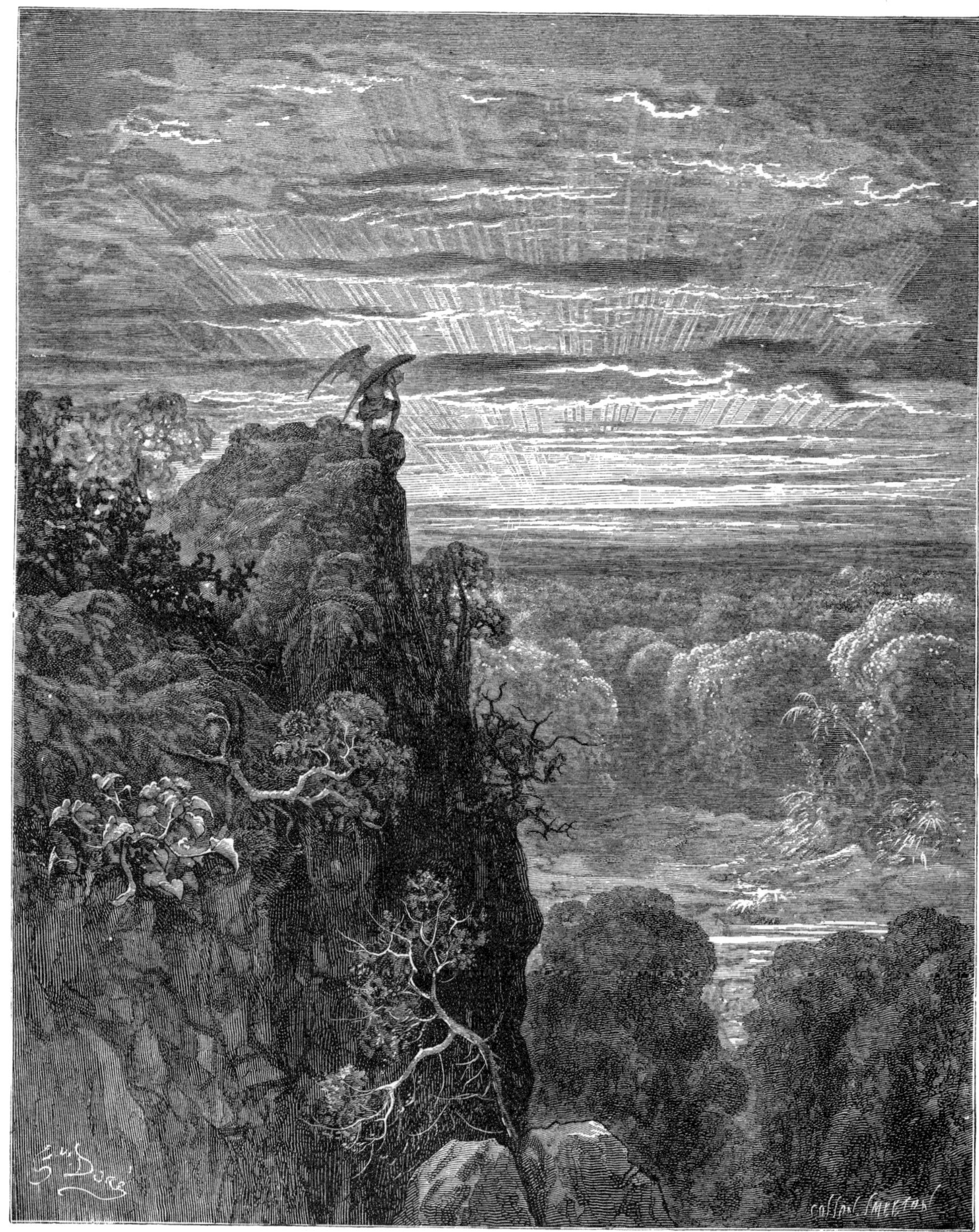

Satan Overlooking Paradise, 1866

Plate 14, *Paradise Lost*, John Milton • Engravers: two British engravers, dates unknown (poss. J. Cosson, J. Burn-Smeeton)

'Thou wast in Eden, the garden of God.' (Ezekiel 28:13) After being cast down to Earth, Satan beholds the beauty of the Creation. Also redrawn for many 1970s black-light posters, this was a major influence on the 1933 *King Kong* jungle scenes.

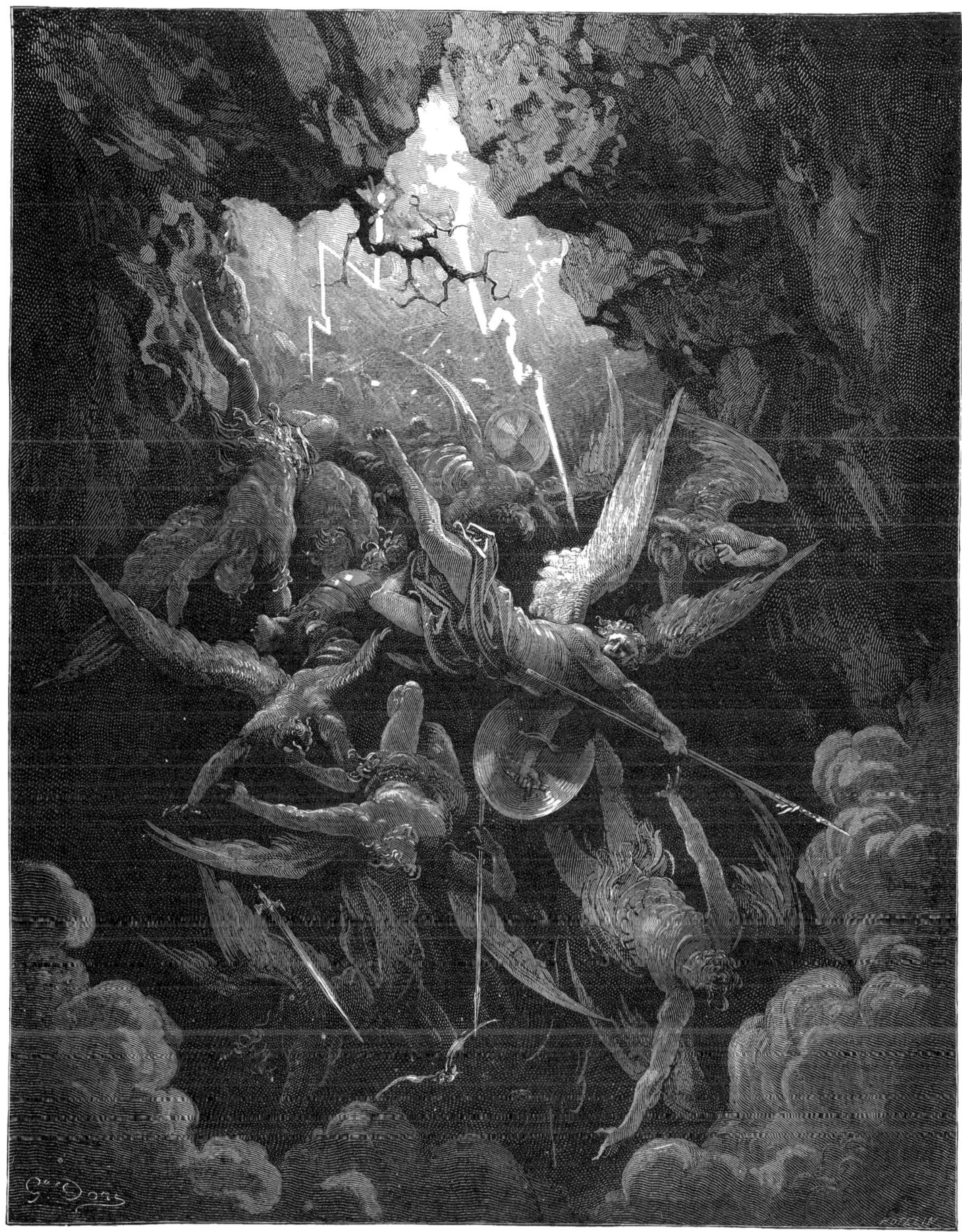

Hell Received Them, 1866

Plate 29, *Paradise Lost*, John Milton • Engraver: L.E. Hotelin (1821–94)

The earth opens up and, with a flash of lightning, the fallen angels are cast into Hell. This is typical of Doré's Milton chaotic angelic conflict scenes. Many reviewers noted the influence of this image on a poster for the 2017 movie *Alien Covenant*.

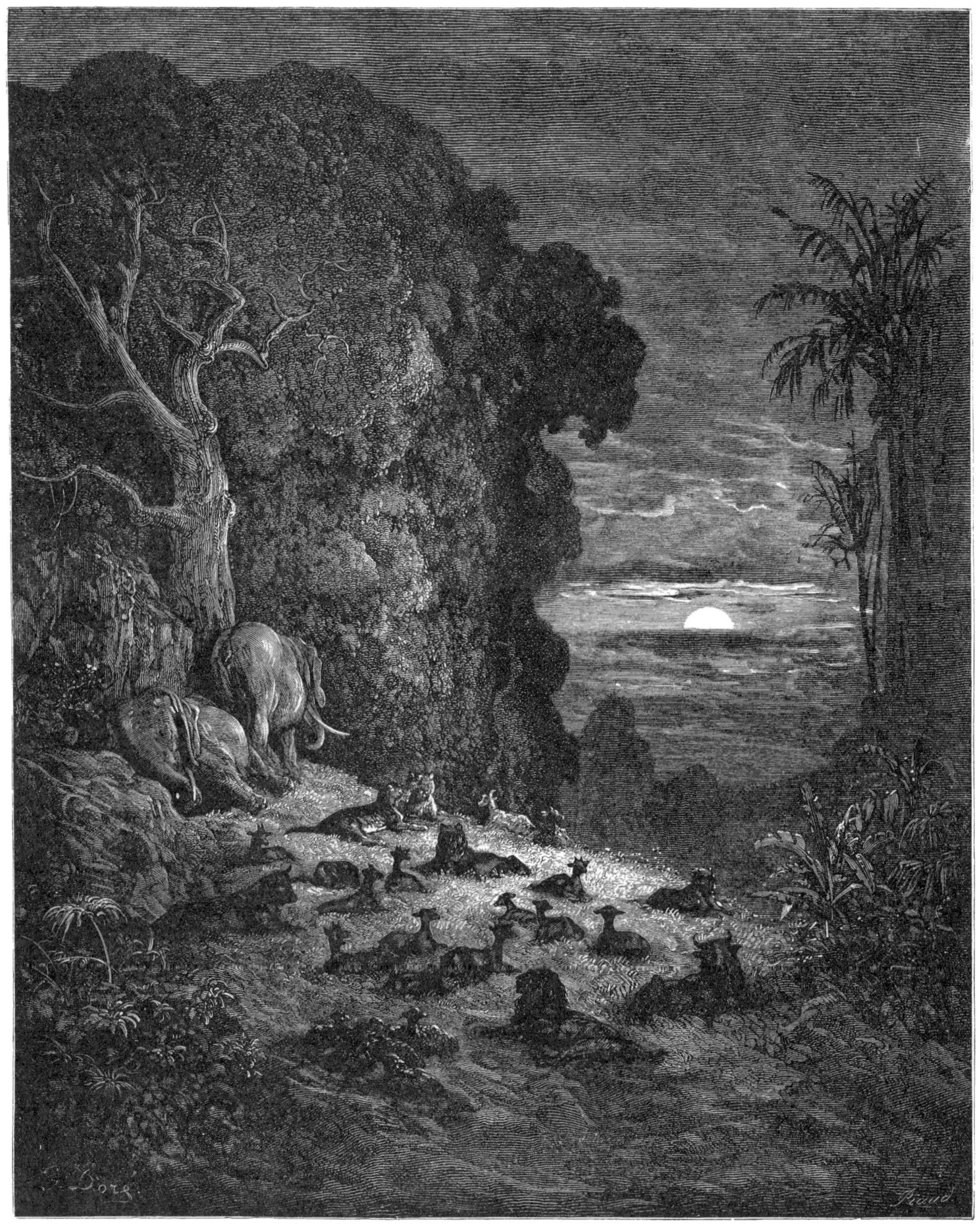

On the Seventh Day God Rested, 1866
Plate 34, *Paradise Lost*, John Milton
• Engraver: Antoine Piaud (*fl.* 1837–1866)

Showing all the animals resting serenely in the setting sun, this image stands in stark contrast to all of the violent, turbulent scenes in Doré's Milton. Few artists have attempted to depict this scene, showing Doré's artistic range.

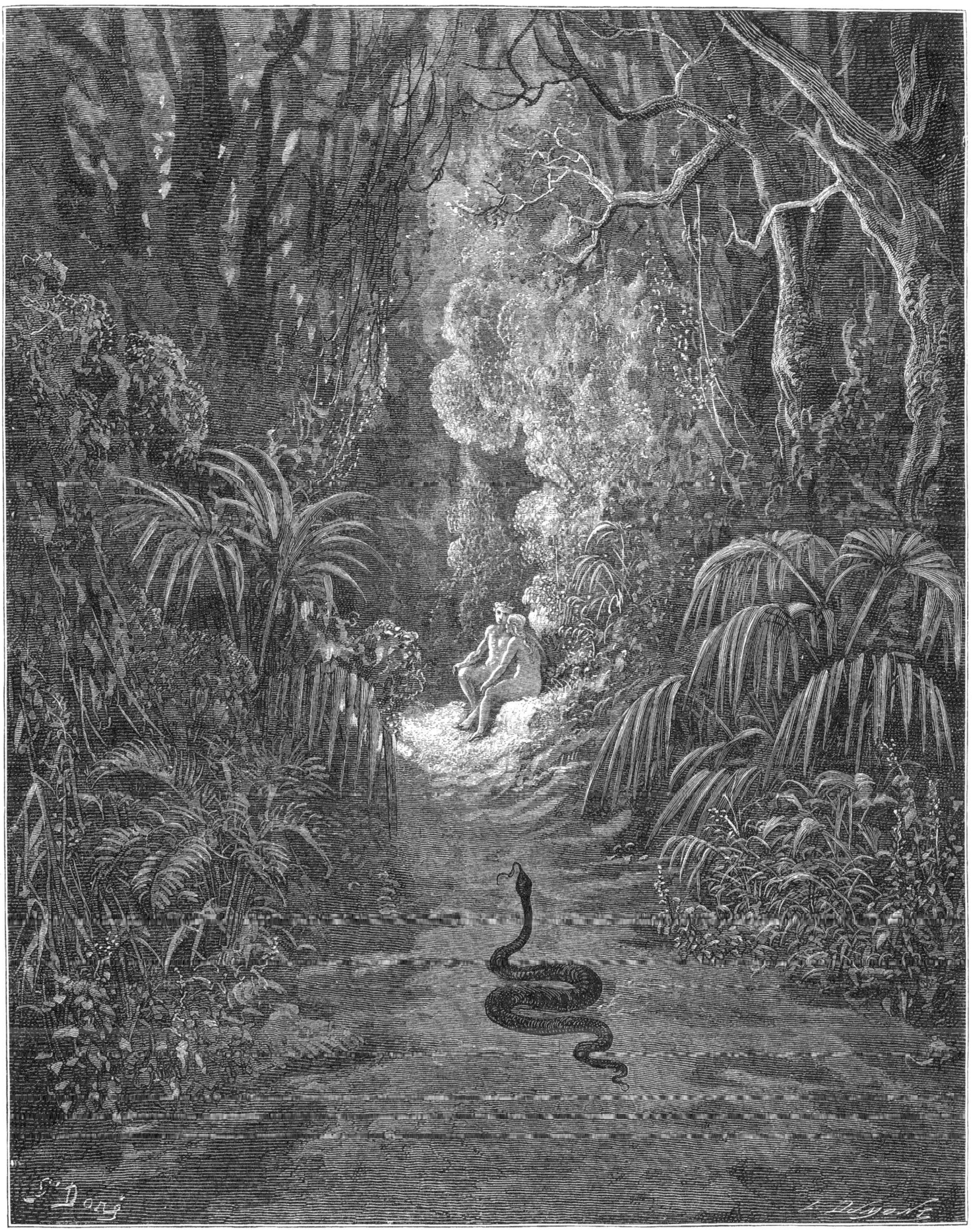

Serpent Approaching Adam and Eve, 1866
Plate 39, *Paradise Lost*, John Milton
• Engraver: Louis Dumont (*c.* 1822–88)

The fiendish serpent slithers in the darkness towards an unsuspecting Adam and Eve – another scene that few artists have ever attempted, especially from the snake's perspective. Harryhausen discussed the influence of this scene on Merian Cooper's *King Kong* (1933).

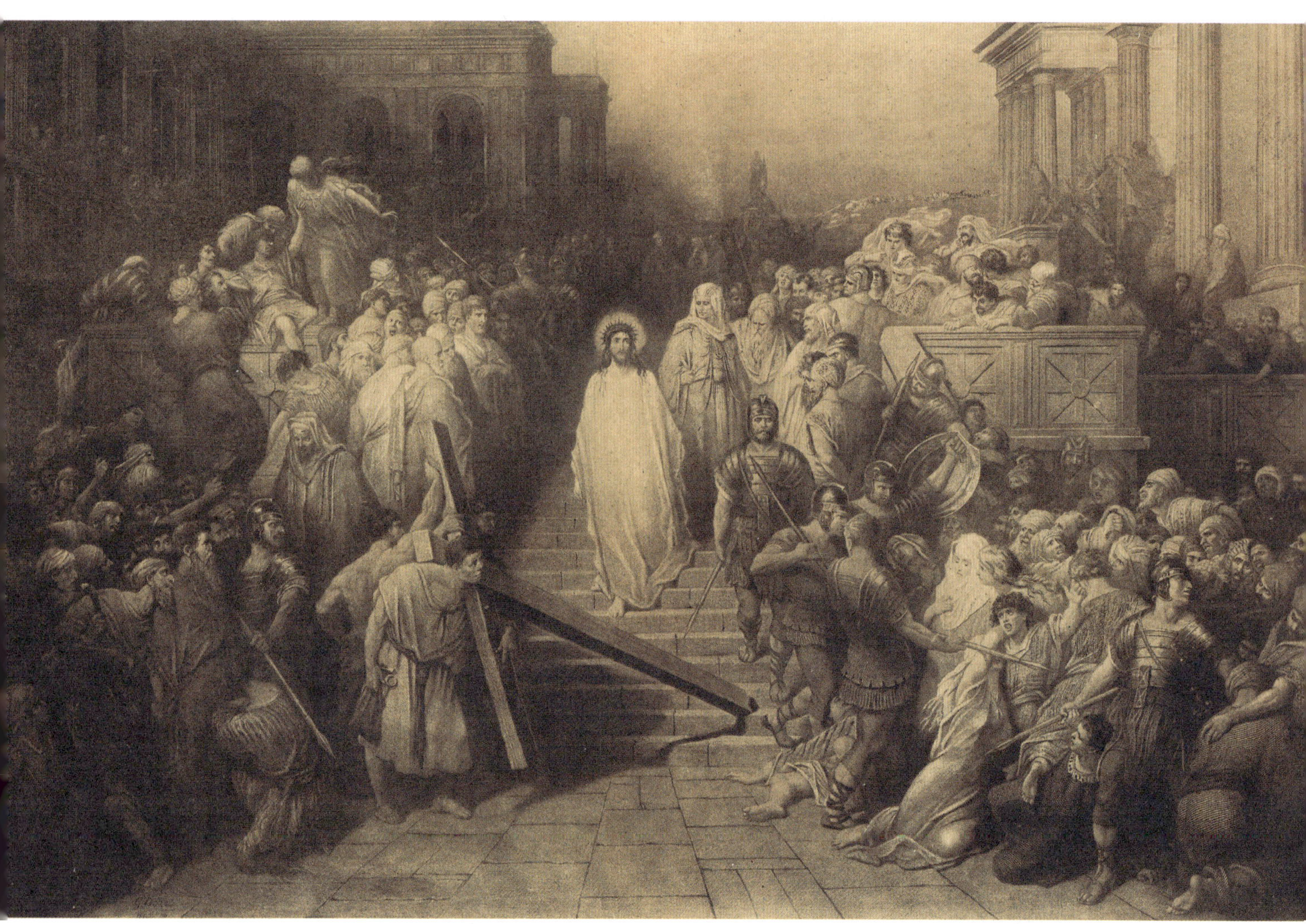

Christ Leaving the Praetorium, 1877
Steel engraving, 55.8 x 83.8 cm (22 x 33 in), of oil painting • Engraver: Herbert Bourne (1826–1907); original painting 6 x 9 m (20 x 30 ft), 1872

Jesus leaves the high priests in the judgment hall, headed for Calvary through the howling mob. This was Doré's most famous painting, reprinted worldwide, of which there are three versions in museums in France and in the US. This image is from the 1896 Chicago Doré Gallery illustrated catalogue.

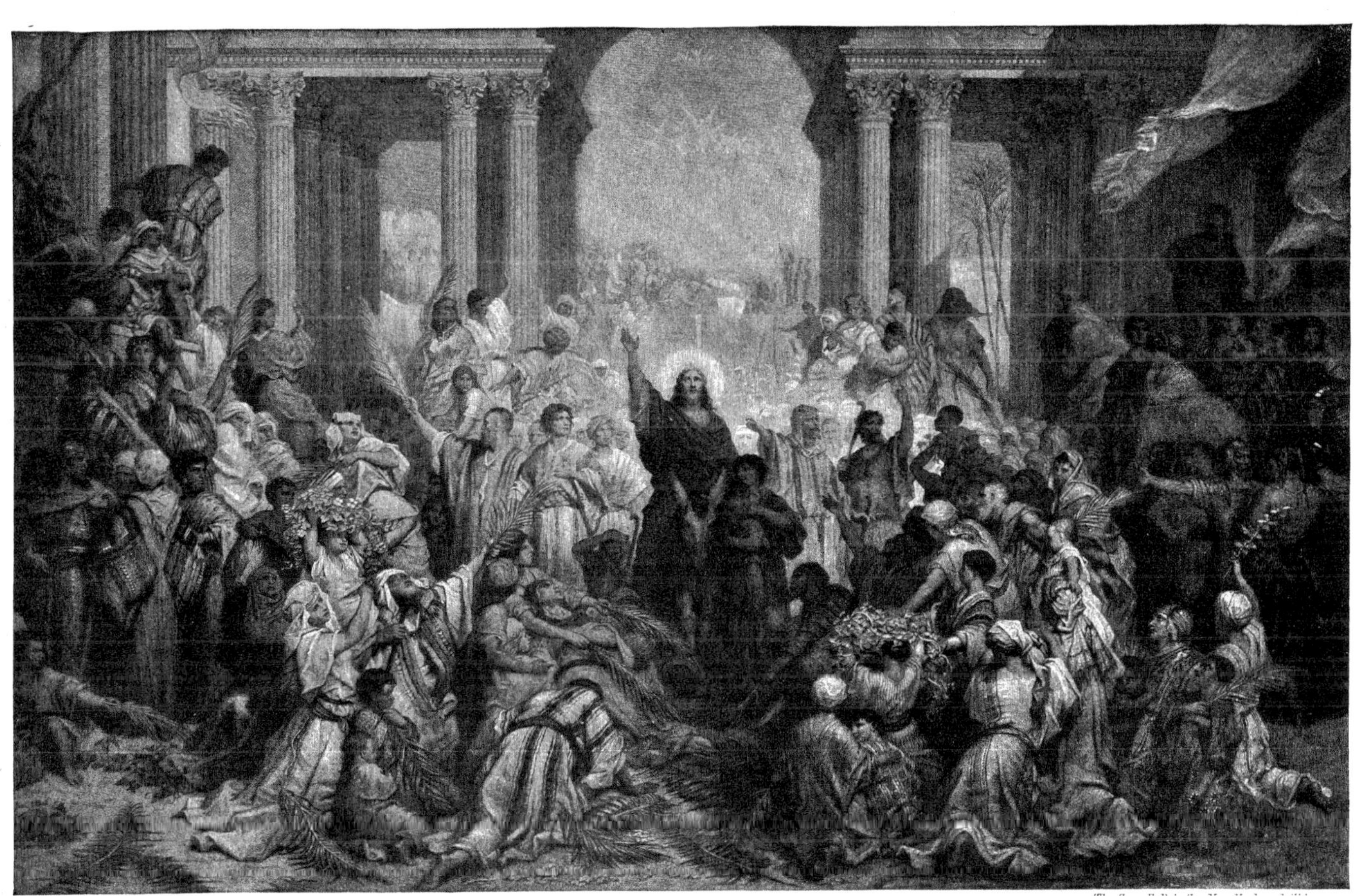

The Triumphal Entry, 1882
Steel engraving, 55.8 x 83.8 cm (22 x 33 in), of oil painting • Engraver: Alphonse François (1814–88); original painting, 6 x 9 m (20 x 30 ft), 1876

A vast panorama of worshippers spreading robes and palm leaves for the Messiah, in a theatrical scene worthy of Cecil B. DeMille (1881–1959). There is only one version of this painting; it was sold in a 1947 New York auction and its location is unknown. This image is from the 1896 Chicago Doré Gallery illustrated catalogue.

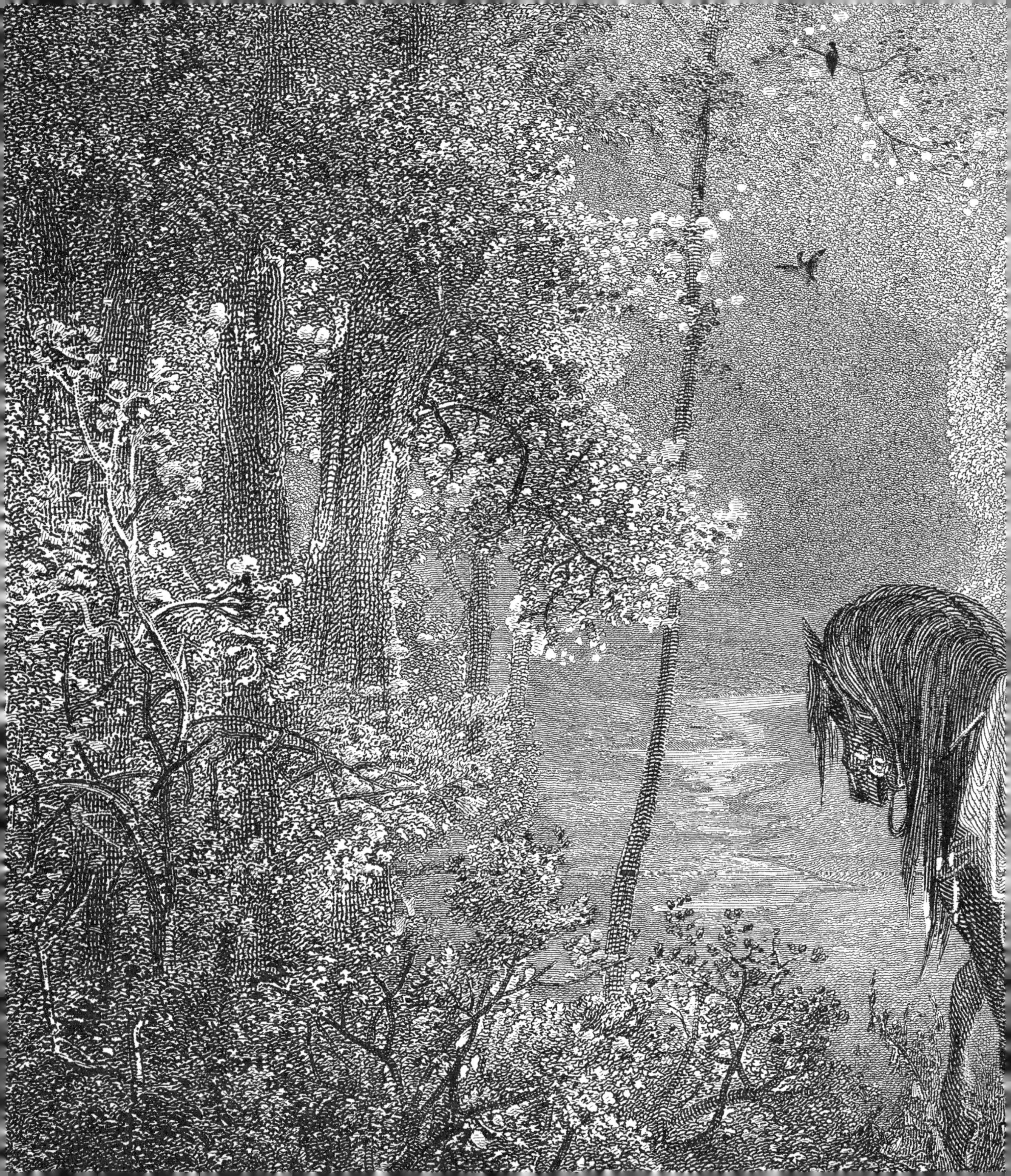

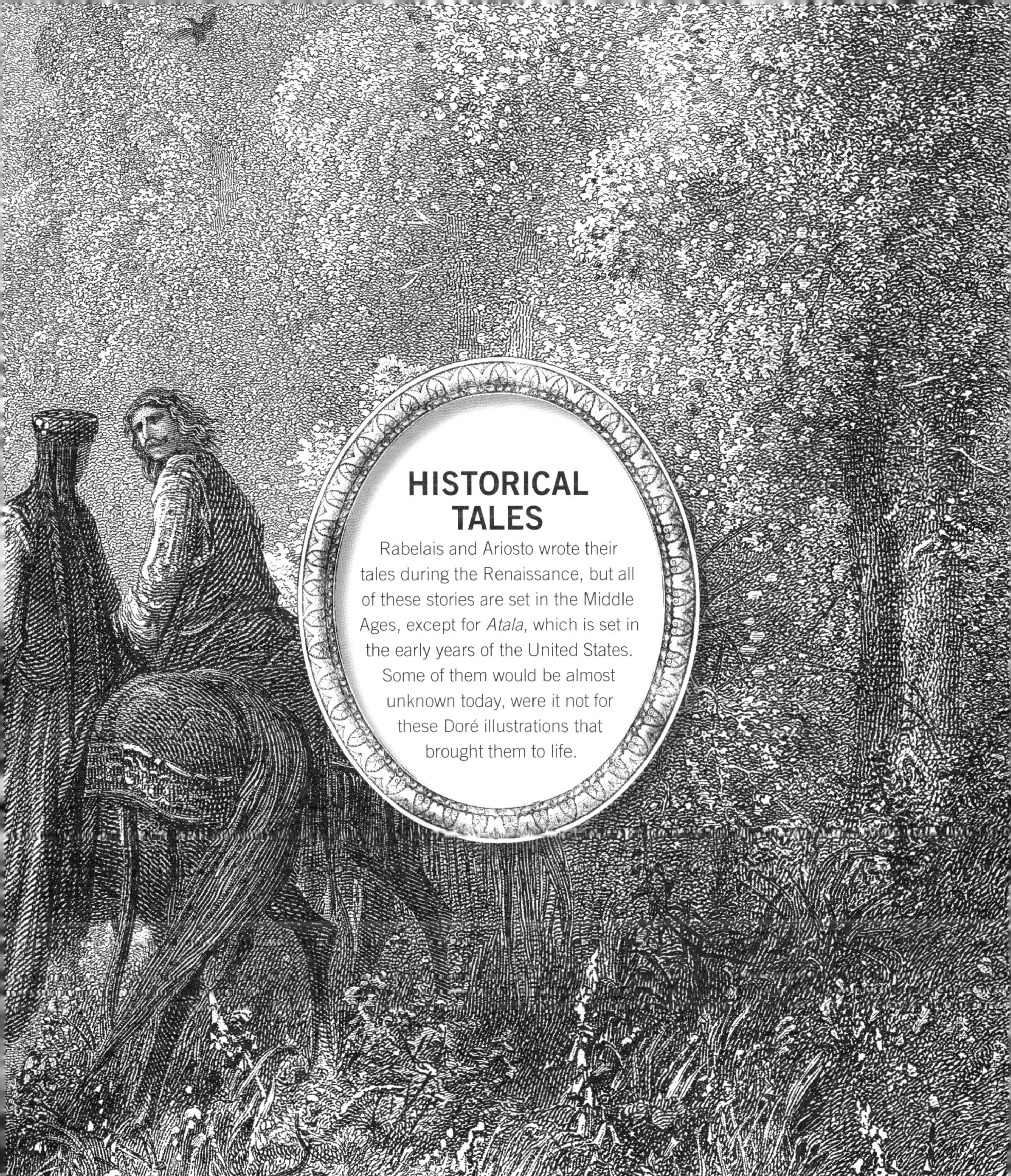

HISTORICAL TALES

Rabelais and Ariosto wrote their tales during the Renaissance, but all of these stories are set in the Middle Ages, except for *Atala*, which is set in the early years of the United States. Some of them would be almost unknown today, were it not for these Doré illustrations that brought them to life.

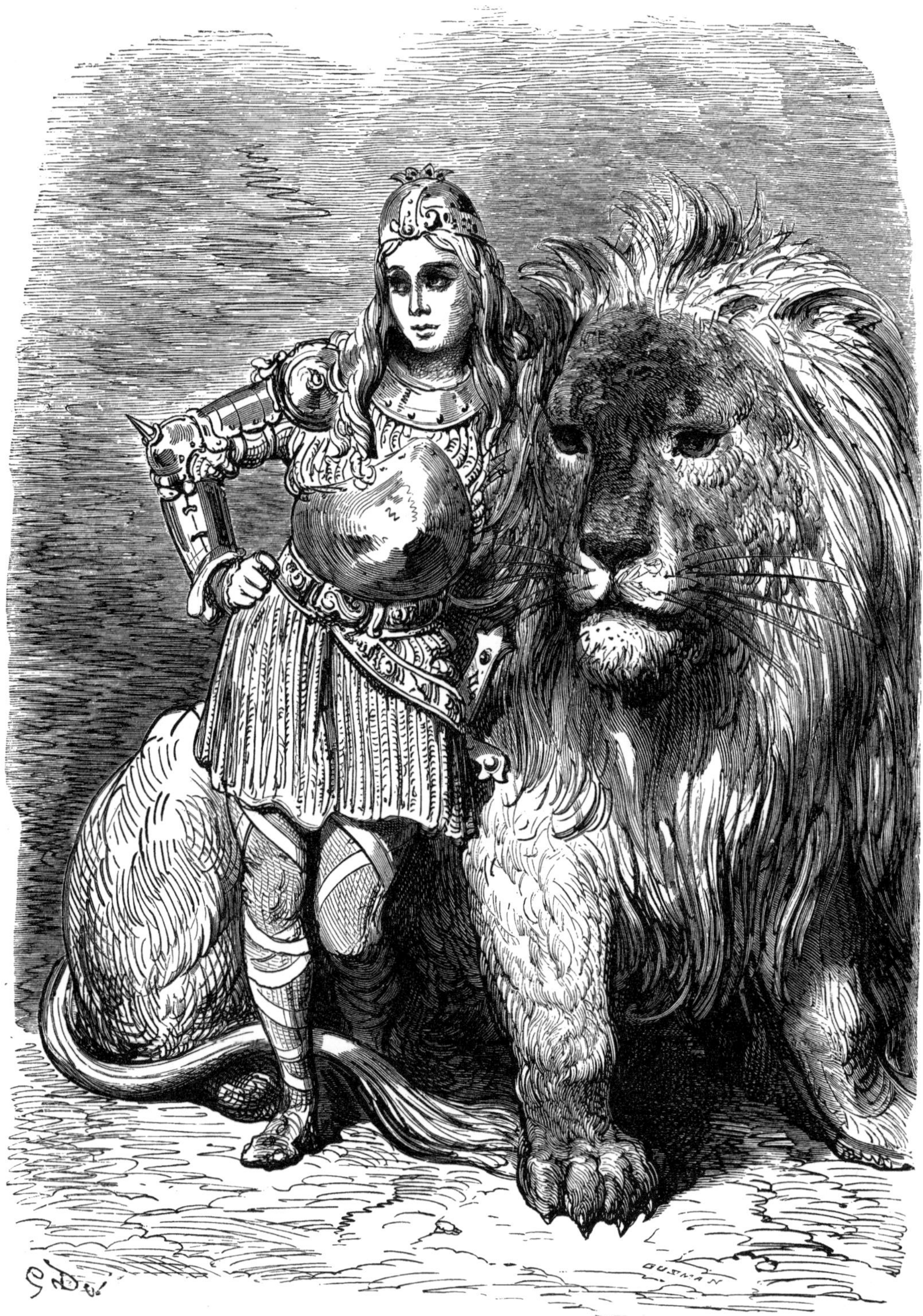

Mitaine and Oghris, 1863
Frontispiece, *La Légende de Croque-Mitaine*, Ernest L'Epine
• Engraver: Adolphe Gusmand (1821–1905)

The armour-clad warrior woman Mitaine and her giant pet lion Oghris, in a French tale set in the times of Charlemagne. This is one of the earliest depictions of a warrior woman, which was a major inspiration to artists like Frank Frazetta a century later.

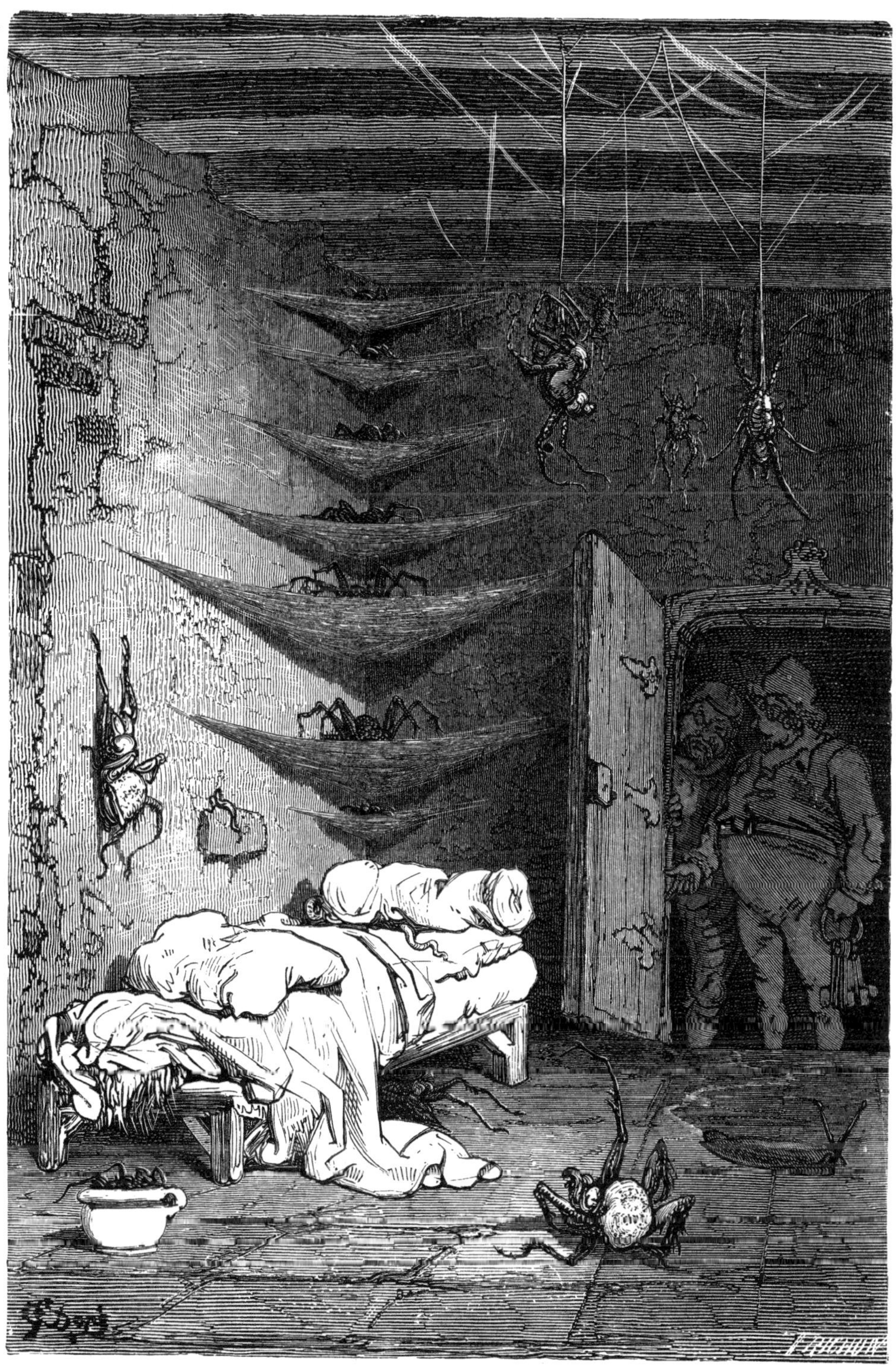

Spare Room at the Inn, 1863

Page 179, *La Légende de Croque-Mitaine*, Ernest L'Epine
• Engraver: A.J.F. Trichon (1814–98)

A brave knight seeking a room at the inn is told there is only one left, which happens to be filled with spiders the size of cats. The look on his face as he peers into the room is priceless; this is one of the best examples of Doré's dark humour.

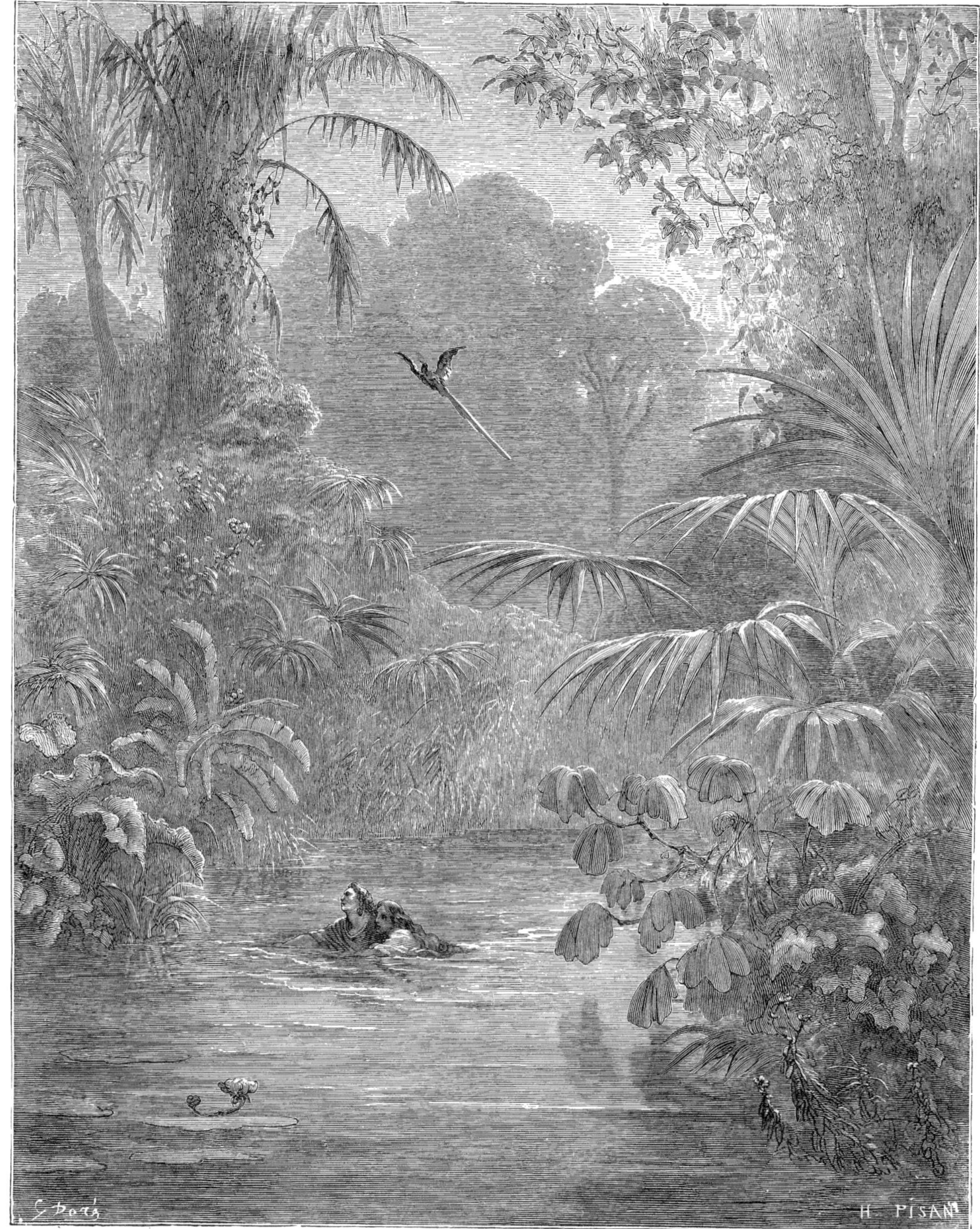

Chactas and Atala Swim Across a Stream, 1863

Plate 3, *Atala*, François-René de Chateaubriand

• Engraver: Heliodore Pisan (1822–1900)

In this scene, a Native American couple are swimming across the stream, fleeing from their captors. This novella is told to Chateaubriand by the elderly Chactas, as he recalls distant memories of his romance with the young maiden Atala. It bears similarities to Shakespeare's *Romeo and Juliet*.

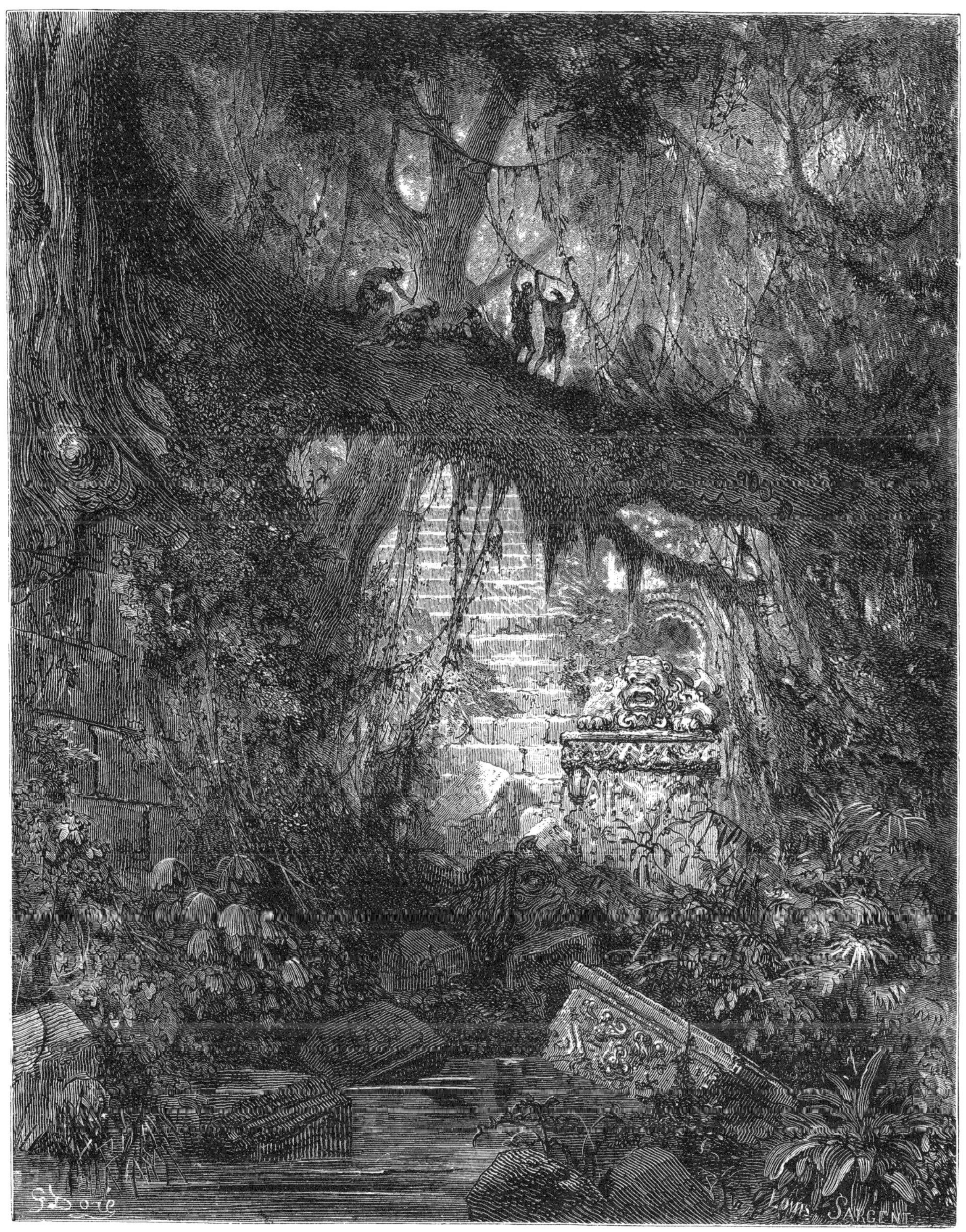

The Log Bridge, 1863

Plate 11, *Atala*, François-René de Chateaubriand

• Engraver: Louis Sargent (1830–unknown)

Native Americans cross a natural log bridge in a dense forest, amidst ruins of unknown origin. This was the primary source for the log bridge in *King Kong* (1933), and this device was borrowed for a dozen other major films, such as *Snow White* (1937).

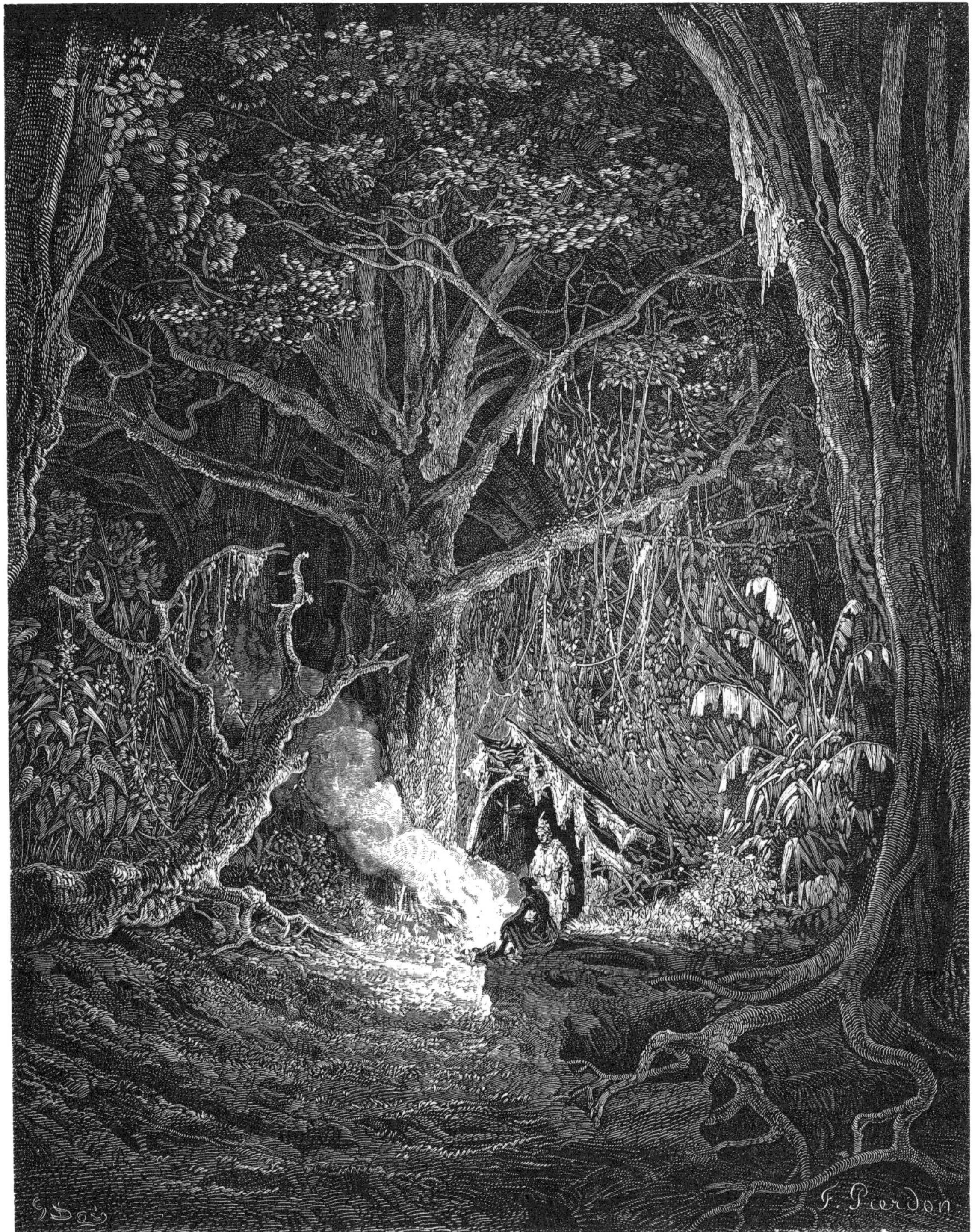

The Lean-to, 1863

Plate 14, *Atala*, François-René de Chateaubriand

• Engraver: François Pierdon (1821–1904)

Chactas and Atala build a tent and a campfire to rest for the night. Amazingly, every detail you see is white-on-black, which became one of Doré's specialities. Scenic views like this showed Doré's artistic range which so amazed writers.

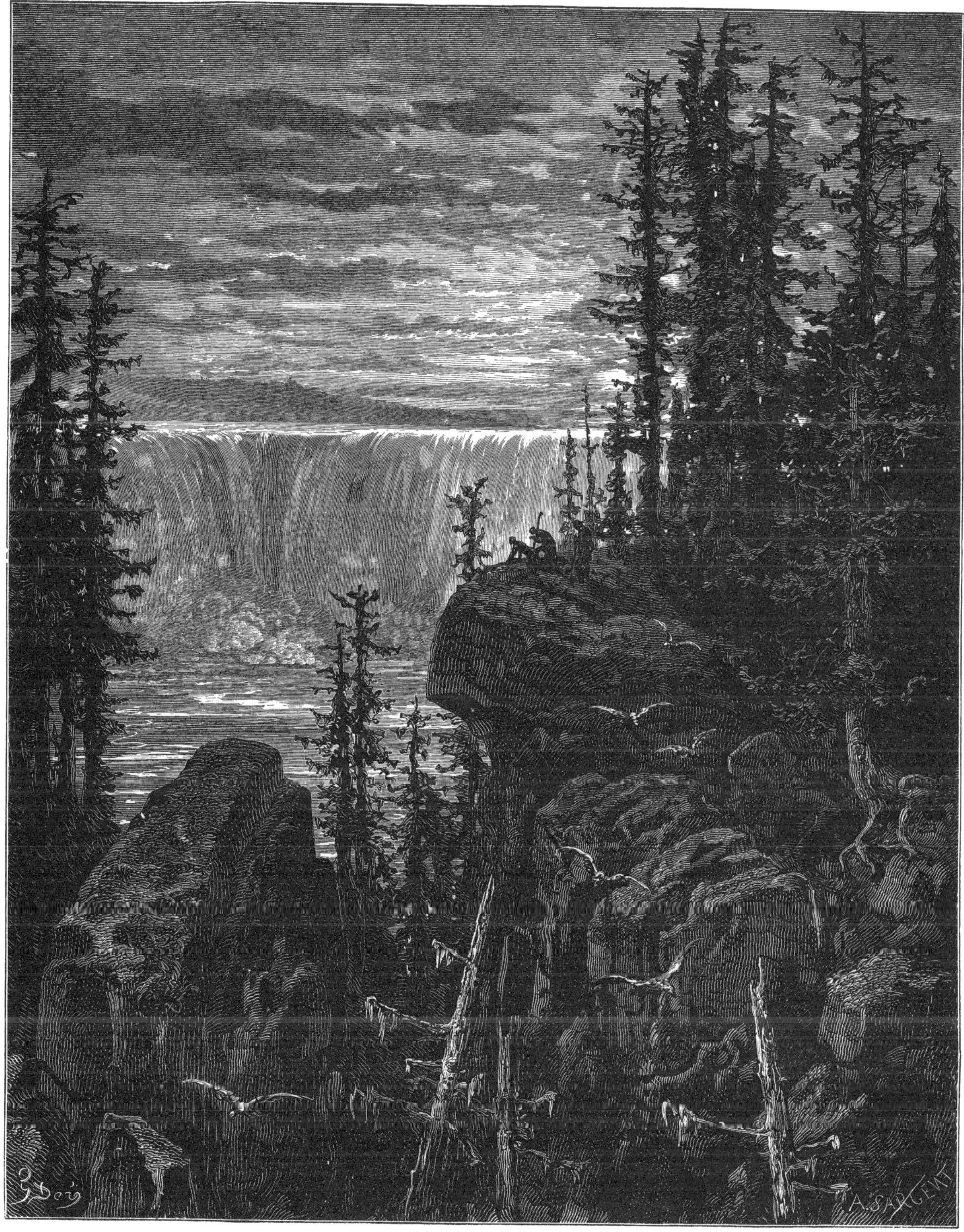

Niagara Falls, 1863

Plate 23, *Atala*, François-René de Chateaubriand

• Engraver: Alfred Sargent (1828–unknown)

Chactas and his party can be seen in the centre as they reach 'the border of the cataract, which announced itself with frightful roarings'. In 1801, Chateaubriand described the mystical fascination of Niagara Falls to French readers.

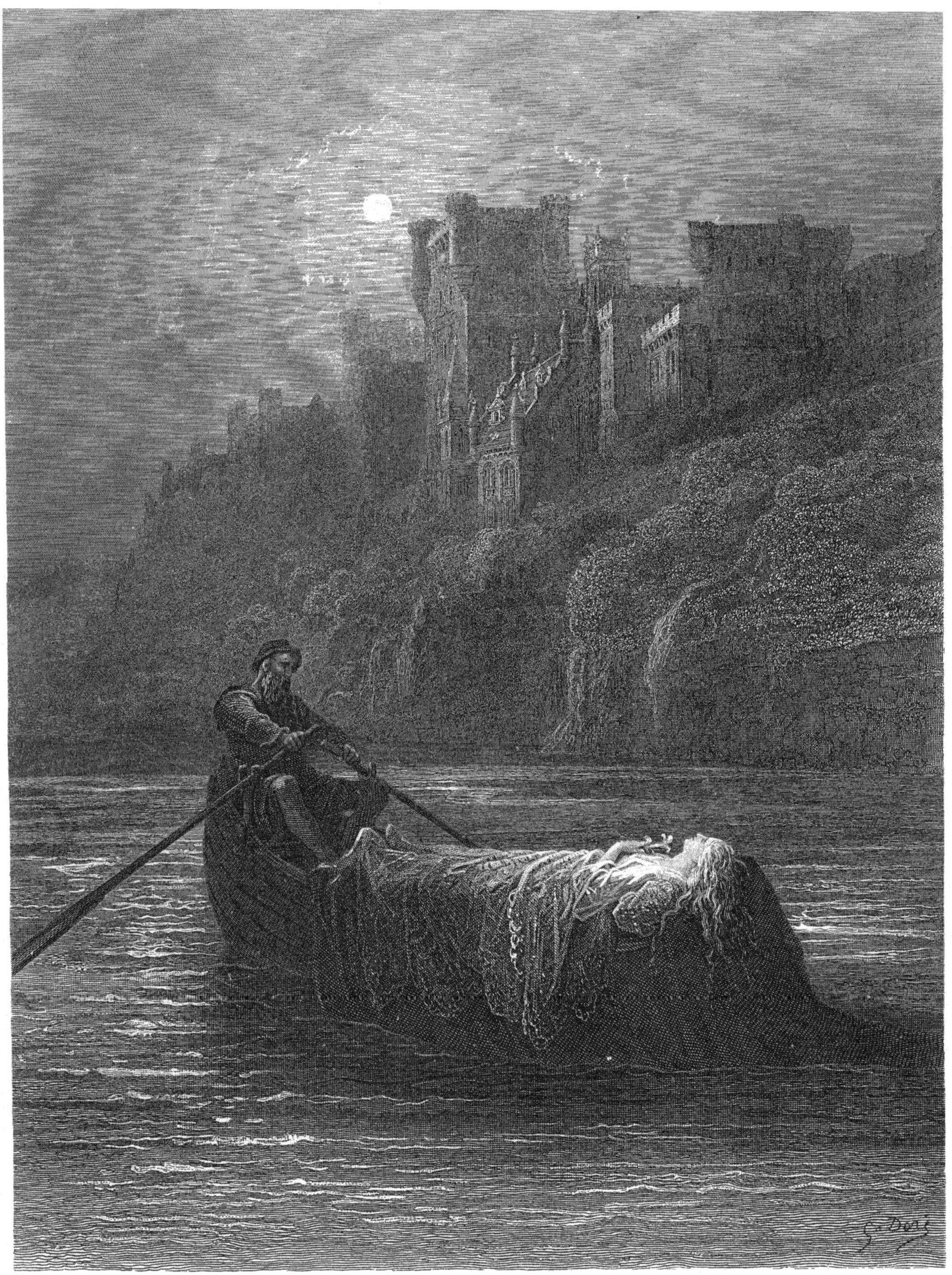

Elaine's Body on a Barge, 1866

Plate 7, *Idylls of the King: Elaine*, Alfred Tennyson

• Engraver: John H. Baker (*c.* 1829–72), steel engraving

The body of Elaine, the Lily Maid of Astolat, floats down the river to Camelot on a barge after her love for Lancelot killed her. This has always been the most popular of Doré's steel engravings for Tennyson, and has been made into many paintings.

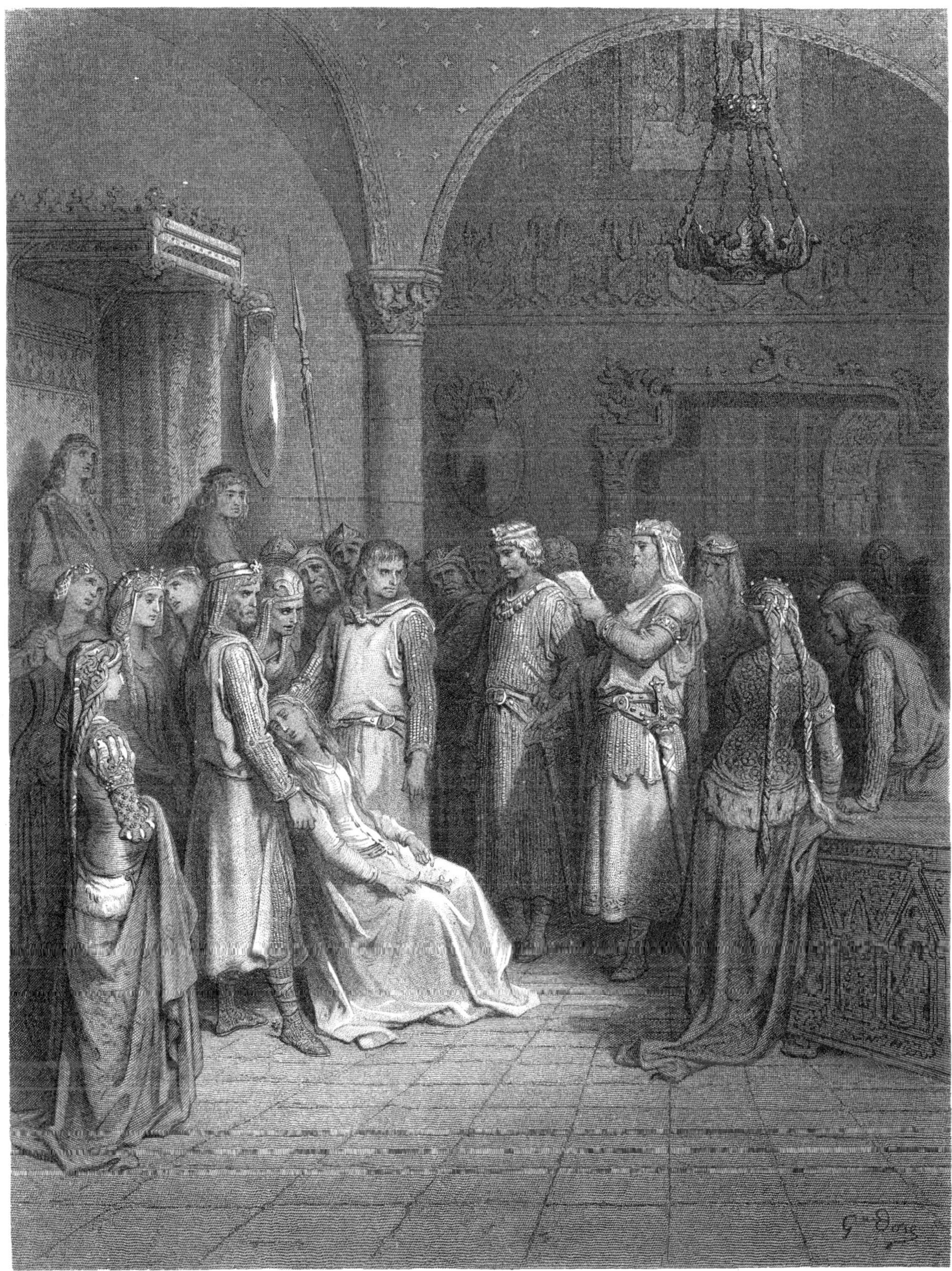

Elaine's Body on a Chair, 1866

Plate 8, *Idylls of the King: Elaine*, Alfred Tennyson
• Engraver: William Holl (1807–71), steel engraving

King Arthur reads Elaine's letter to Lancelot in the hall at Camelot. This was one of Doré biggest errors, since he 'forgot' that Elaine was dead and depicted her corpse seated on a chair, as though she had fainted. It is also the image Tennyson said he hated.

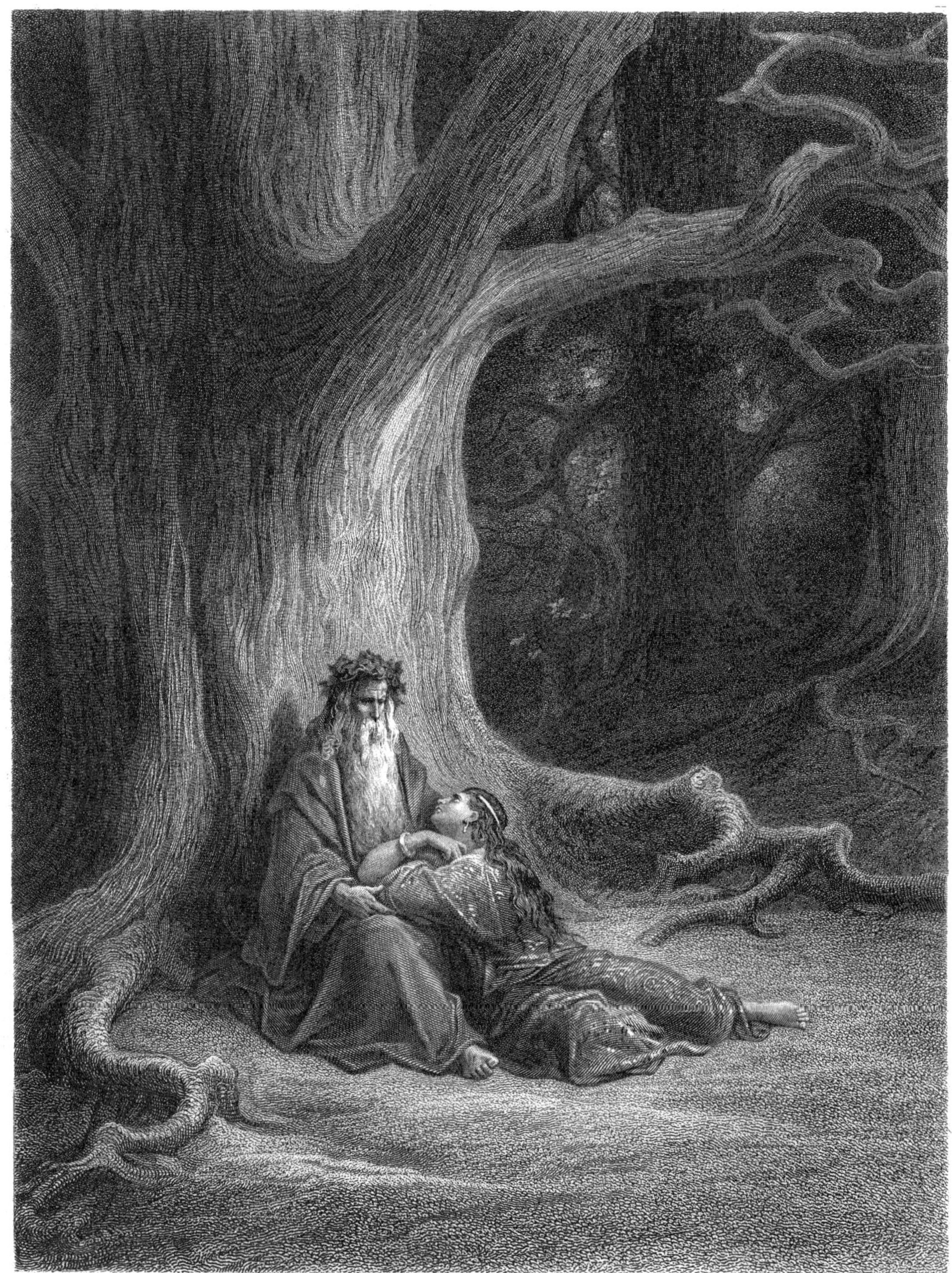

Merlin and Vivien Repose Under Tree, 1867

Plate 1, *Idylls of the King: Vivien*, Alfred Tennyson

• Engraver: William Ridgway (*fl.* 1855–85), steel engraving

This peaceful scene of a man and a woman lounging under a beautiful tree disguises the conflict between the wizard Merlin and the enchantress Vivien. Eventually, the young lover would destroy the older wizard through a magical charm.

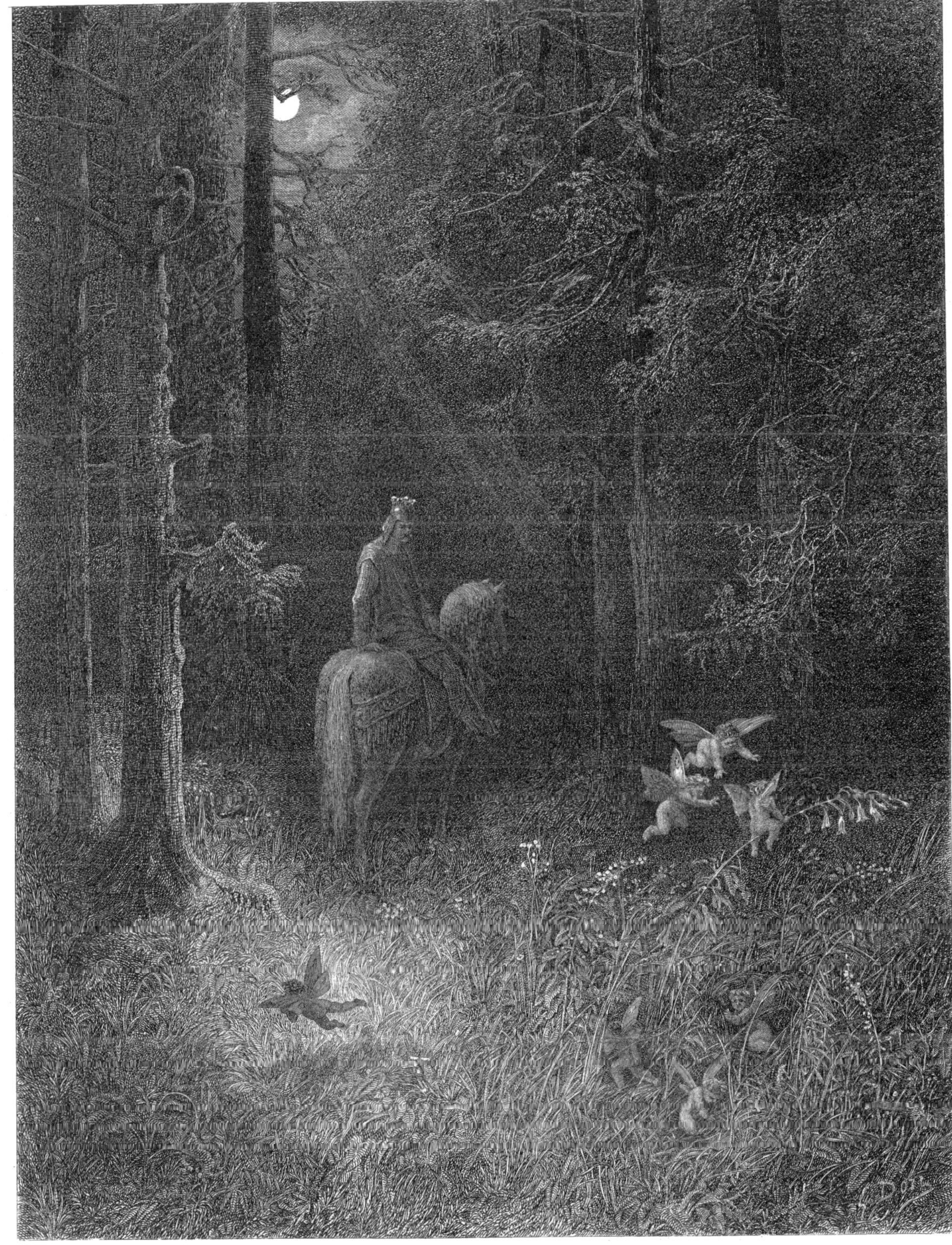

The Joyous Sprites, 1867

Plate 5, *Idylls of the King: Guinevere*, Alfred Tennyson

• Engraver: G.C. Finden (1811–85), steel engraving

A mystical scene of a knight pausing in the forest in the moonlight, with seven tiny winged creatures fluttering about in the bushes, which today we would call spirits or fairies. Doré was constantly intertwining the physical with the mystical.

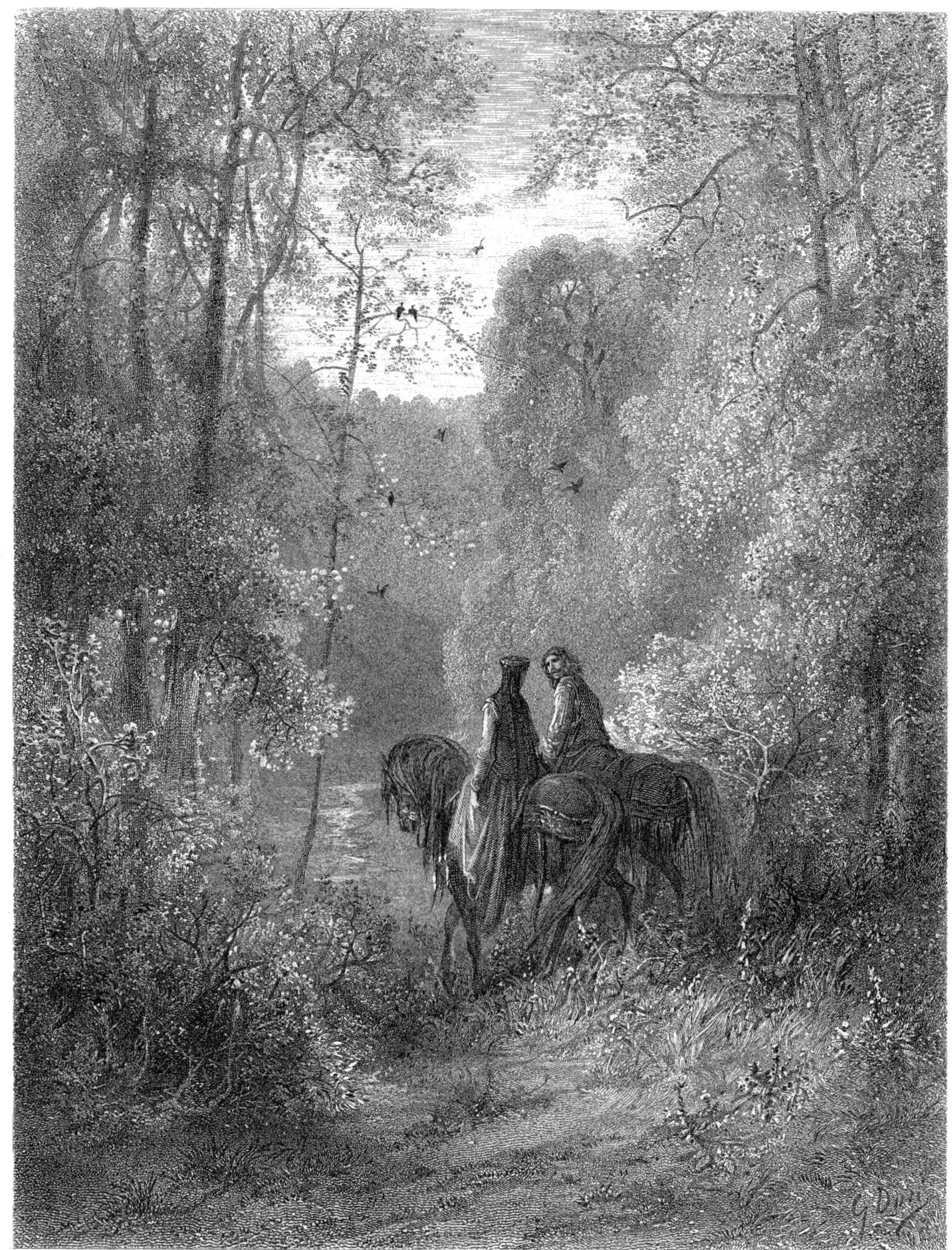

Lancelot and Guinevere, 1867

Plate 8, *Idylls of the King: Guinevere*, Alfred Tennyson

• Engraver: E.P. Brandard (1819–98), steel engraving

What could be more serene than a knight and a lady riding in the meadow? The original scene title was 'The Dawn of Love' – an illicit love that would eventually destroy Camelot. The fabulous artistic effects for the foliage were created by the engraver.

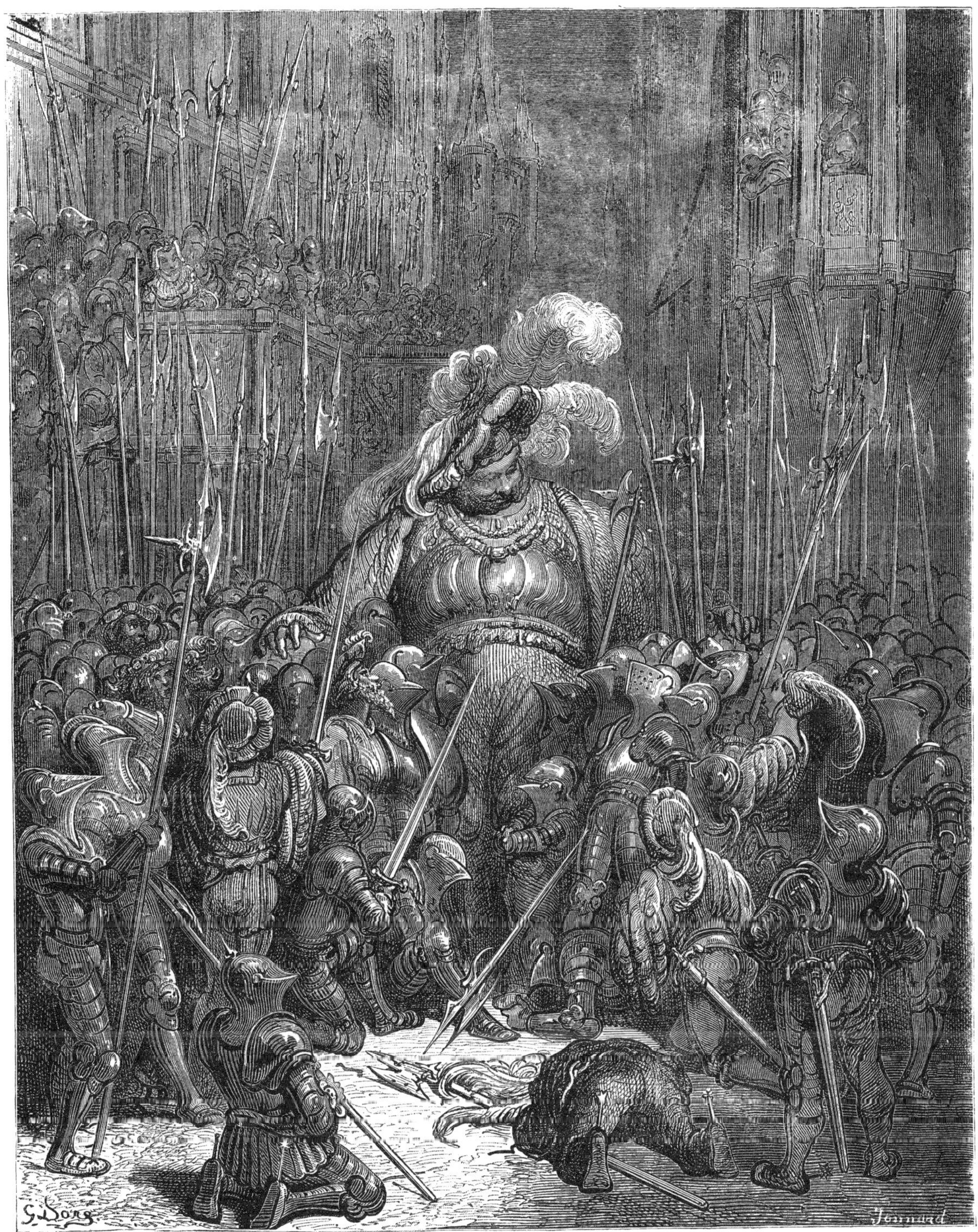

Gargantua and Soldiers, 1873

Book 1: Chapter 51, *Gargantua and Pantagruel*, François Rabelais

• Engraver: Paul Jonnard (1840–1902)

Gargantua thanks his soldiers after a victorious battle. Doré varied the sizes of Gargantua and Pantagruel compared to normal humans: in this scene, the soldiers come up to Gargantua's waist, while in some scenes, they are below his knees.

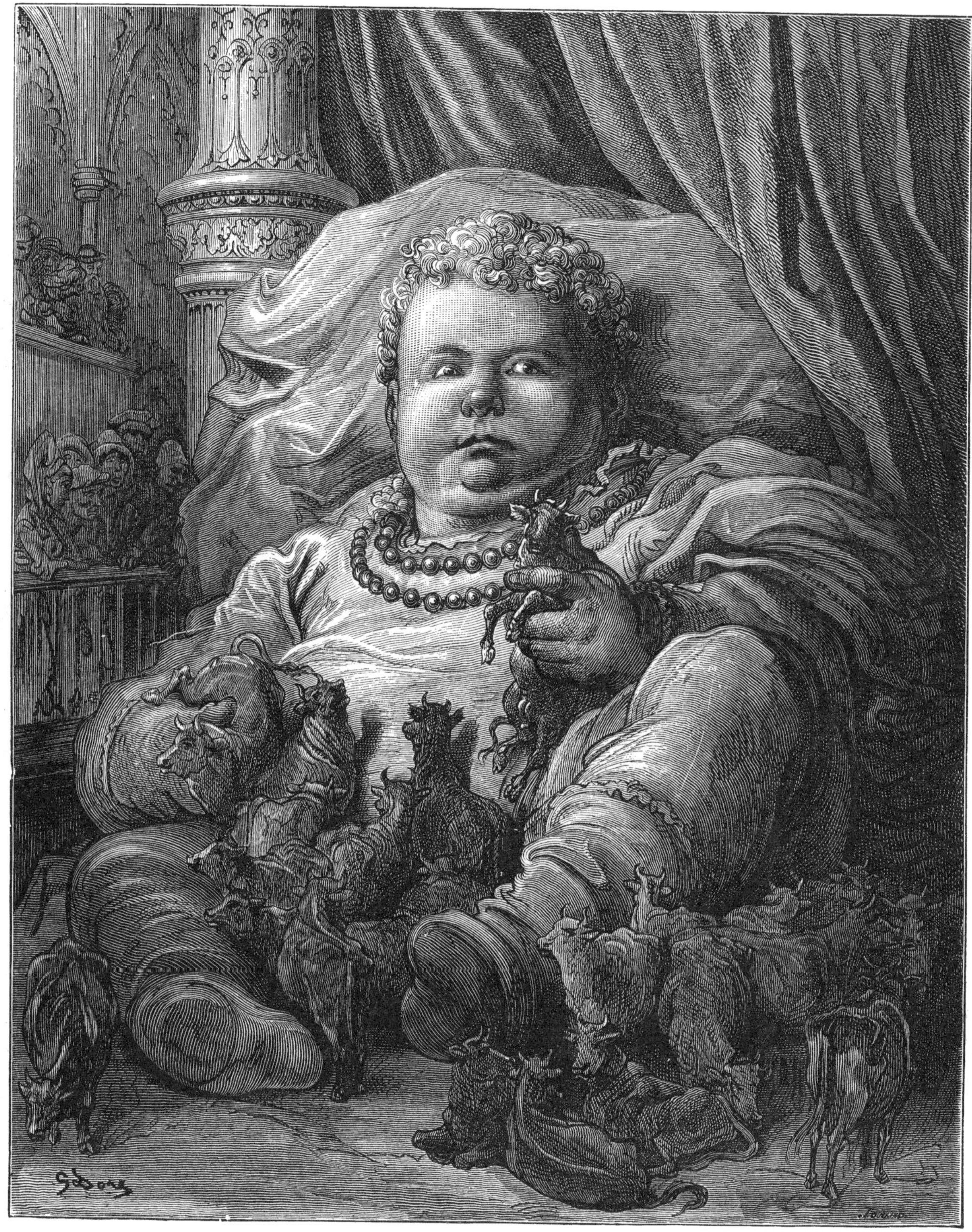

Pantagruel with 4,600 Cows, 1873

Book 2: Chapter 4, *Gargantua and Pantagruel*, François Rabelais

• Engraver: Paul Jonnard (1840–1902)

Gargantua's young son, Pantagruel, requires the milk from 4,600 cows for nourishment. Notice how large Pantagruel is in this scene: each cow is no bigger than his foot. The ludicrousness of many of these scenes is quite amusing.

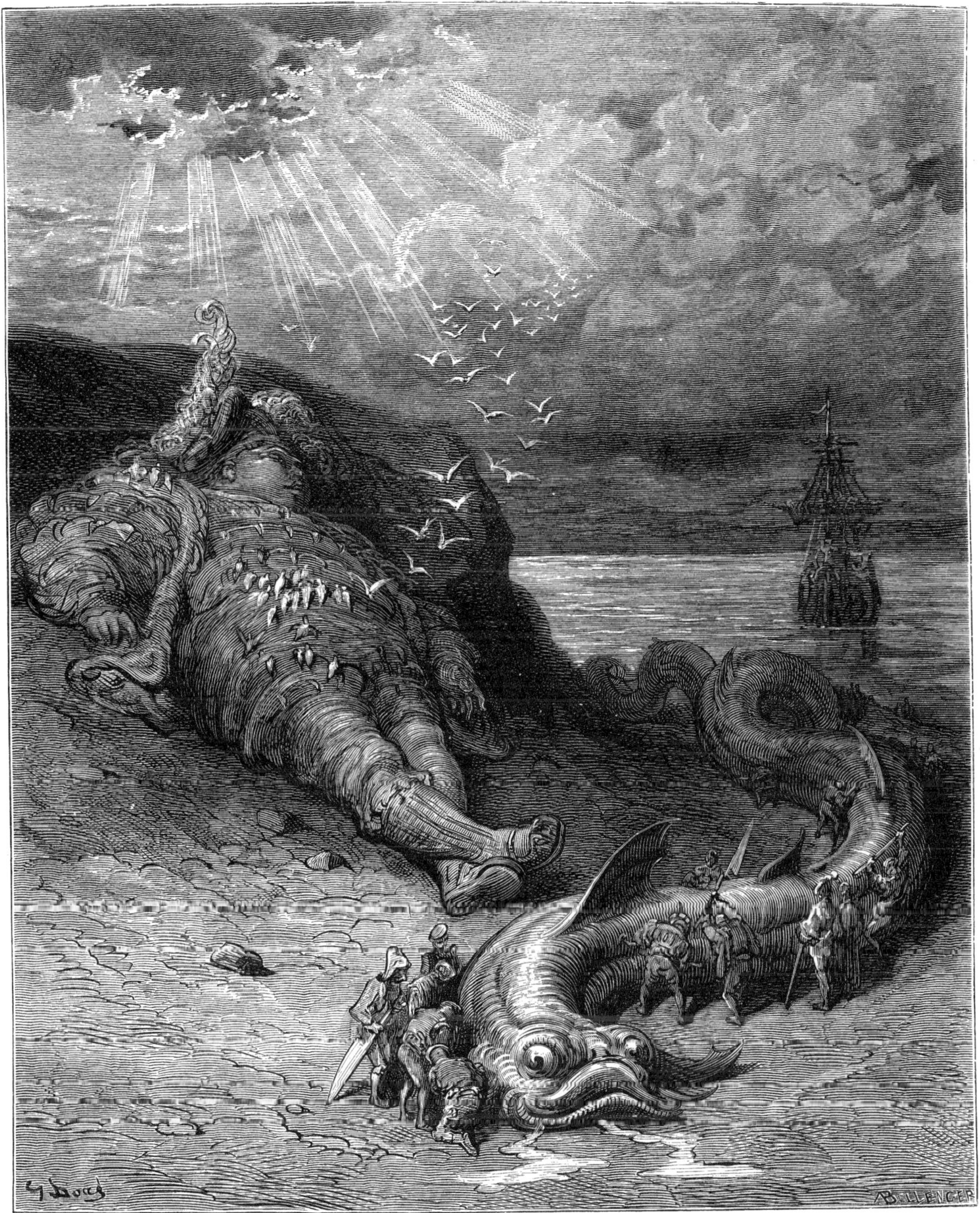

Pantagruel and the Sea Monster, 1873

Book 4: Chapter 35, *Gargantua and Pantagruel*, François Rabelais
• Engraver: Albert Bellenger (1846–1914)

Pantagruel rests on an island, as his men drag up the sea monster that he has just vanquished; it is a strange one, but the men will eat well that night. Pantagruel is now so enormous that a large flock of birds land on his torso.

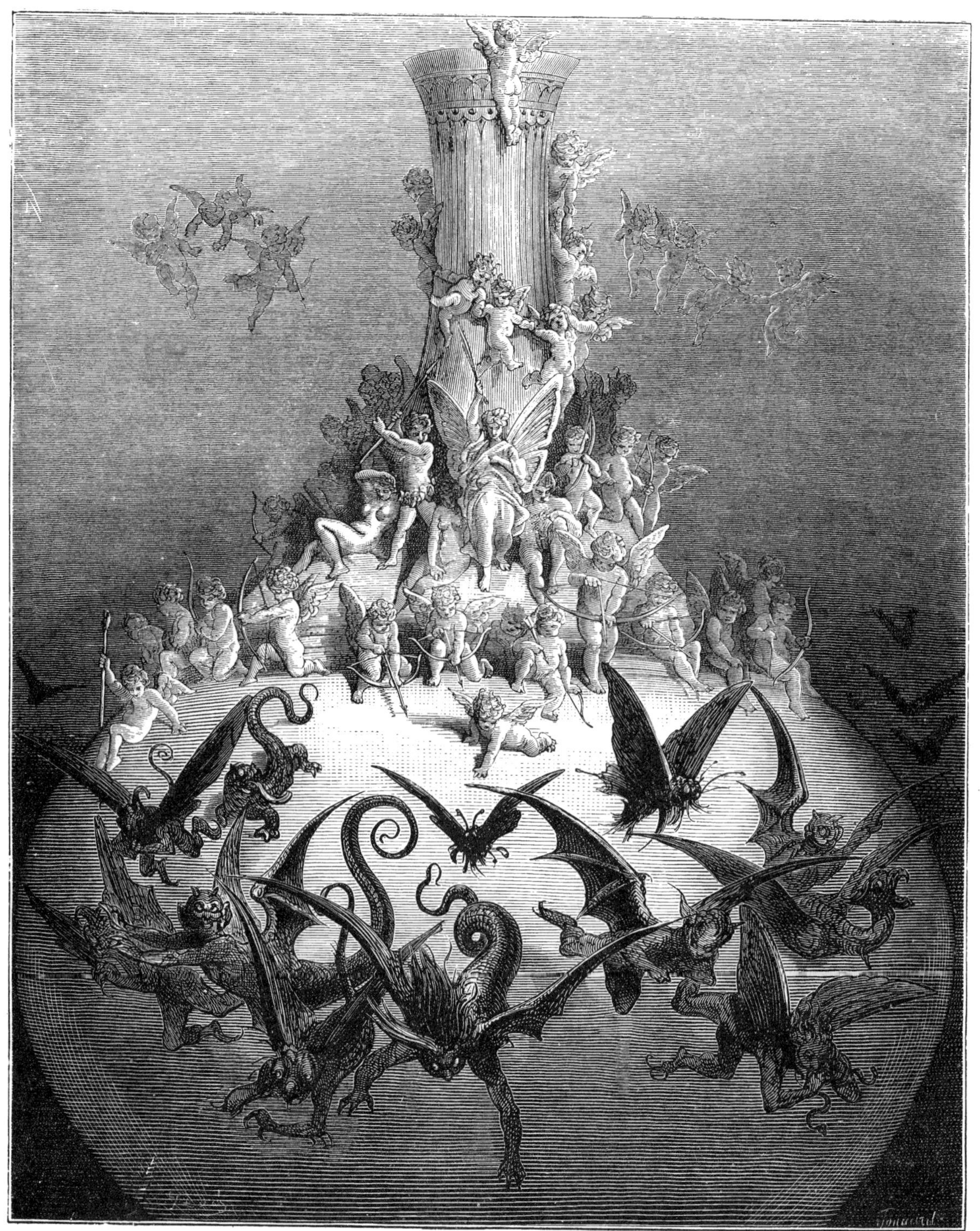

The Divine Bottle, 1873

Book 5: Chapter 45, *Gargantua and Pantagruel*, François Rabelais
• Engraver: Paul Jonnard (1840–1902)

Pantagruel and his men consult the oracle of the Divine Bottle. This is the origin of the famous Doré vase, but here, the good creatures are using bows and arrows to drive away the evil flying creatures. However, on the vase, all of the creatures are benign, playing and frolicking, with none of them flying off.

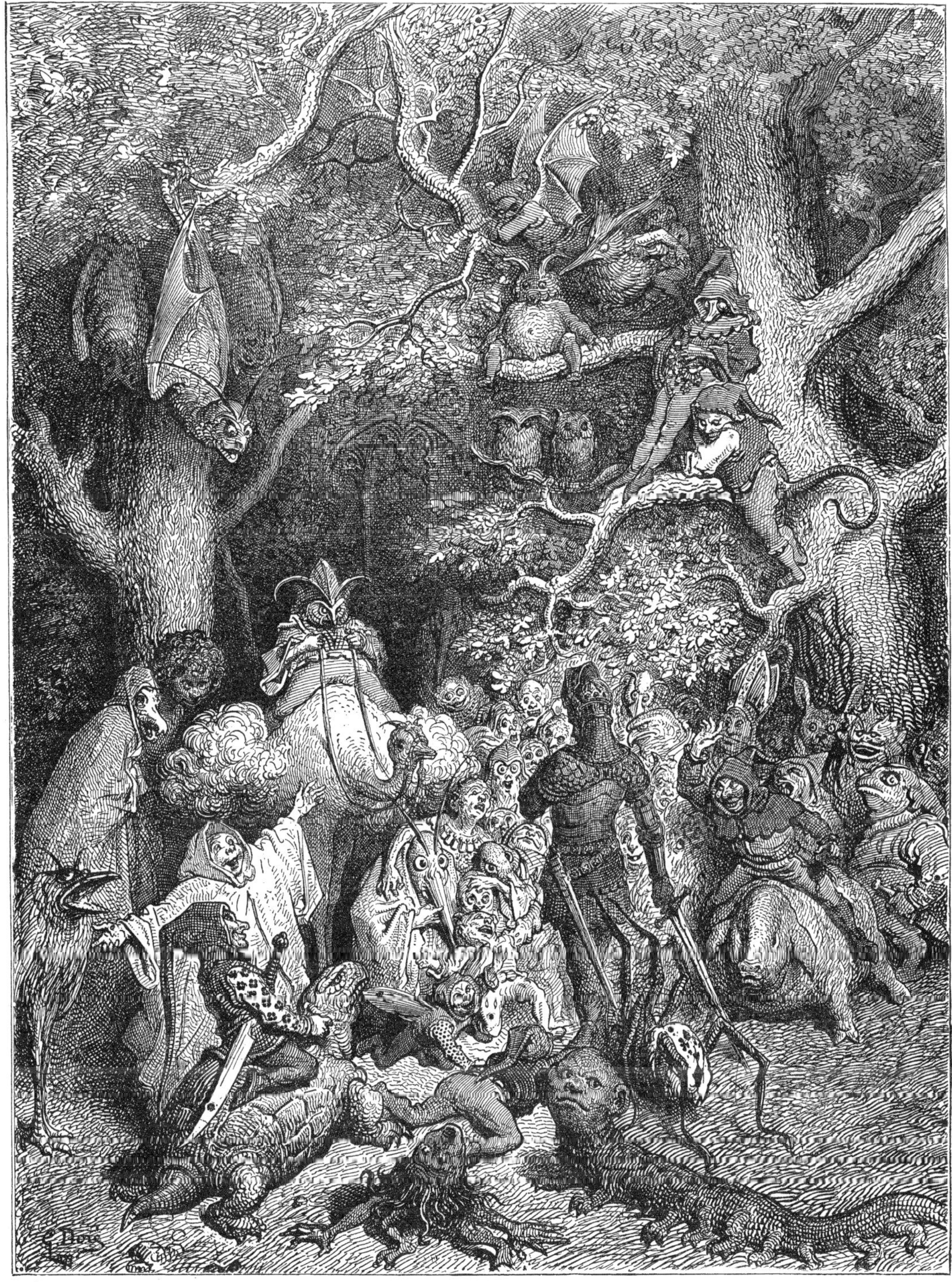

Creatures Greeting Ruggiero, 1879

Canto 6: Stanza 60, *Orlando Furioso*, Ludovico Ariosto

• Engraver unknown

How brave Ruggiero must have been to have a spider the size of a large dog right behind him! In his lifetime, Doré must have created thousands of creatures purely from his imagination, bewildering his viewers, and so many of them have been borrowed in popular culture in the last century.

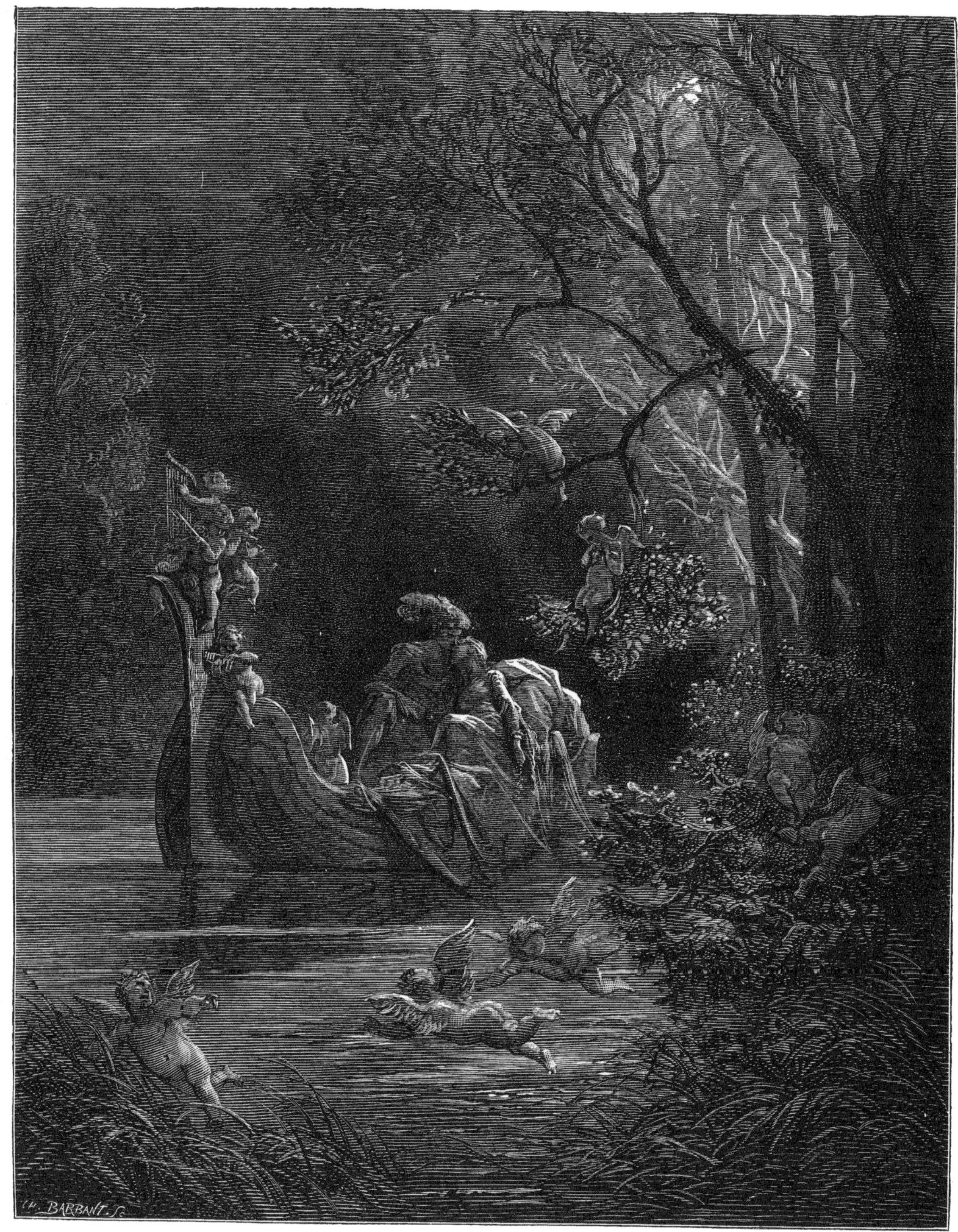

Lovers in Boat, 1879

Canto 7: Stanza 32, *Orlando Furioso*, Ludovico Ariosto

• Engraver: Charles Barbant (1844–1922)

The horror genre gives way to pure romance, as Alcina and Ruggiero glide on this peaceful stream, surrounded by cupids. When asked what he illustrated, Doré replied, 'I illustrate everything.' He illustrated every genre imaginable.

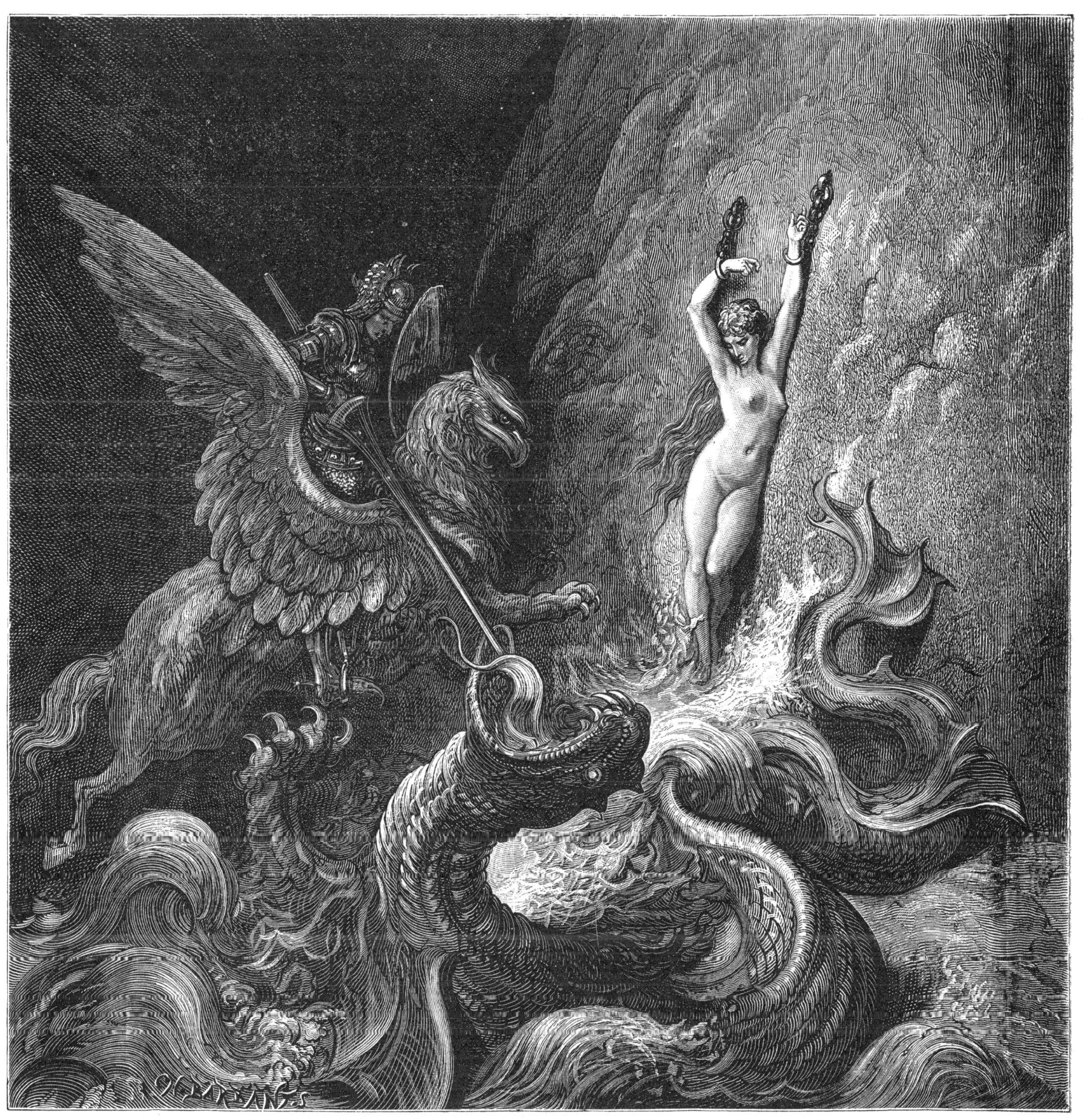

Ruggiero Spearing Sea Monster, 1879

Canto 10: Stanza 104, *Orlando Furioso*, Ludovico Ariosto

• Engraver: Charles Barbant (1844–1922)

Doré created many artistic works of brave knights rescuing nude maidens, chained to rocks, from sea monsters. Here, we see Ruggiero rescuing Angelica. This hippogriff is now available on the internet as *a* bronze statue – not by Doré, but 'after' Doré.

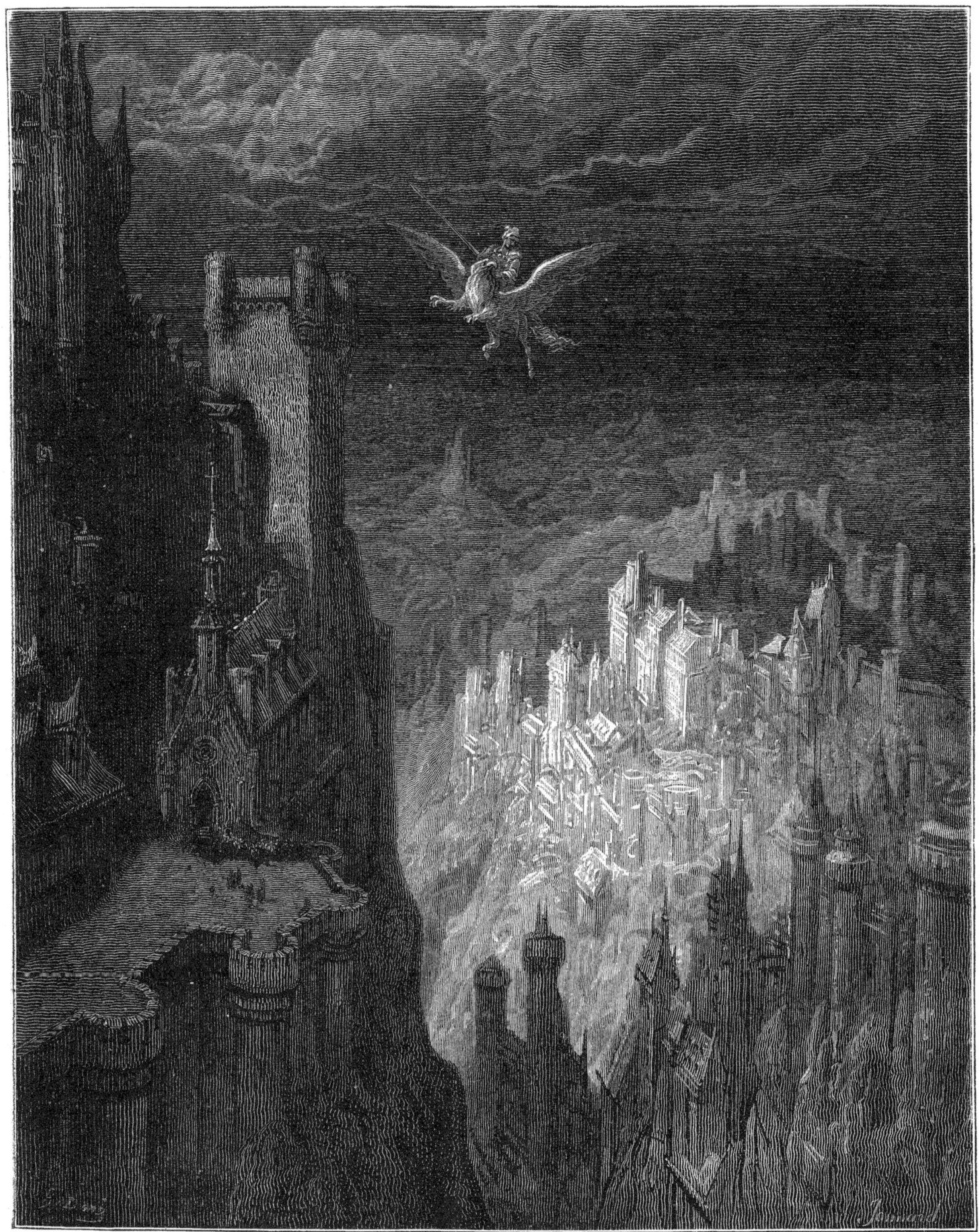

Astolfo on Hippogriff over Castle, 1879

Canto 33: Stanza 96, *Orlando Furioso*, Ludovico Ariosto

• Engraver: Paul Jonnard (1840–1902)

Is this a movie still of Harry Potter flying on Buckbeak the hippogriff over Hogwarts? No, this is an 1879 Doré engraving of Astolfo on his hippogriff. Doré is indeed 'fated to being eternally revived for the popular culture of succeeding generations'.

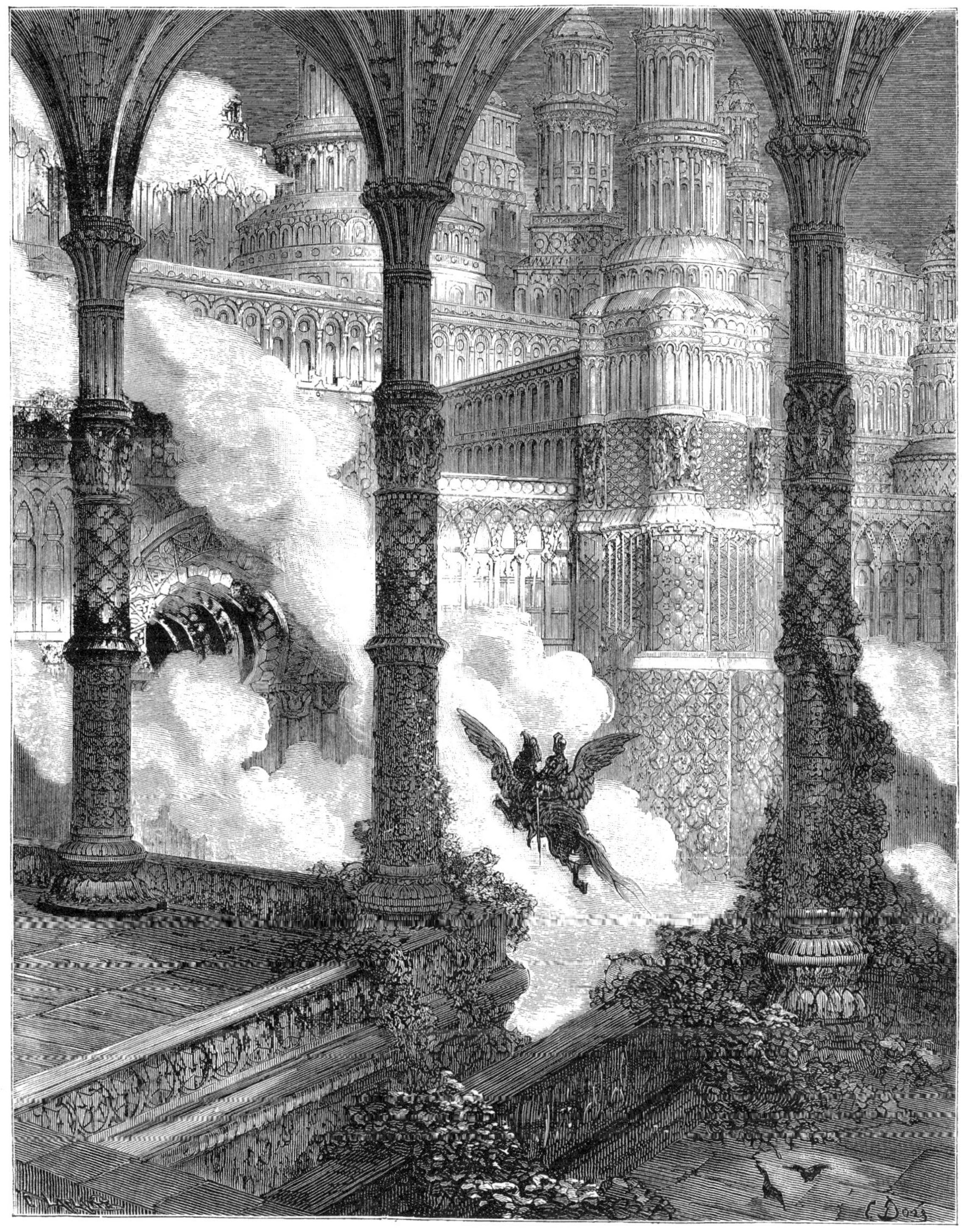

Astolfo on Hippogriff Arrives at Palace, 1879
Canto 34: Stanza 52, *Orlando Furioso*, Ludovico Ariosto
• Engraver: Charles Laplante (1837–1903)

Doré's mind was a world of fantasy – here, we see Astolfo on his hippogriff, arriving at a palace that seems to have been built in the clouds. This scene was tinted blue and used in a very different film: Karel Zeman's 1961 *The Fabulous Baron Munchausen*.

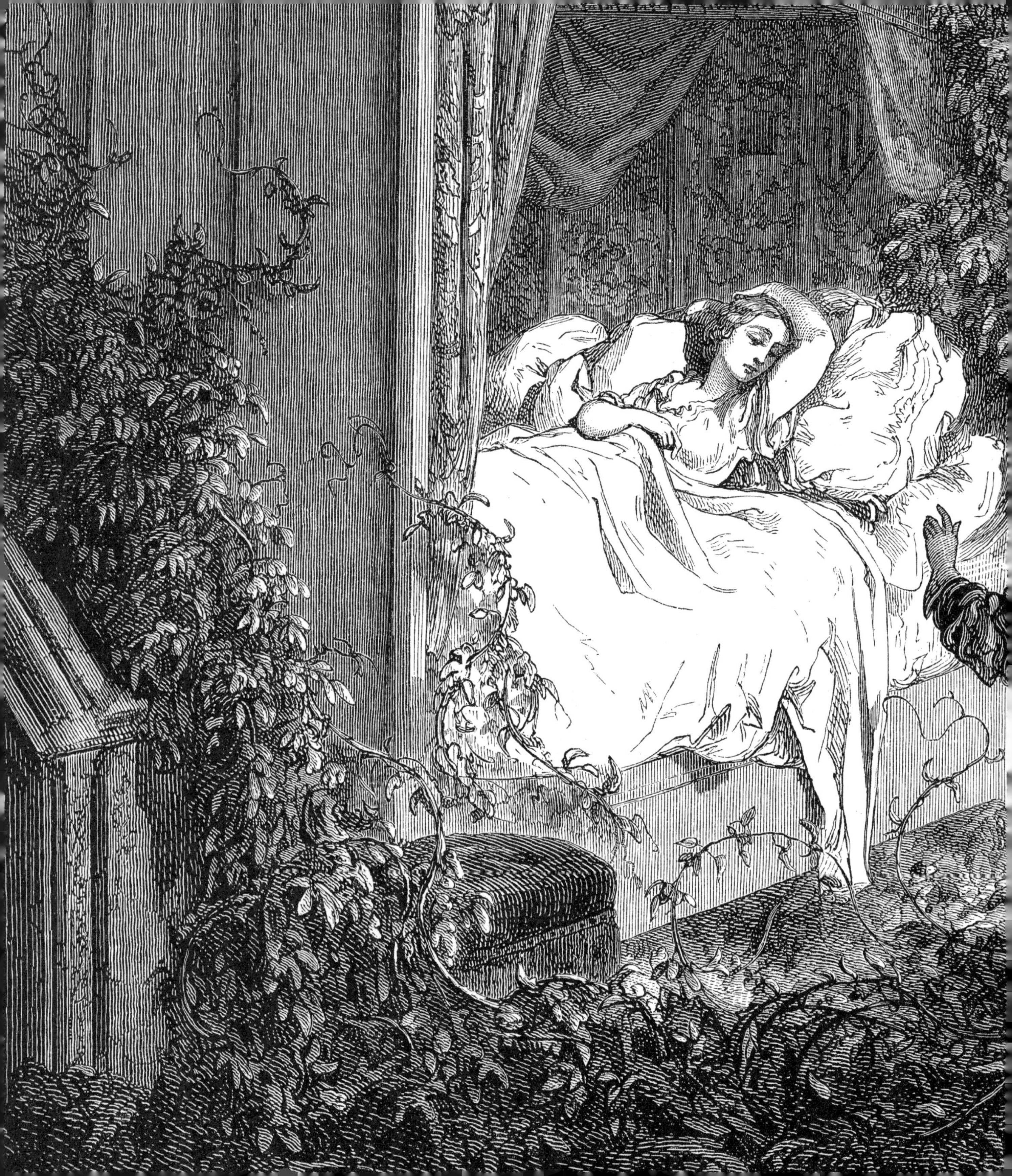

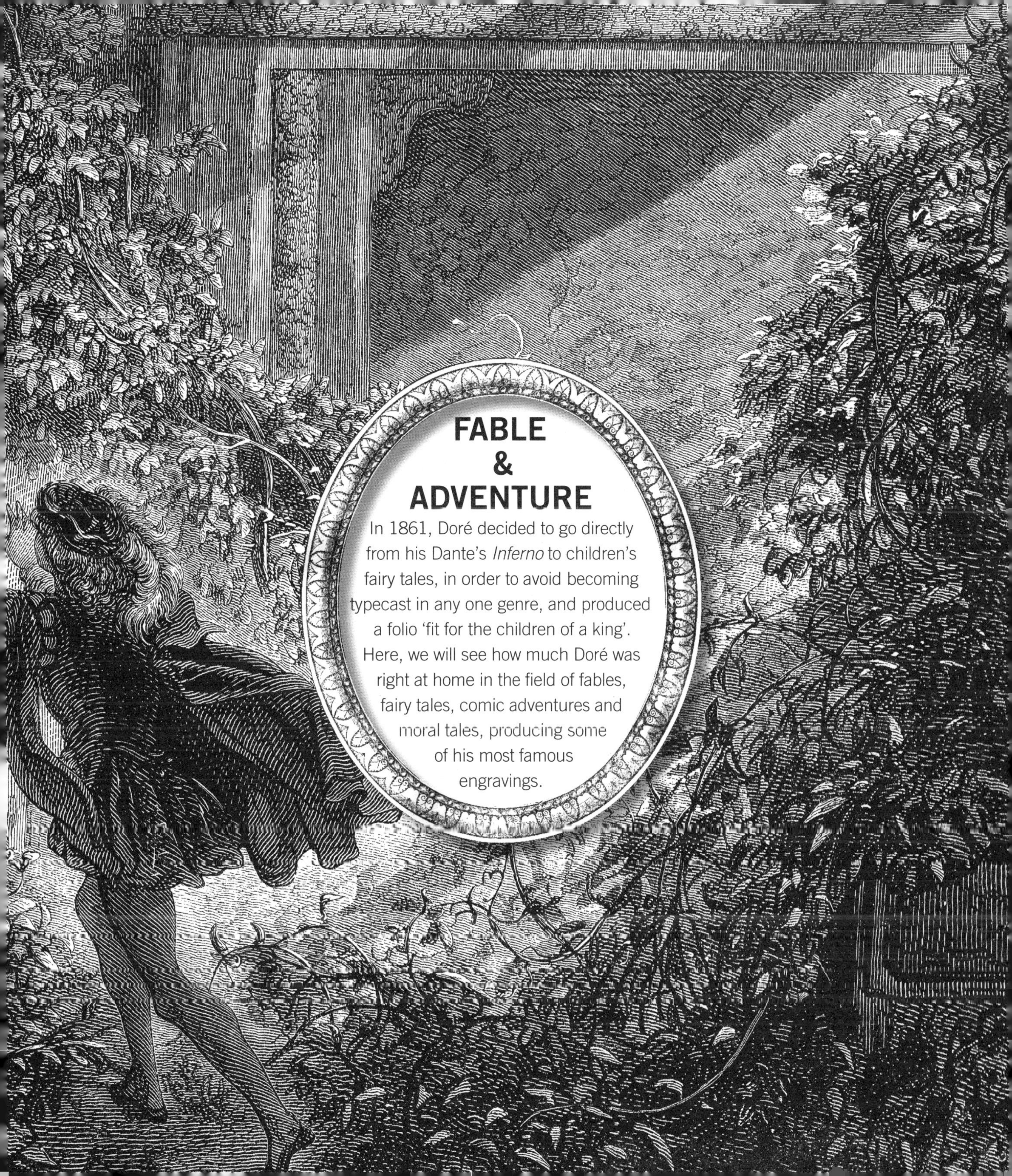

FABLE
&
ADVENTURE

In 1861, Doré decided to go directly
from his Dante's *Inferno* to children's
fairy tales, in order to avoid becoming
typecast in any one genre, and produced
a folio 'fit for the children of a king'.
Here, we will see how much Doré was
right at home in the field of fables,
fairy tales, comic adventures and
moral tales, producing some
of his most famous
engravings.

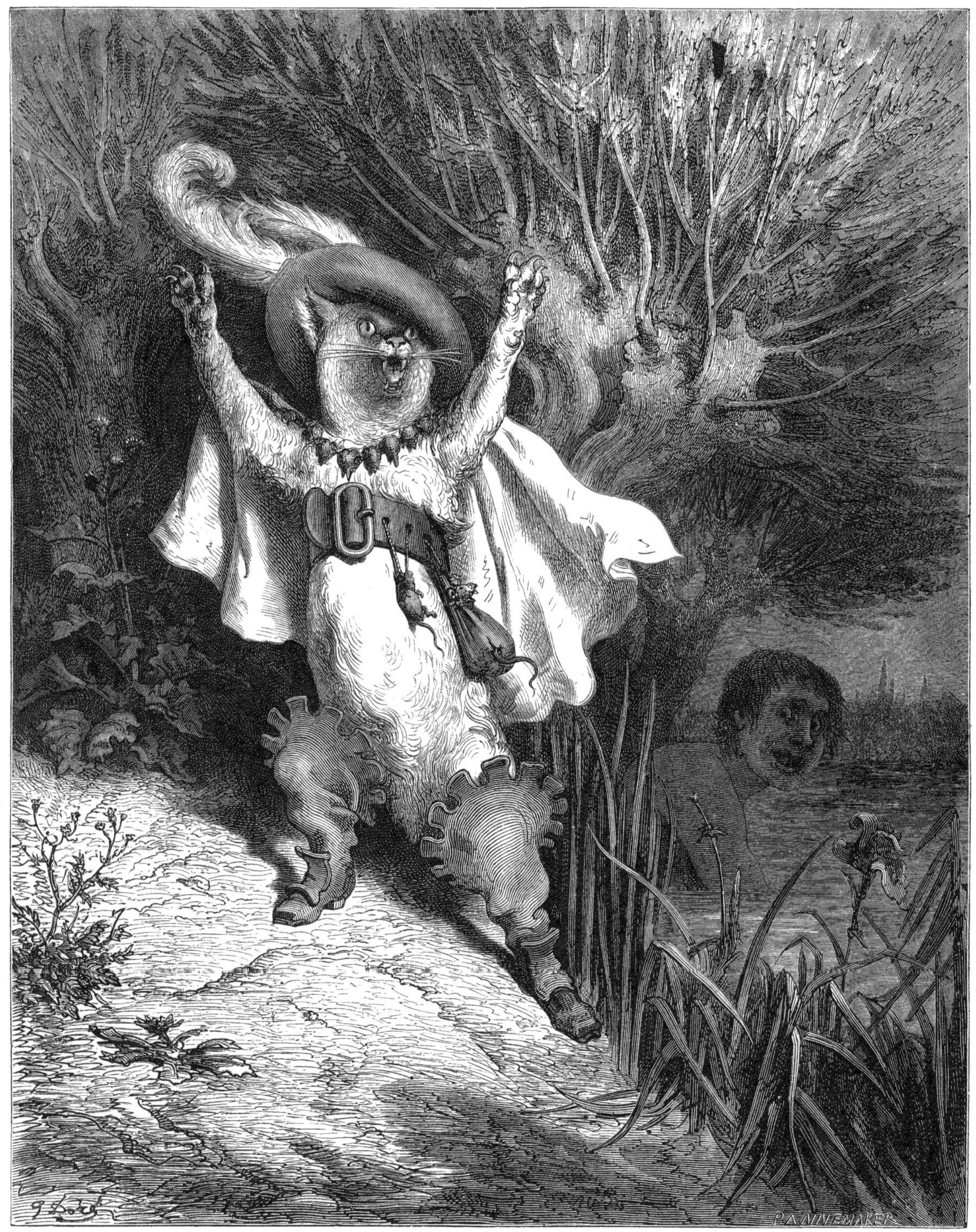

Puss in Boots, 1861

Plate 1 of 4, *Fairy Tales: Puss in Boots*, Charles Perrault
• Engraver: A.F. Pannemaker (1822–1900)

Doré made the heroic feline into a swashbuckling cavalier. Used for a 1997 French postage stamp, it became Doré's most widely recognized art after it was used for the *Shrek* films and the 2011 spin-off *Puss in Boots*. It was also used for promotional materials for a major 2014 Doré exhibition.

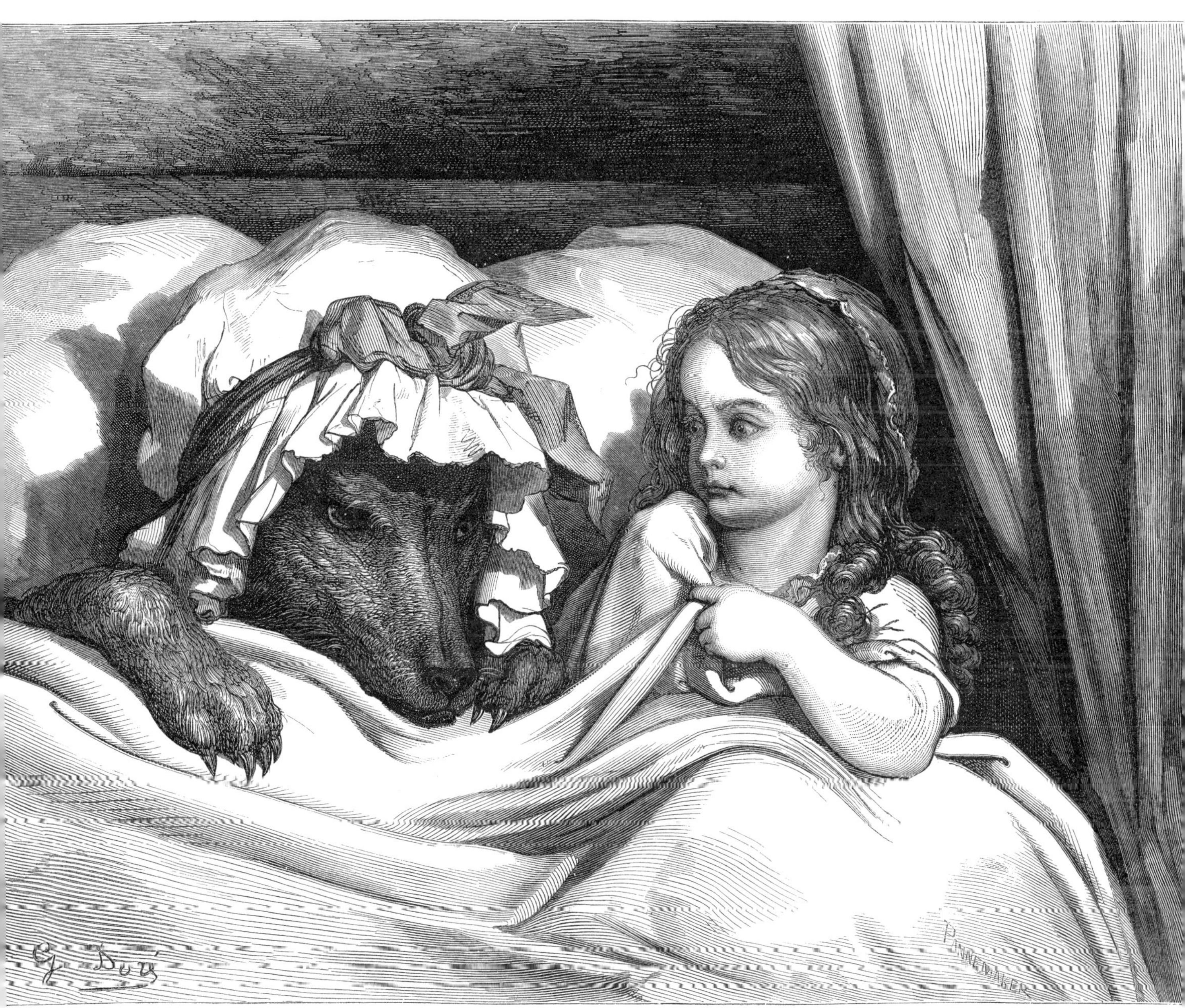

Little Red Riding Hood in Bed with Wolf, 1861

Plate 3 of 3, *Fairy Tales: Little Red Riding Hood*, Charles Perrault
• Engraver: A.F. Pannemaker (1822–1900)

The close-up facial expressions of innocent puzzlement and fiendish aggression are priceless in this popular Doré scene. This engraving has been widely borrowed visually and textually in psychology books. Christina Ricci was selected for the 1997 film *Little Red Riding Hood* because she resembled the Doré heroine.

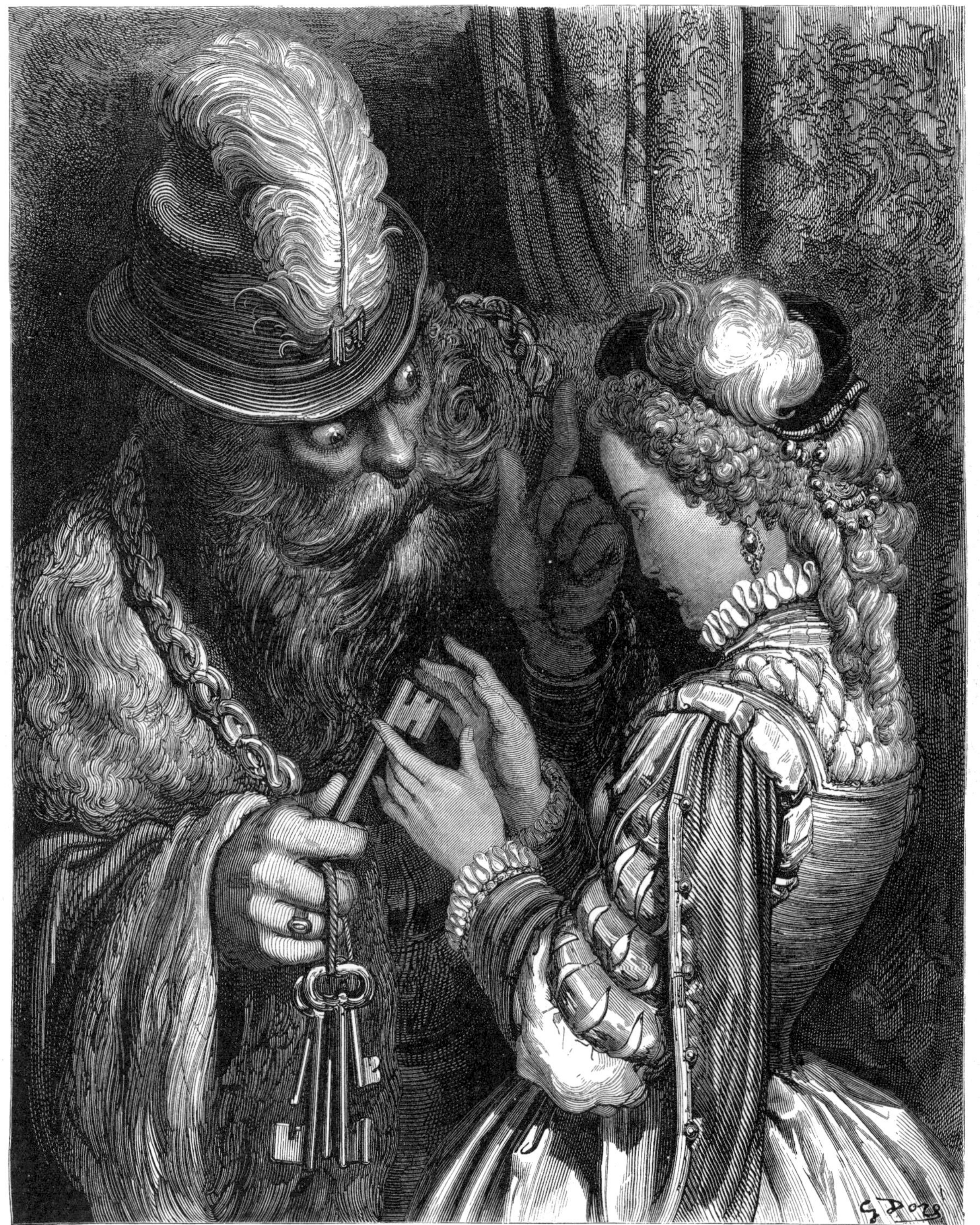

Bluebeard Showing His Wife the Keys, 1861
Plate 1 of 4, *Fairy Tales: Bluebeard*, Charles Perrault
• Engraver unknown

The evil Bluebeard shows his wife the key to the one door she is never to open. Psychologists have had a field day, looking for sexual innuendos in this Doré scene. Jean Cocteau borrowed this scene for his 1946 film *La Belle et la Bête* and it was also used for a French postage stamp in 1983.

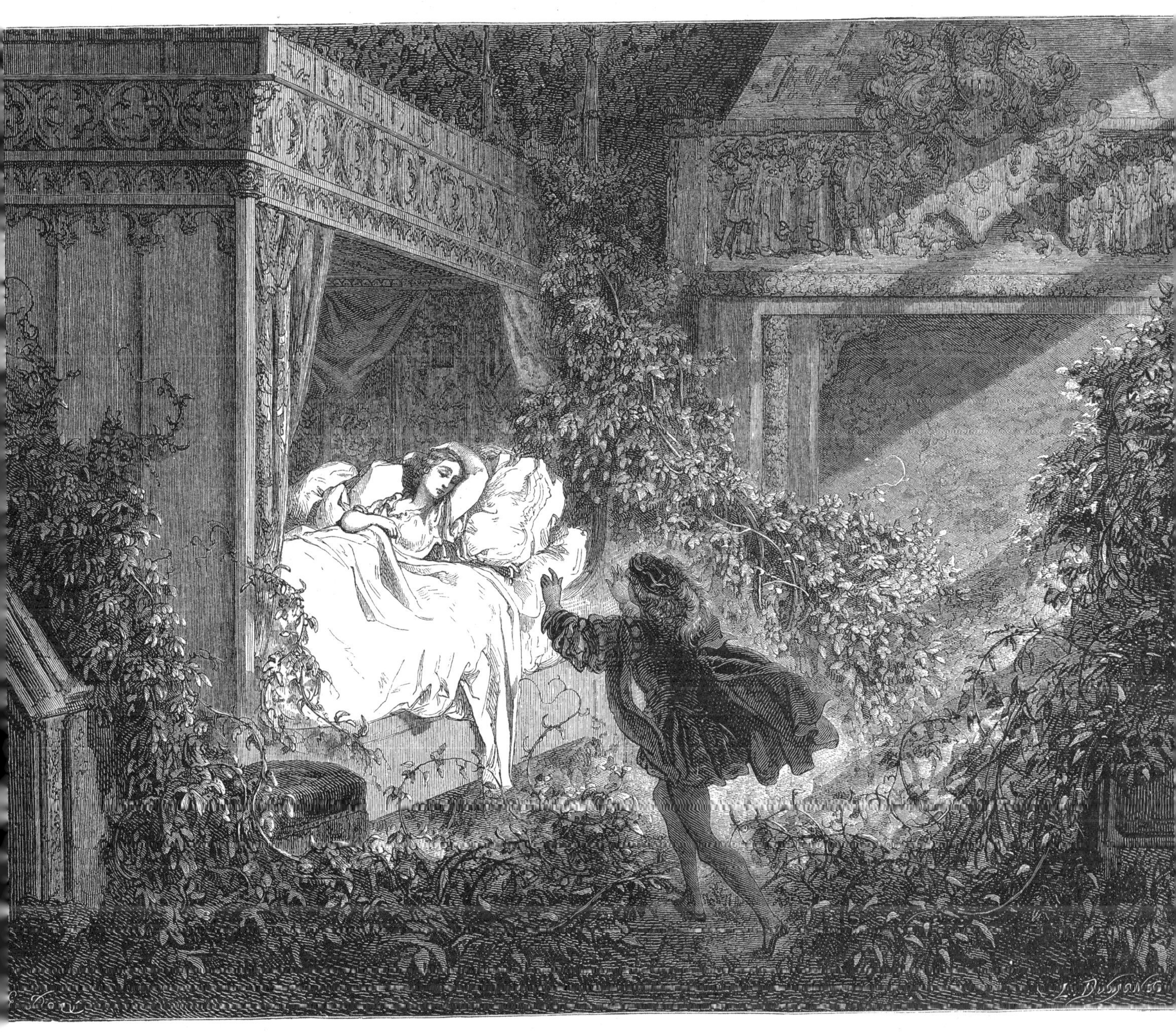

Prince Charming Finding Sleeping Beauty, 1861
Plate 6 of 6, *Fairy Tales: Sleeping Beauty*, Charles Perrault
• Engraver: Louis Dumont (1822–98)

In one of Doré's most romantic scenes, the prince comes out of dark shadows into the bright sunshine that is bathing Sleeping Beauty, with dazzling detail in the overgrown foliage, canopy and sunrays. It is hard to believe this was the same artist who had just shown all the hellish horrors of Dante's *Inferno*.

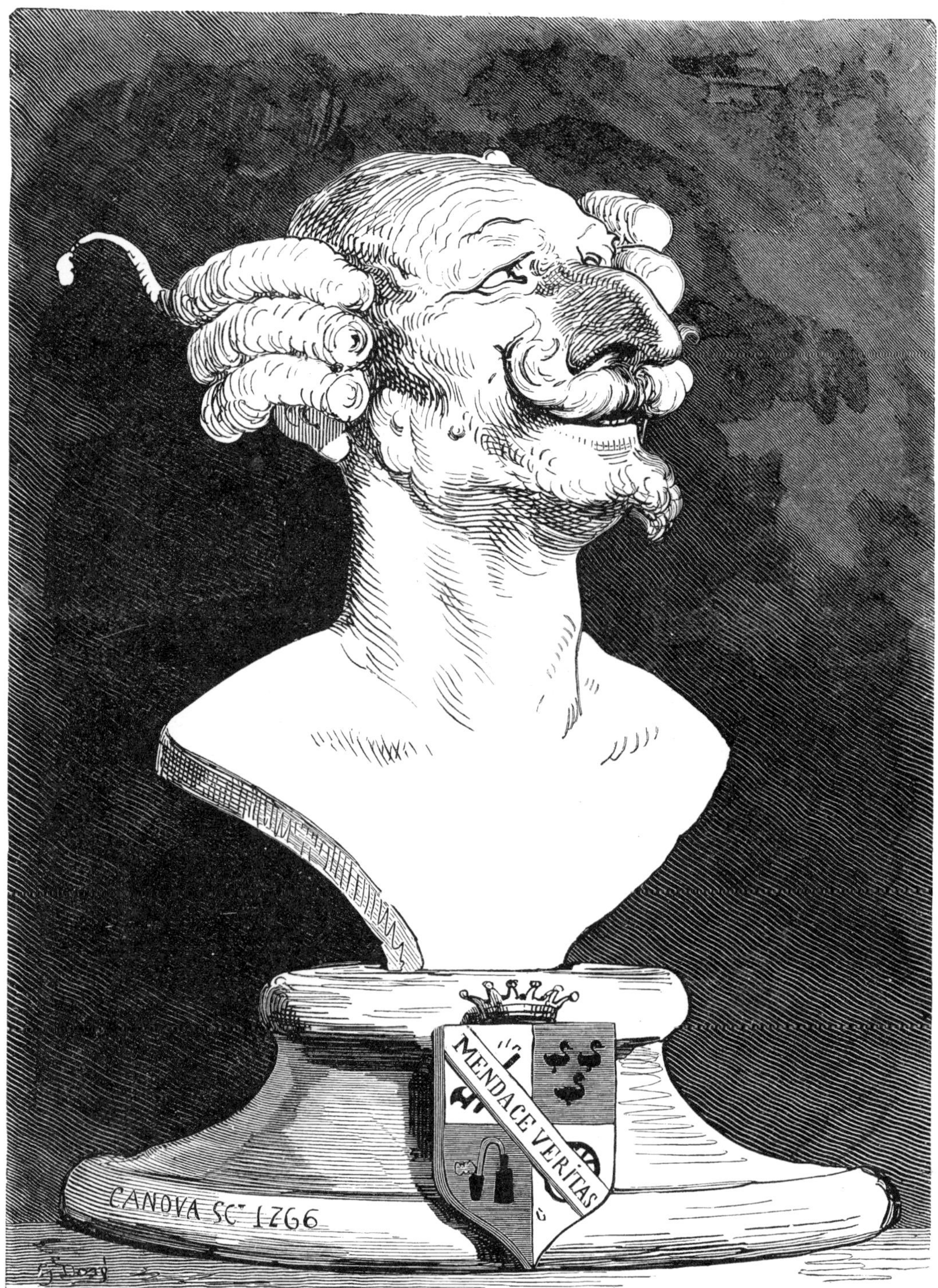

Baron Munchausen (bust), 1862
Frontispiece, *The Adventures of Baron Munchausen* (anon.)
• Engraver: A.F. Pannemaker (1822–1900)

Doré drew the Baron as a bust, and this iconic image was made into a bronze bust in 1988 by artist Bill Basso, based on the 1984 Terry Gilliam film (*The Adventures of Baron Munchausen*) that borrowed Doré's character.

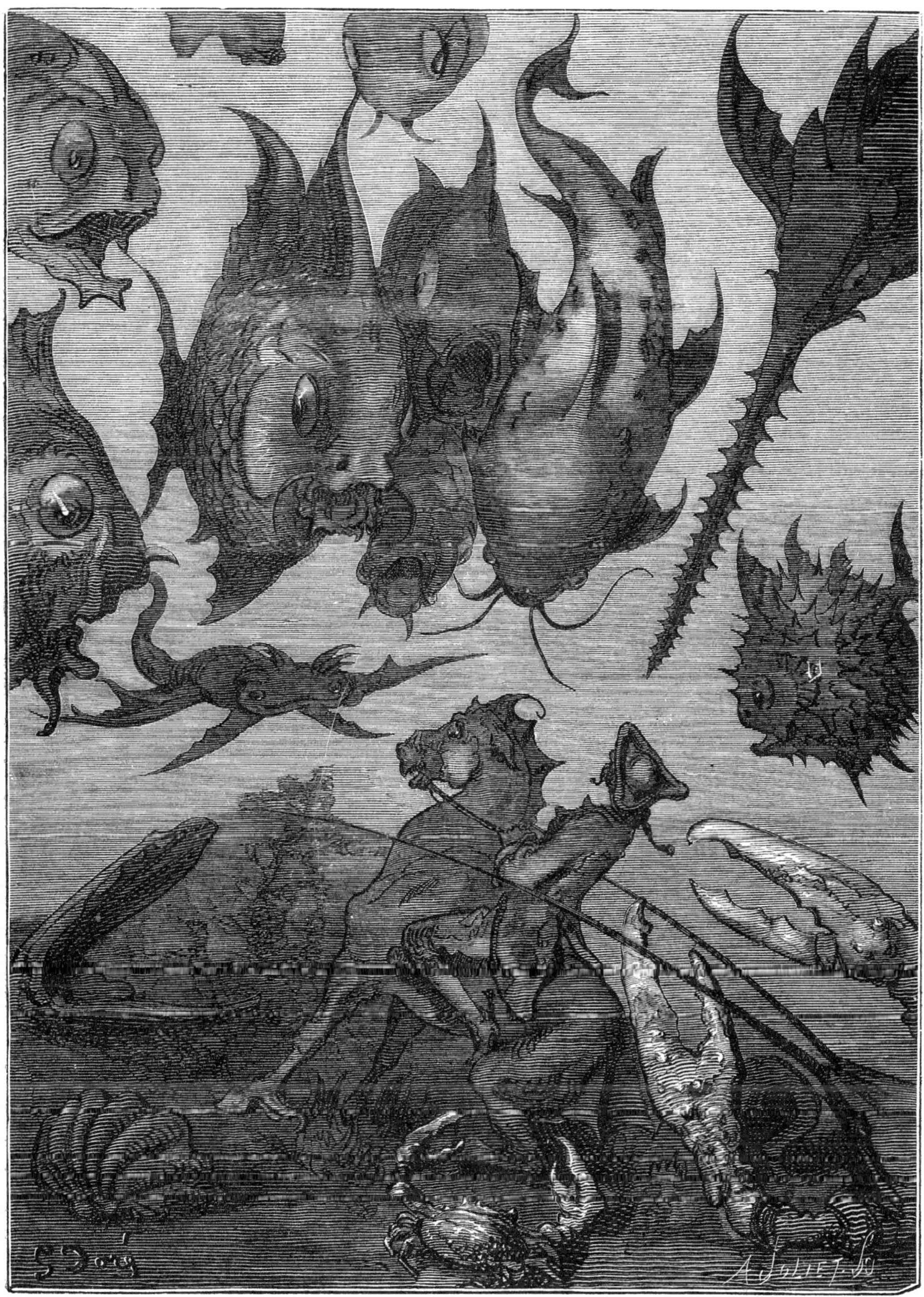

Munchausen Riding Horse Underwater, 1862
Plate 24, *The Adventures of Baron Munchausen* (anon.)
• Engraver: Auguste Joliet (1839–1915)

For the Baron, it was not enough to describe being able to ride his horse underwater: big fish and other sea creatures also crowded around him and his steed to observe such a curious spectacle. Doré took great delight in infusing his animals, fish and other creatures with human personality traits.

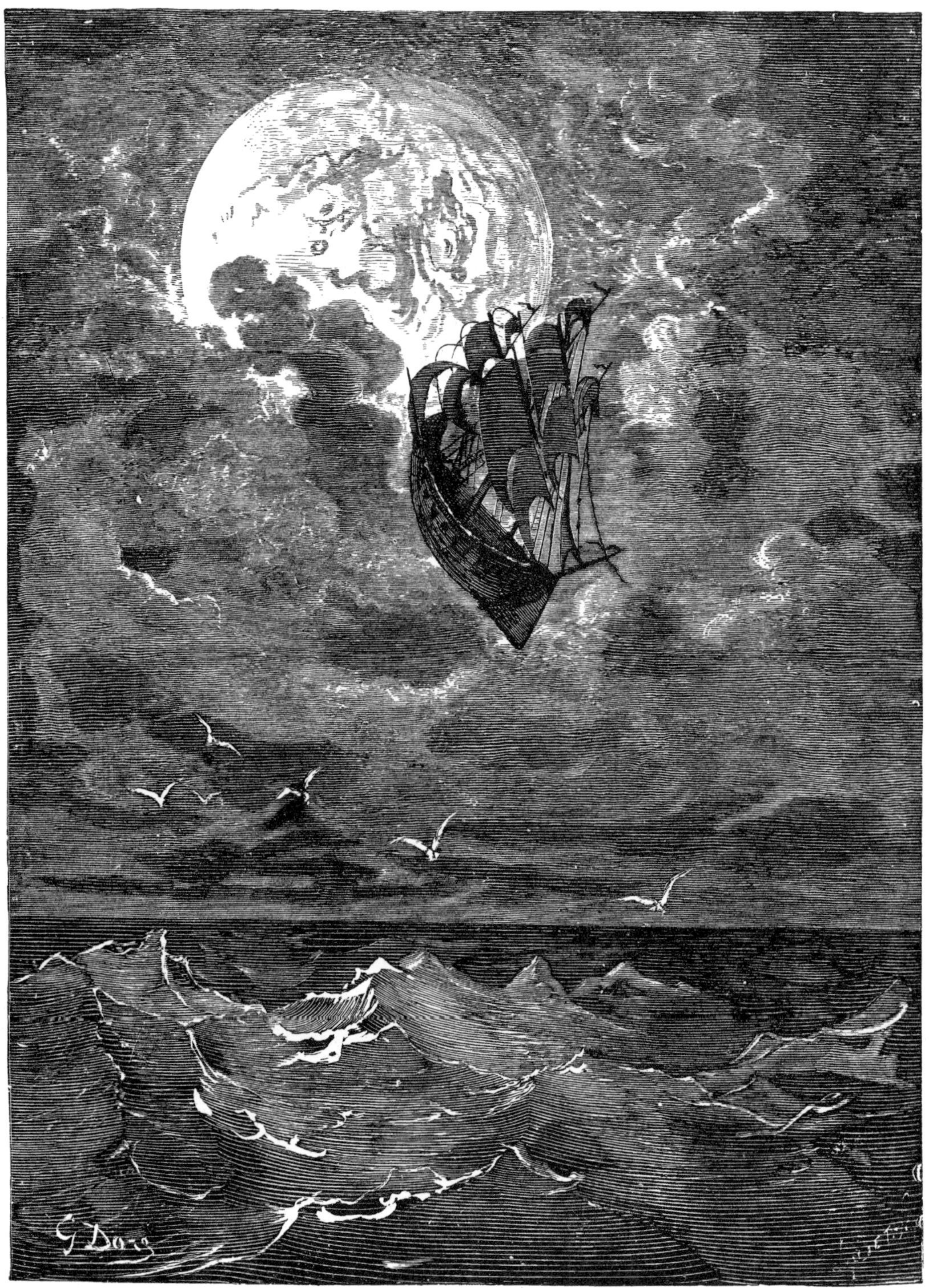

Munchausen Riding to the Moon, 1862
Plate 28, *The Adventures of Baron Munchausen* (anon.)
• Engraver: Auguste Joliet (1839–1915)

For Doré, space was the final frontier: Here, the Baron flies to the moon in a sailing ship. It is a similar engraving to the one for Ariosto, where they fly to the moon in Elijah's chariot. This Munchausen image was made into a beautiful black-light poster in the 1970s.

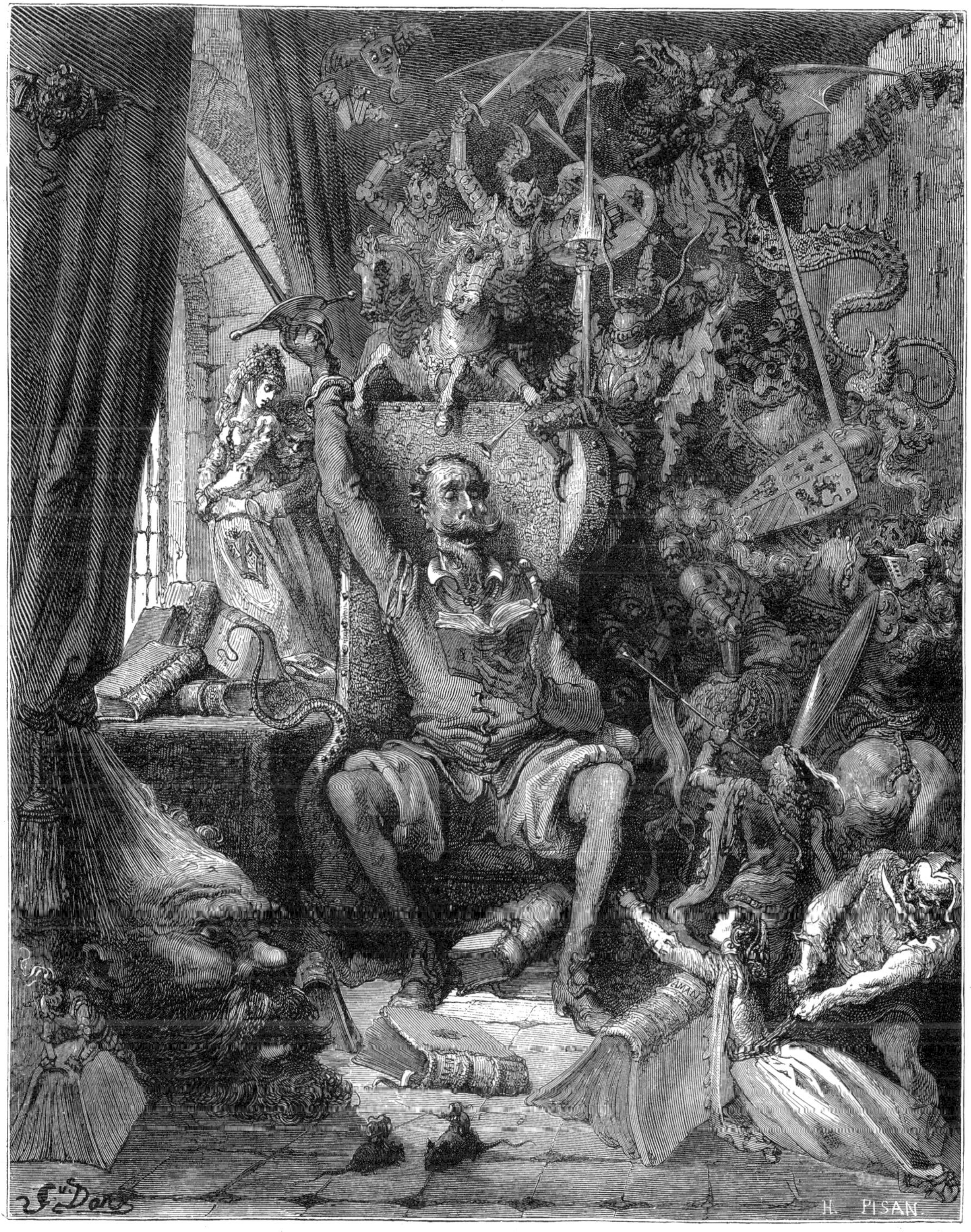

Don Quixote in His Study, 1863

Frontispiece, *Don Quixote*, Miguel de Cervantes

• Engraver: Heliodore Pisan (1822–1900)

As the elderly Don Quixote immerses himself in old chivalry tomes, the humans, creatures and objects in the books come to life all around him. This is the most spectacular and famous illustration from *Don Quixote* – widely borrowed, it was on the front cover of almost all the programmes for the Broadway production of *Man of La Mancha*.

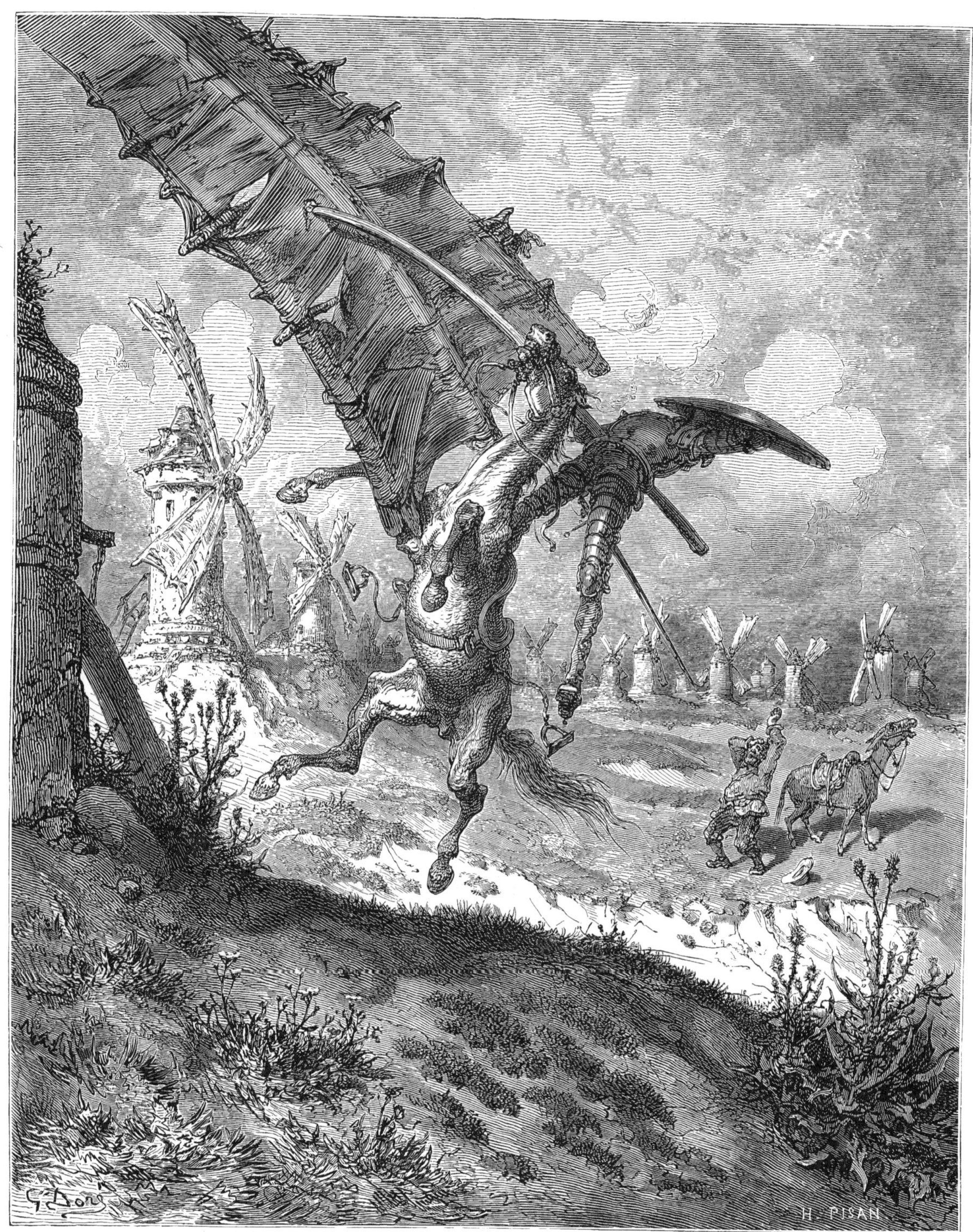

Don Quixote Tilting at Windmill, 1863

Plate 9, *Don Quixote*, Miguel de Cervantes

• Engraver: Heliodore Pisan (1822–1900)

Doré depicts falling horse and ejected rider frozen in mid-air, as Don Quixote spears a giant monster in the form of an old windmill. This is the second most famous and most borrowed Don Quixote image ever created; all 377 of these illustrations were engraved by Pisan.

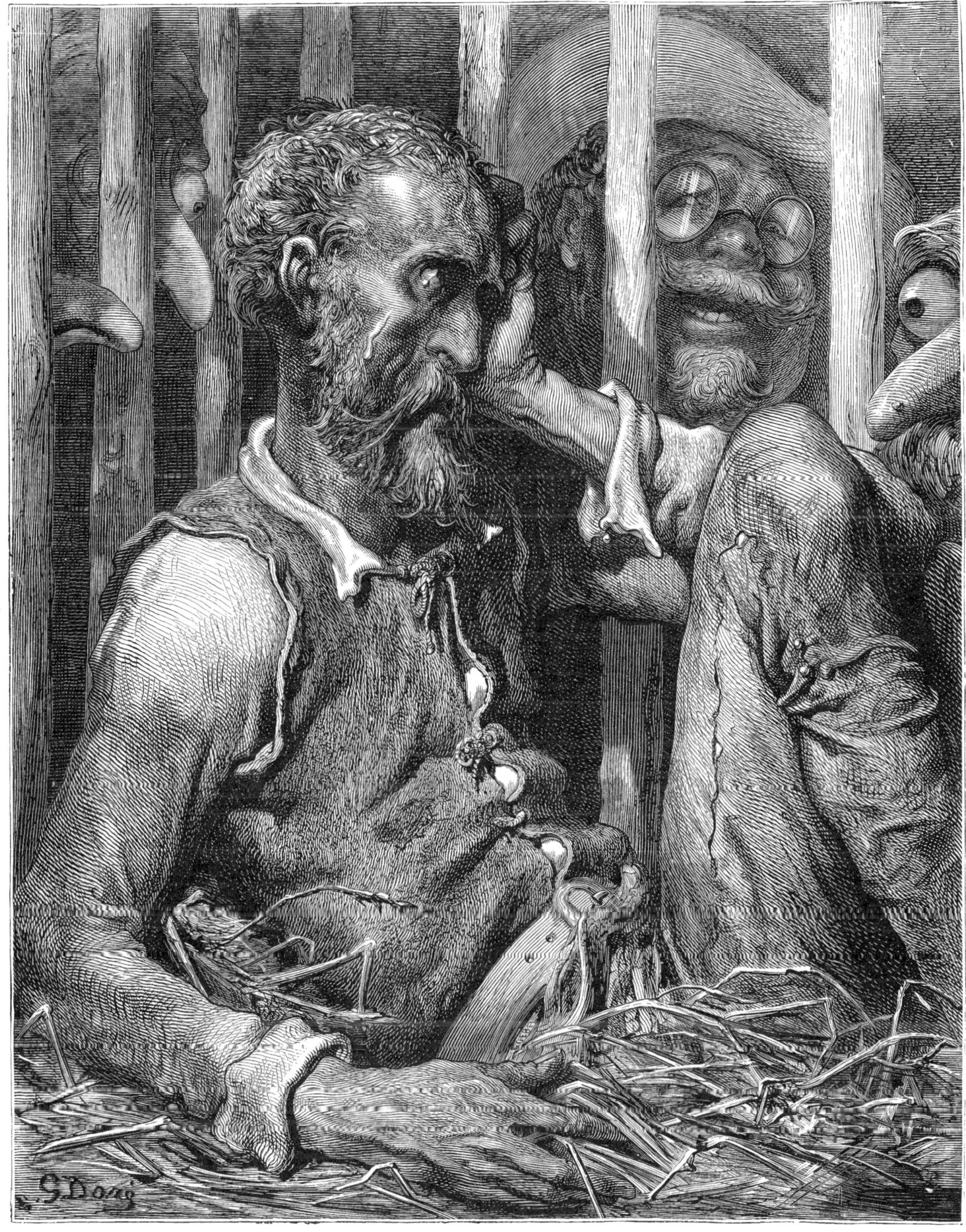

Don Quixote in Cage, 1863

Plate 53, *Don Quixote*, Miguel de Cervantes

• Engraver: Heliodore Pisan (1822–1900)

In his caricaturist years when he was a teenager, Doré loved to depict facial close-ups. He hearkens back to that time in this scene, depicting curious onlookers poking their long noses through the bars to heckle Don Quixote in a cage after a brawl at an inn.

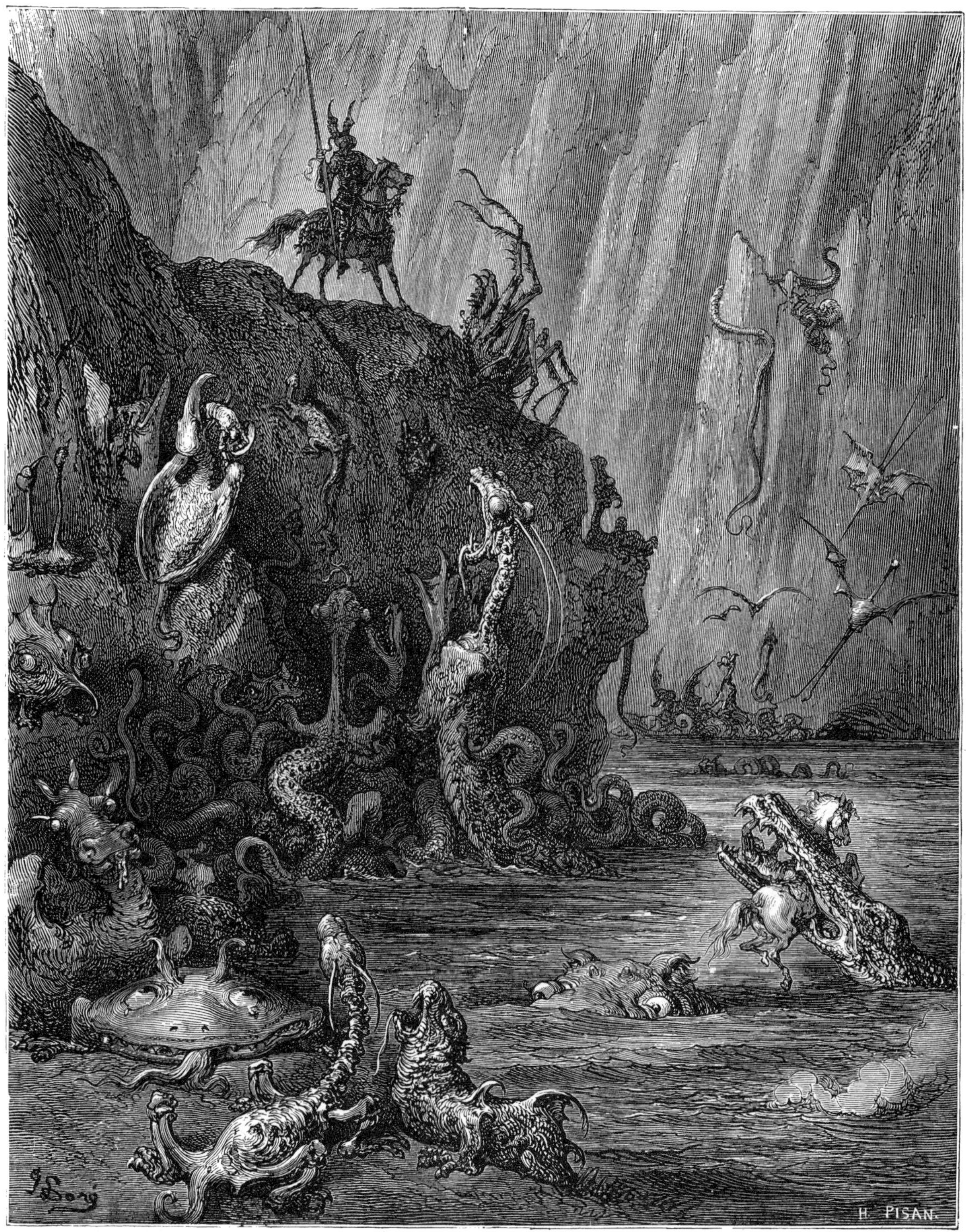

Knight Approaching Lake, 1863

Plate 55, *Don Quixote*, Miguel de Cervantes

• Engraver: Heliodore Pisan (1822–1900)

As an aside from the narrative, Doré depicts a knight approaching a boiling lake filled with giant monsters. The huge spiders have grown from the size of cats to the size of horses, and also notice the crocodile so large that it has a horse and its rider in its mouth.

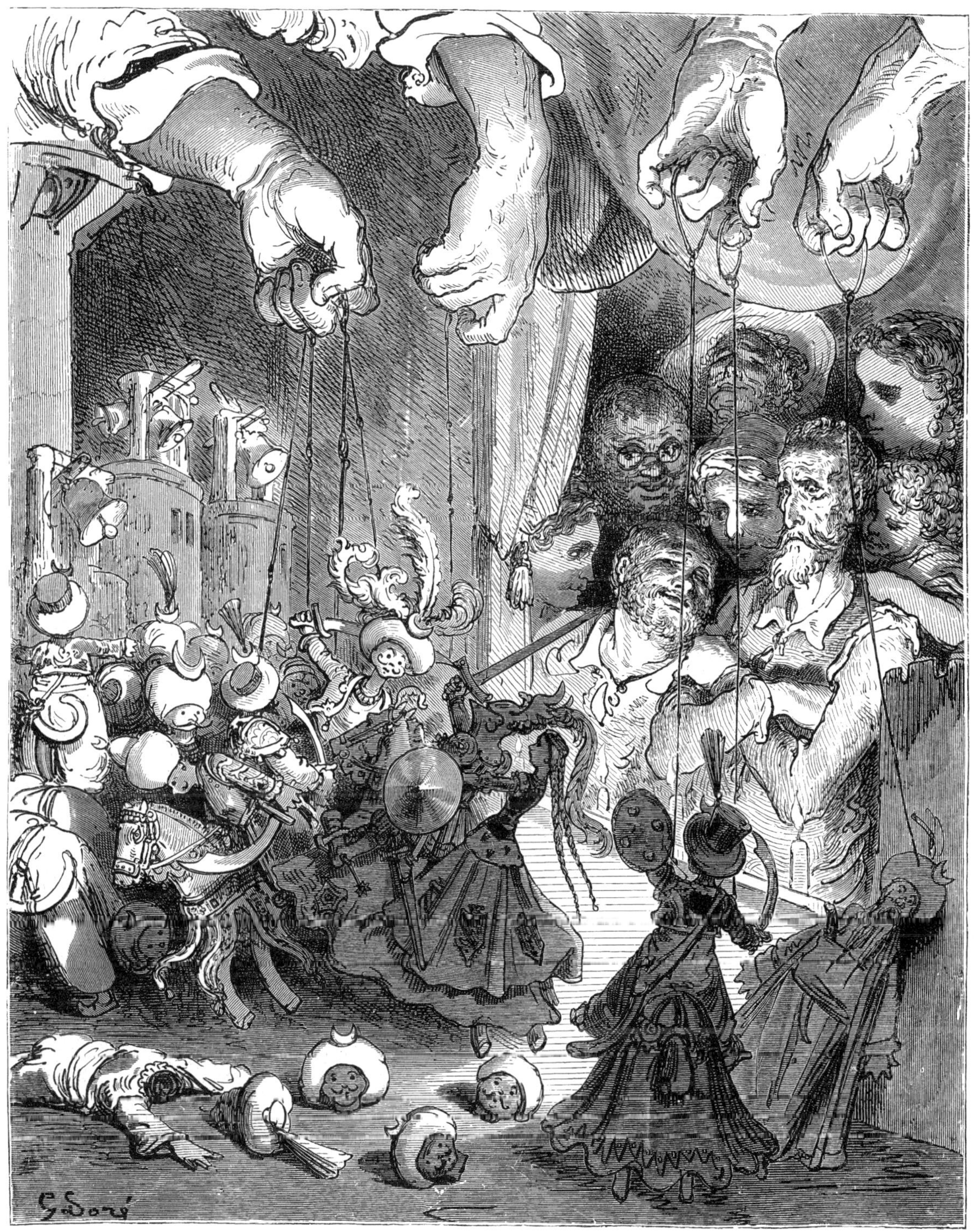

The Puppet Show, 1863

Plate 81, *Don Quixote*, Miguel de Cervantes
• Engraver: Heliodore Pisan (1822–1900)

Don Quixote and friends watch a puppet show, which everyone enjoys while his imagination runs wild, thinking that the wooden figures must be real and somehow hostile. In the following scene, he whips out his sword and destroys the stage, blaming the puppet master for making the marionettes too realistic.

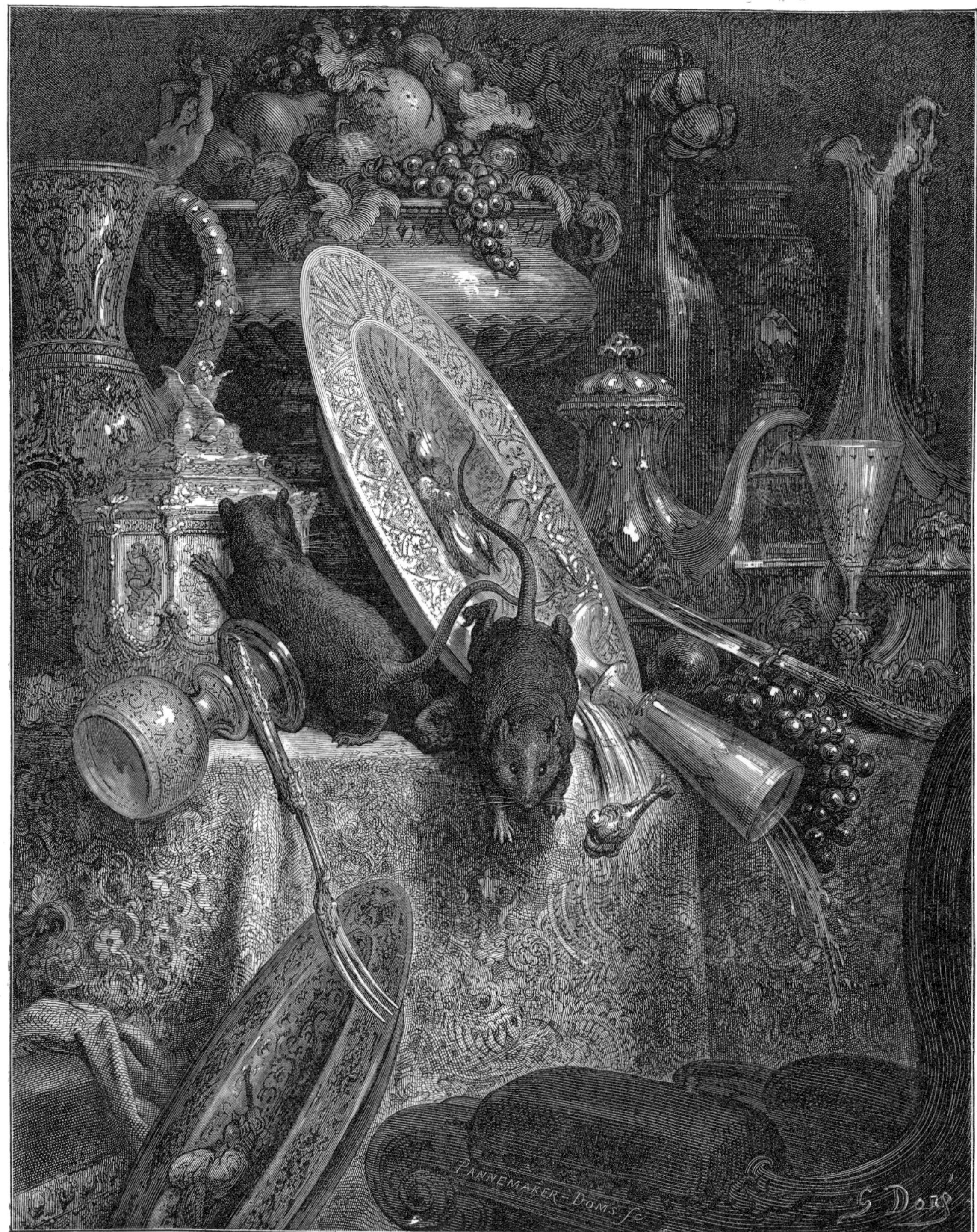

Town Rat and Country Rat, 1867
Plate 4, *Fables*, Jean de La Fontaine,
• Engraver: A.F. Pannemaker (1822–1900)

Victorian readers were amazed at the detail that Doré put into his backgrounds, which most illustrators kept plain. Here, a rat from the countryside visits its cousin in a fancy house in the city, but increased luxury also brings more danger. This was made into a beautiful chromolithograph trade card.

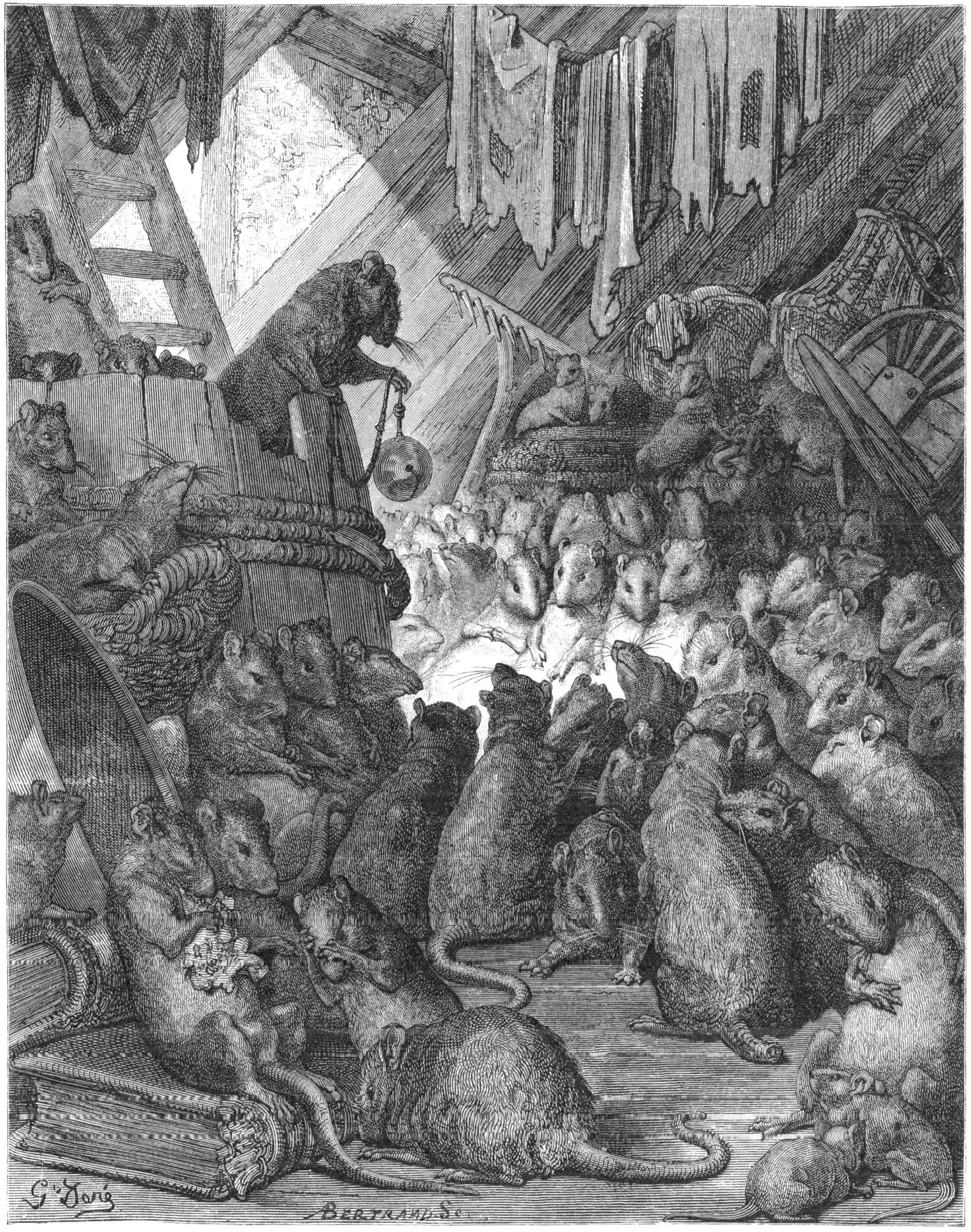

Council of Rats, 1867

Plate 8, *Fables*, Jean de La Fontaine

• Engraver: Antoine Bertrand (1828–88)

In an all-too-human gathering of rats in an attic, the leader proposes a bell around a cat's neck to warn them of approaching danger, but none of them can figure out how to get the feline to wear it. Doré spent months at the Paris zoo, studying animals for this folio.

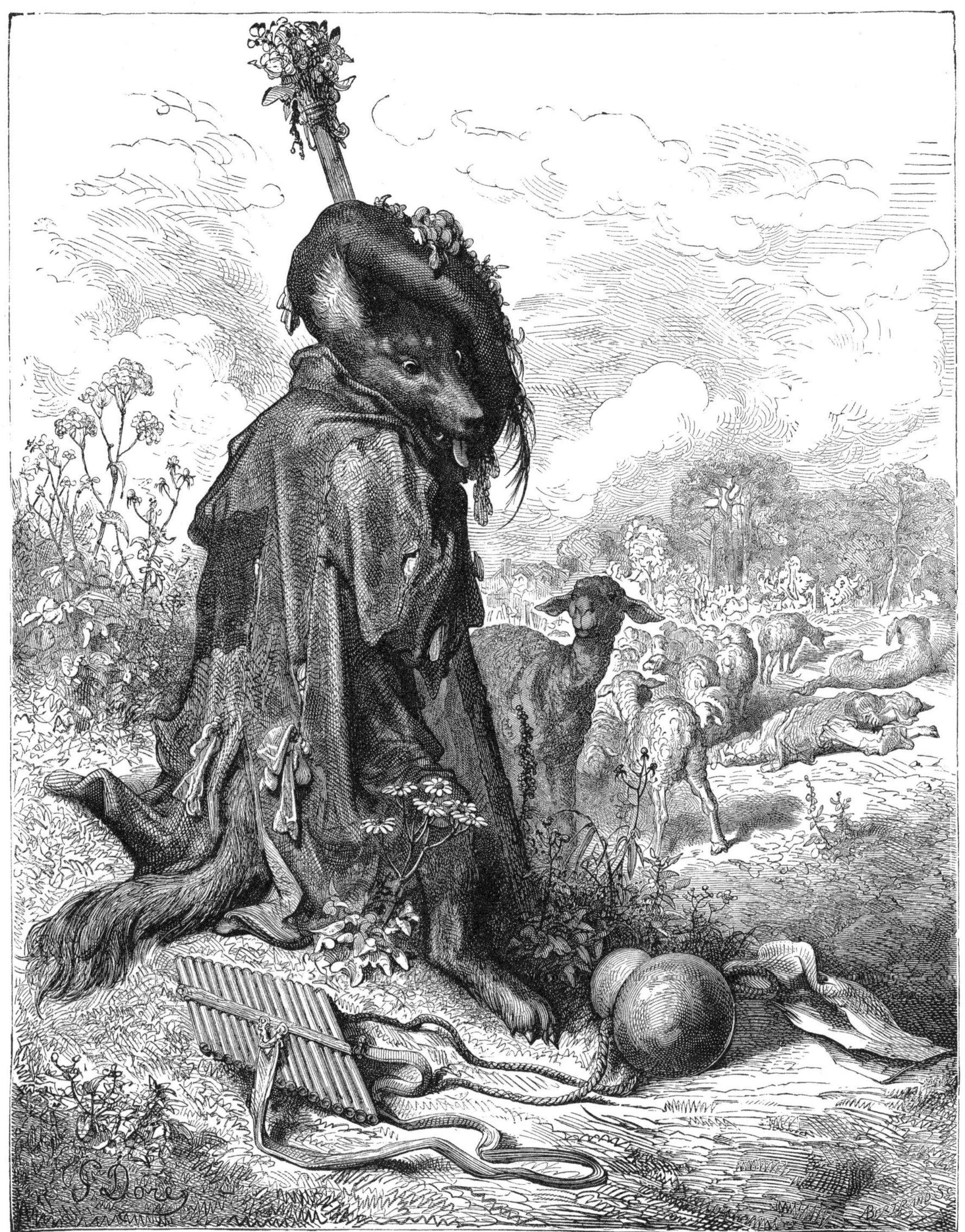

Wolf Turned Shepherd, 1867

Plate 14, *Fables*, Jean de La Fontaine

• Engraver: Antoine Bertrand (1828–88)

A wolf figures out how to sneak up on sheep by donning clothing stolen from the shepherd, who lies asleep in the distance. One sheep is intrigued by the strange creature. Doré loves wolves and rats, and several of these animals have been depicted in this folio.

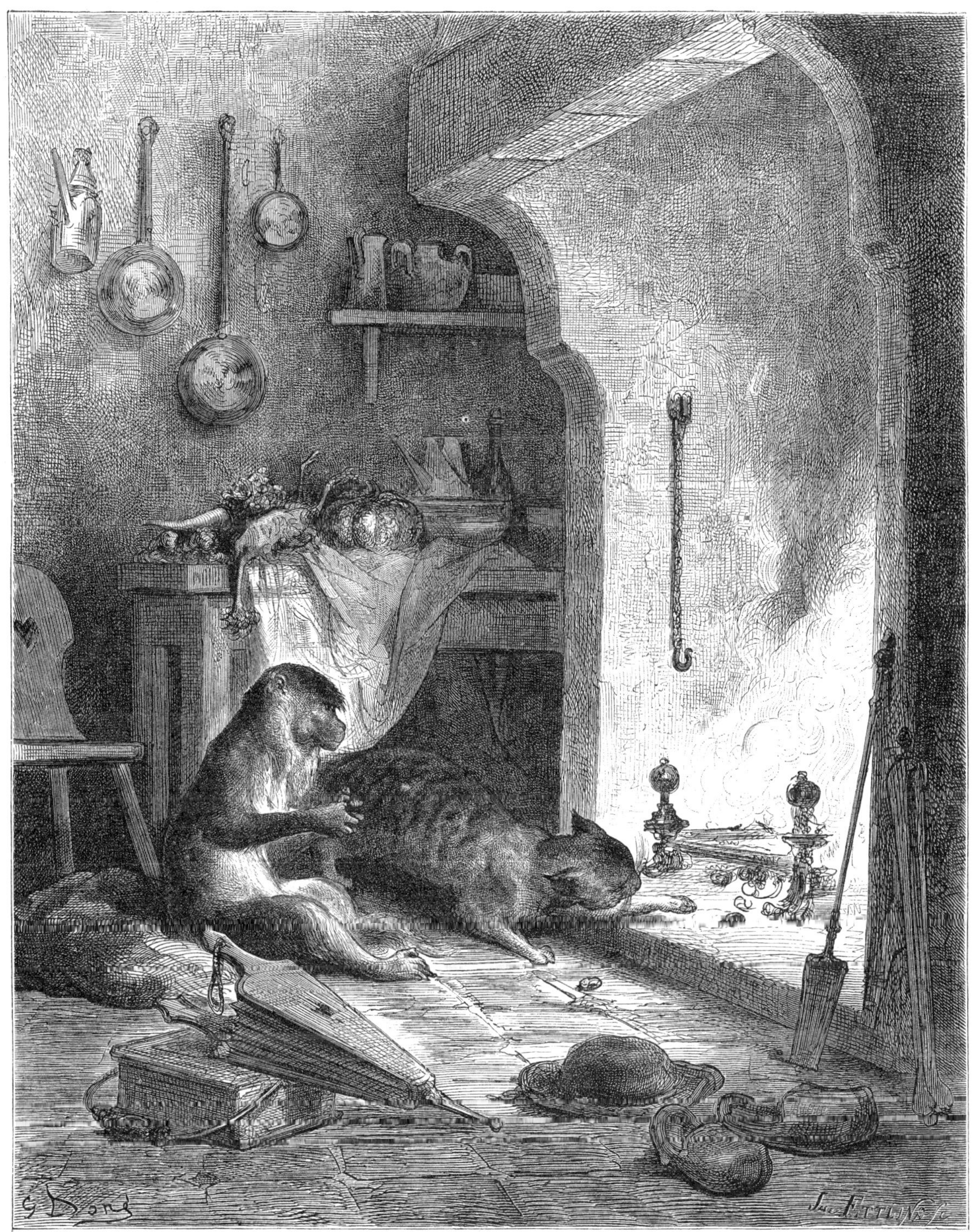

The Monkey and the Cat, 1867

Plate 63, *Fables*, Jean de La Fontaine

• Engraver: Jean-Jacob Ettling (dates unknown)

A monkey and a cat seek chestnuts from the fire; the latter risks getting burned, while the former eats them. This folio was criticized for not being as spectacular as other Doré folios, but these plates have a quaint charming quality and are still popular.

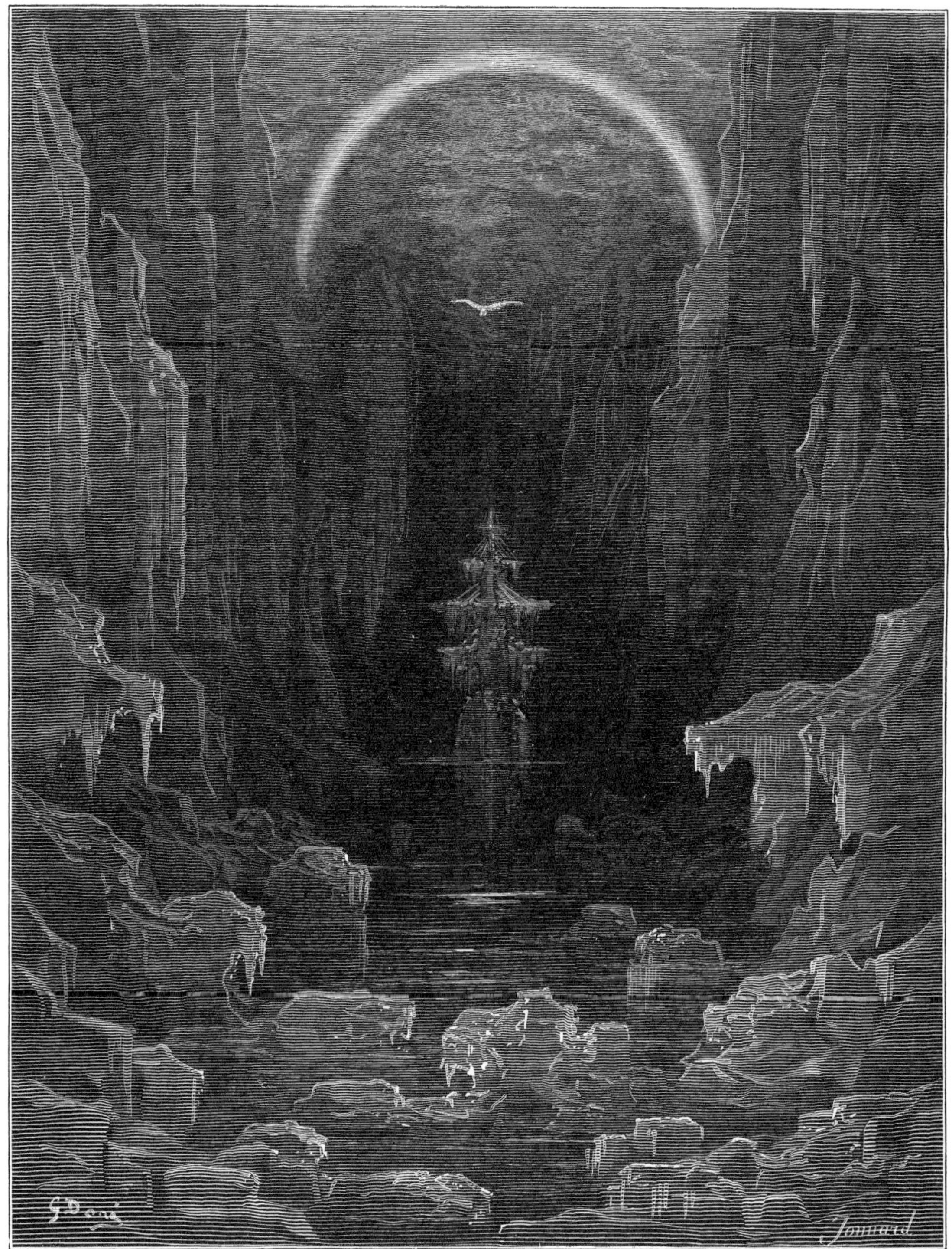

The Ice Ship, 1875

Plate 6, *The Rime of the Ancient Mariner*, Samuel Taylor Coleridge

• Engraver: Paul Jonnard (1840–1902)

'The ice was here, the ice was there / The ice was all around.' Doré adds more symbolism with the albatross and rainbow above the ship. This image has been borrowed for several beautiful posters and for the pipe organ in *Pirates of the Caribbean: Dead Man's Chest* (2006).

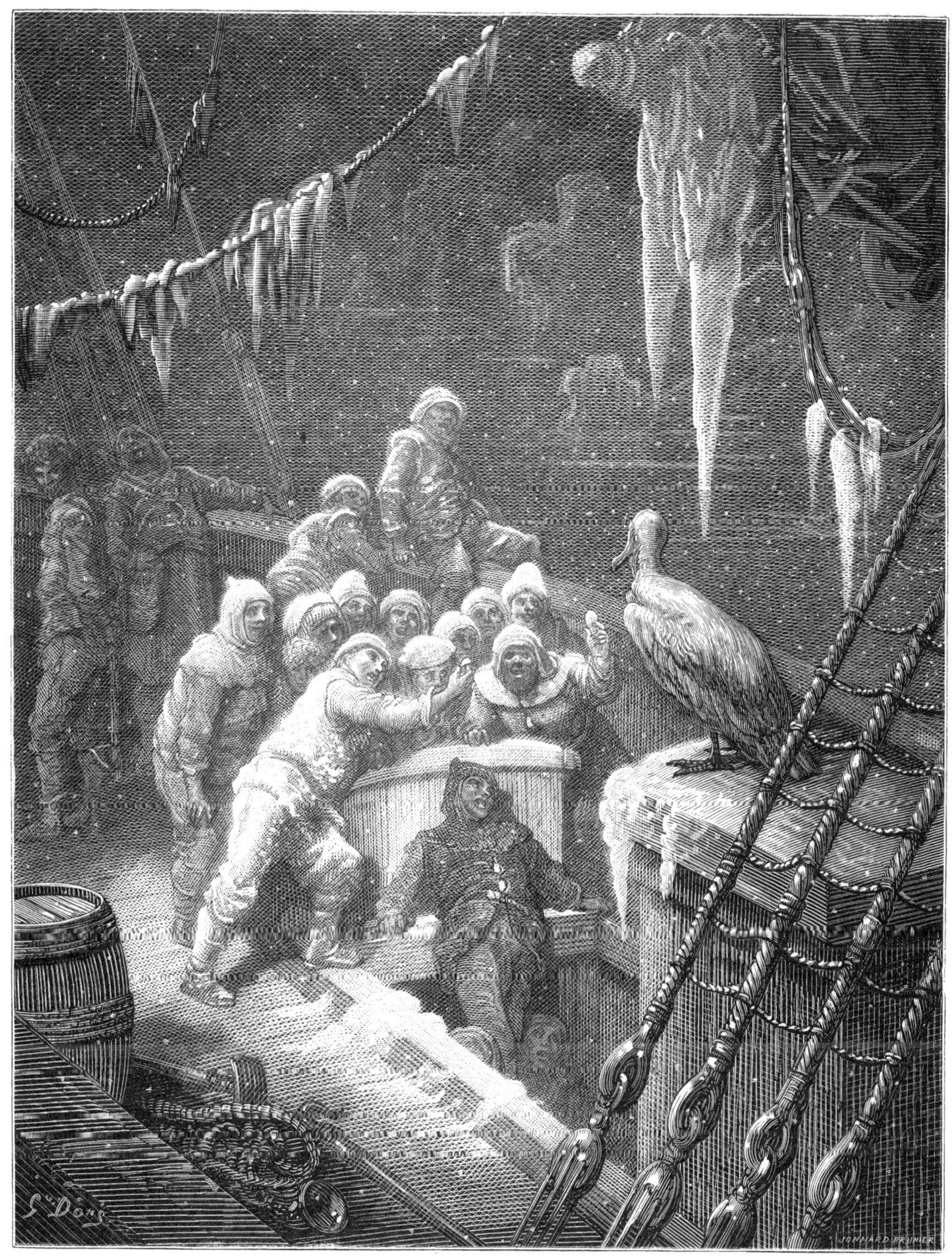

Sailors Feeding Albatross, 1875

Plate 7, *The Rime of the Ancient Mariner*, Samuel Taylor Coleridge
• Engraver: Paul Jonnard (1840–1902)

An albatross – a bird of good omen – arrives, the ship is freed from the ice, and snow-covered sailors feed the animal; it shows Doré at the height of his creative ability. This 22.8 x 30.4 cm (9 x 12 in) original, seen through major magnification, shows beautiful cross-hatching patterns that create dazzling effects.

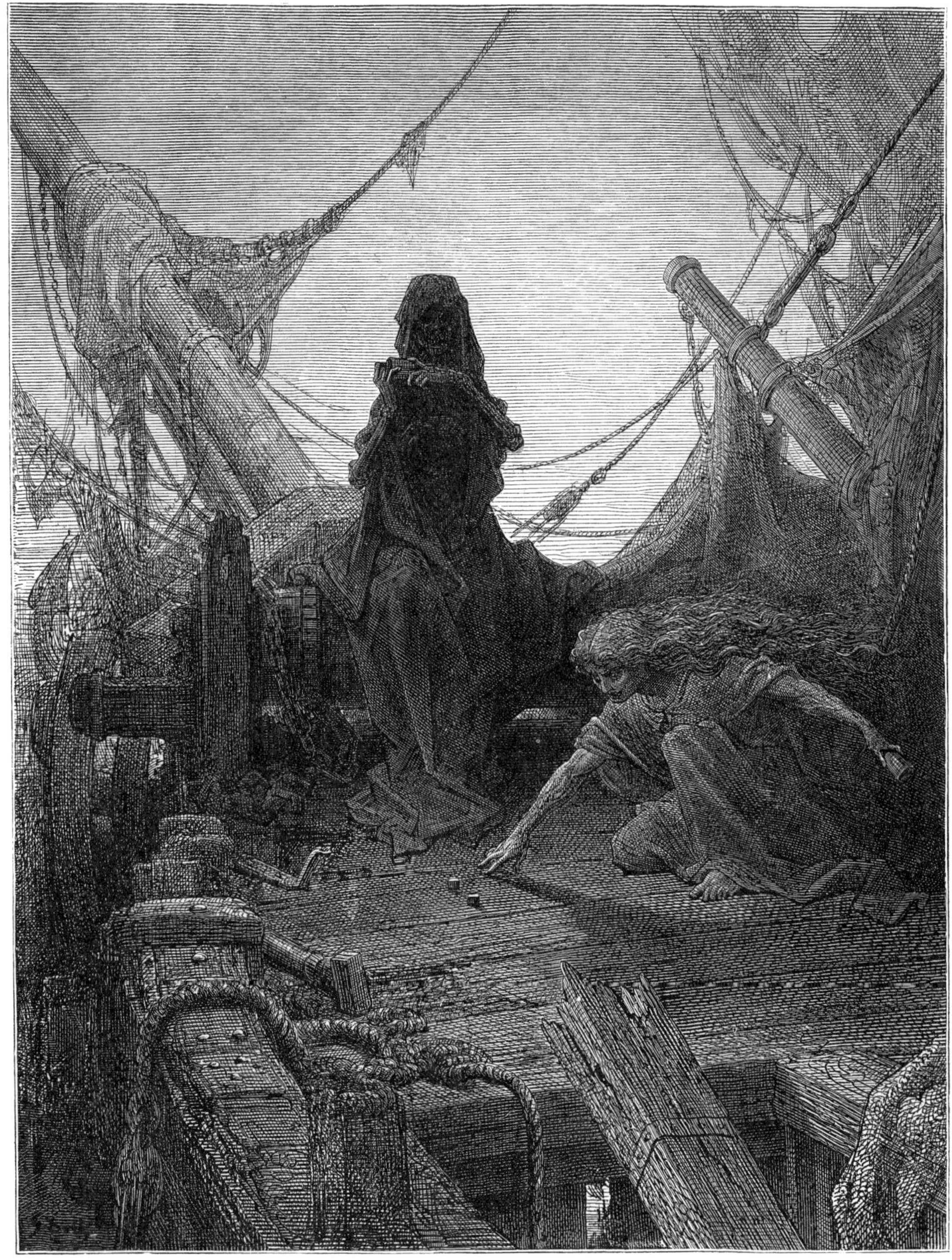

Death on the Ghost Ship, 1875

Plate 14, *The Rime of the Ancient Mariner*, Samuel Taylor Coleridge

• Engraver: A.F. Pannemaker (1822–1900)

Another ship appears, but proves to be a lifeless ghost ship. Doré depicts two allegorical figures casting lots for the souls of the sailors – 'Death' (a skeleton) and a witch-like 'Life-in-Death' who exclaims, 'The game is done! I've won, I've won!'

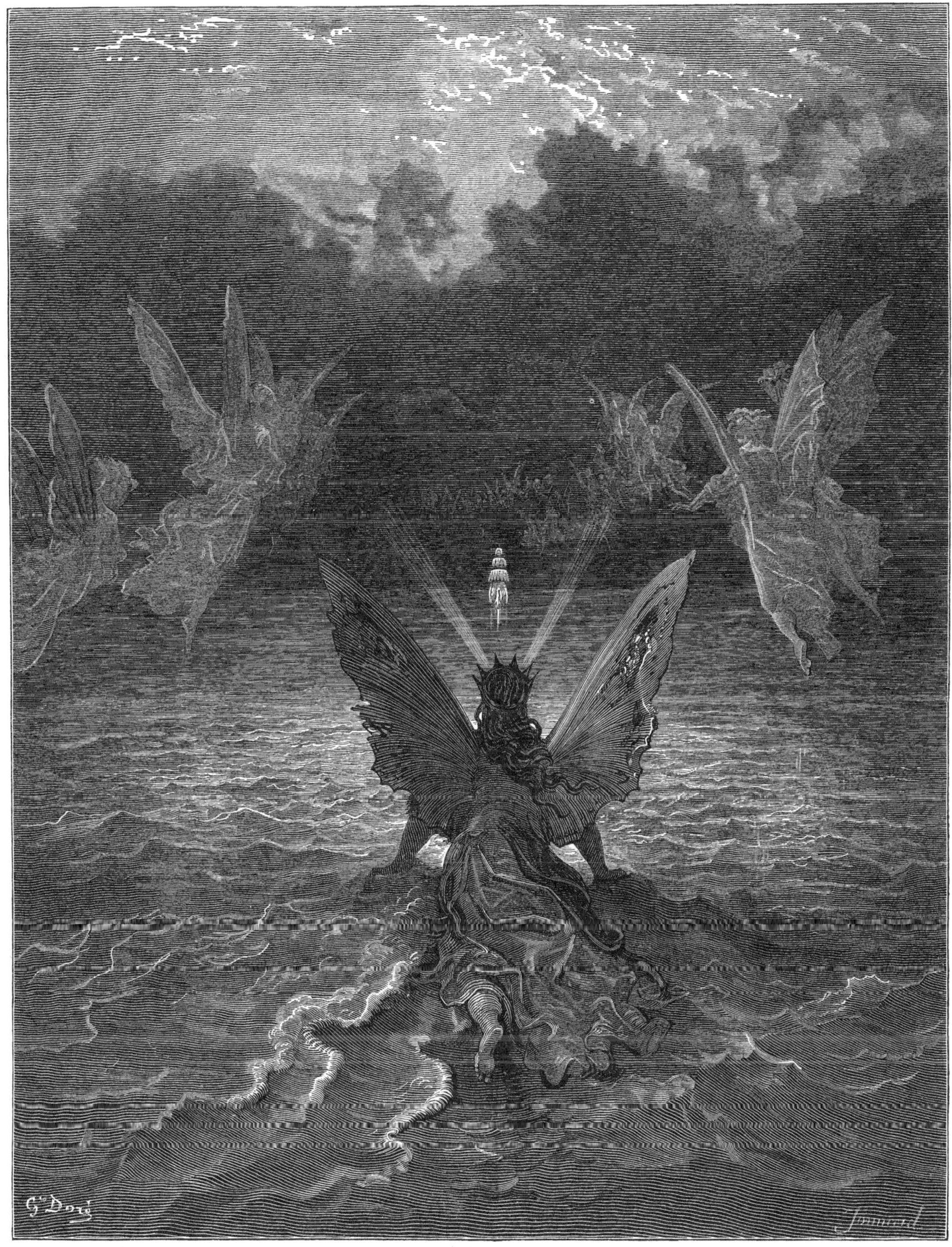

Angels Approaching Ship, 1875

Plate 23, *The Rime of the Ancient Mariner*, Samuel Taylor Coleridge
• Engraver: Paul Jonnard (1840–1902)

The mariner, all alone amidst his dead sailor mates, does not realize that a group of angels are flying and skimming the waters towards the tiny doomed ship in the distance. Doré's angels alternated between butterfly and feathered wings.

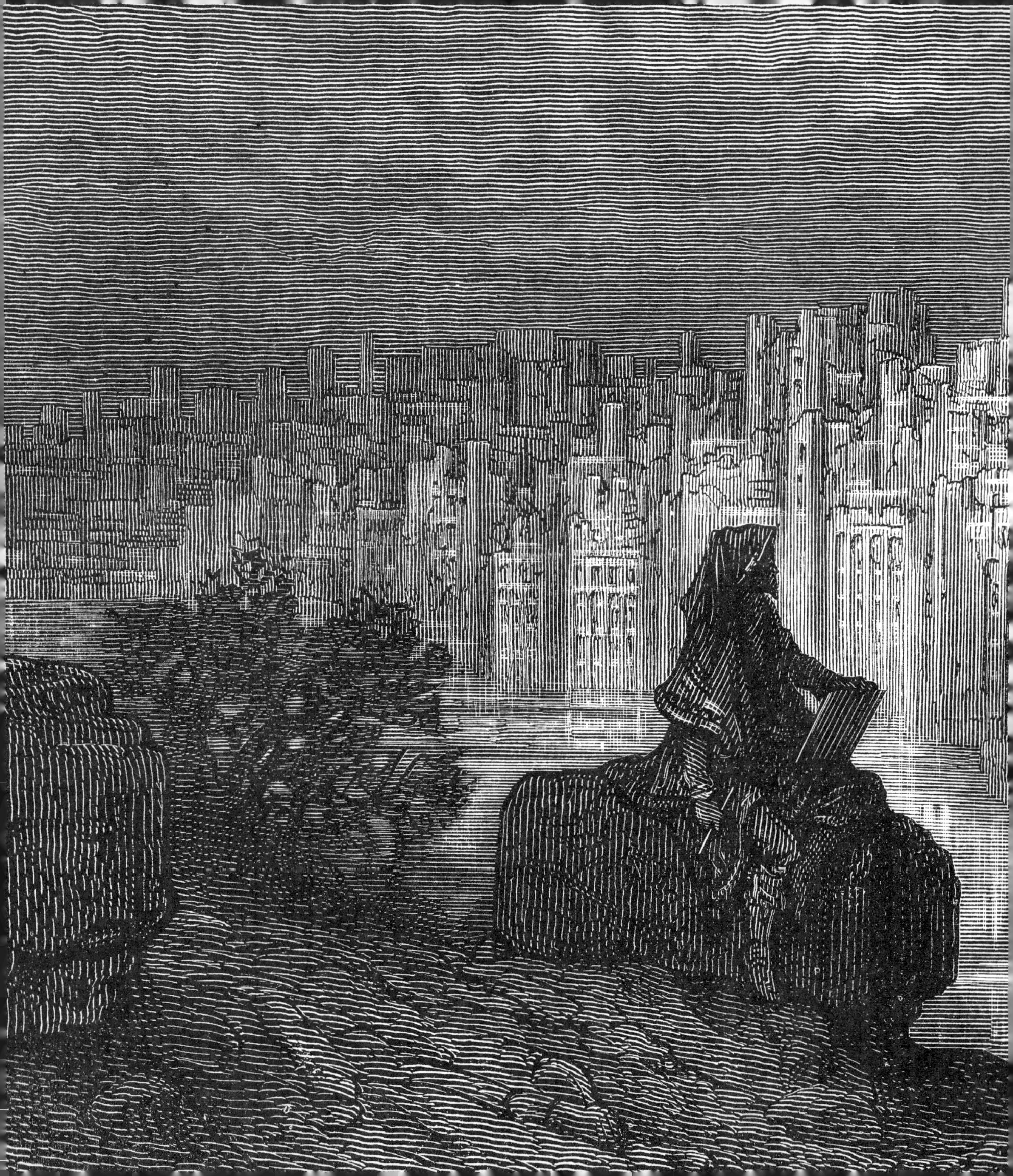

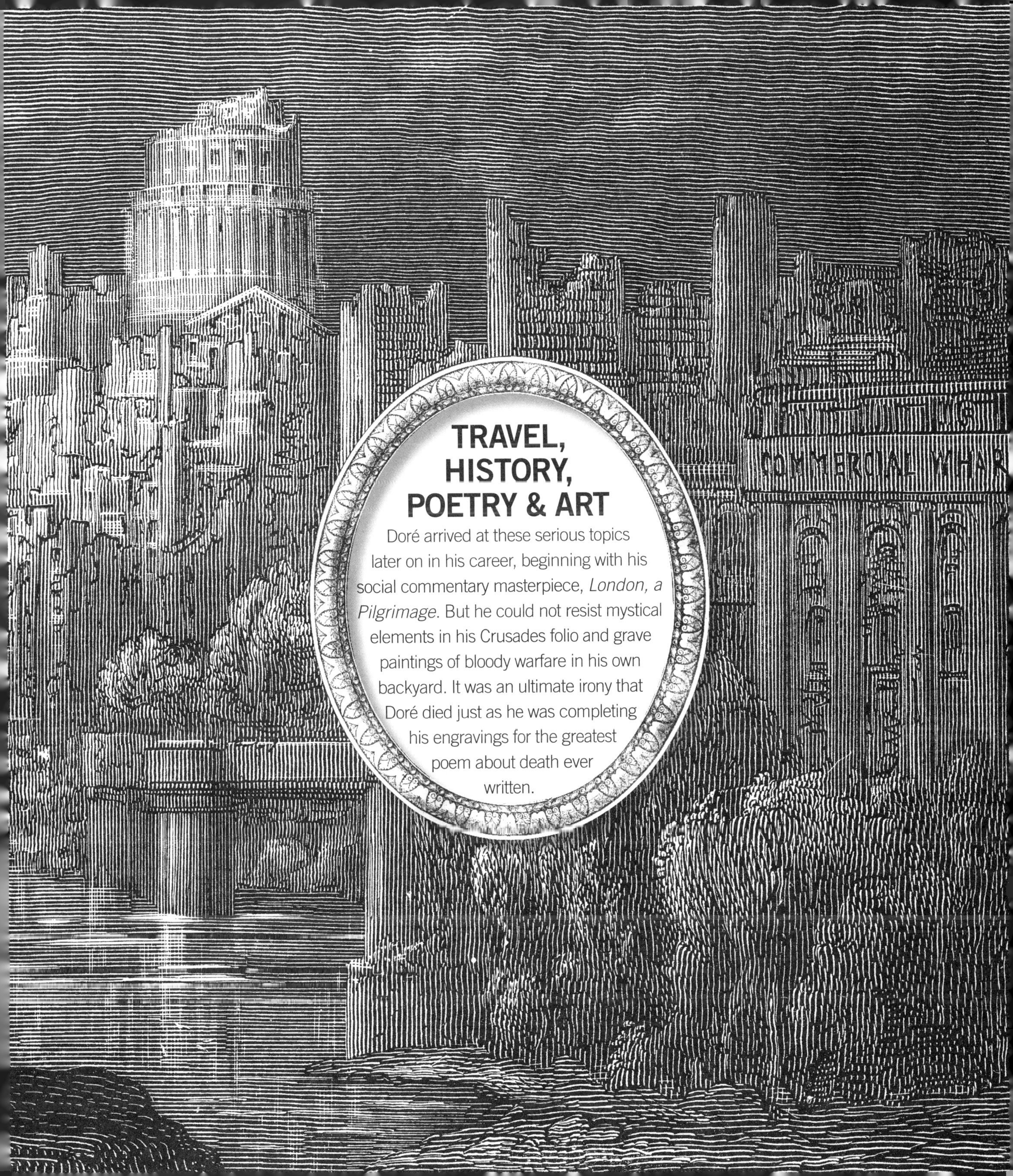

TRAVEL, HISTORY, POETRY & ART

Doré arrived at these serious topics later on in his career, beginning with his social commentary masterpiece, *London, a Pilgrimage*. But he could not resist mystical elements in his Crusades folio and grave paintings of bloody warfare in his own backyard. It was an ultimate irony that Doré died just as he was completing his engravings for the greatest poem about death ever written.

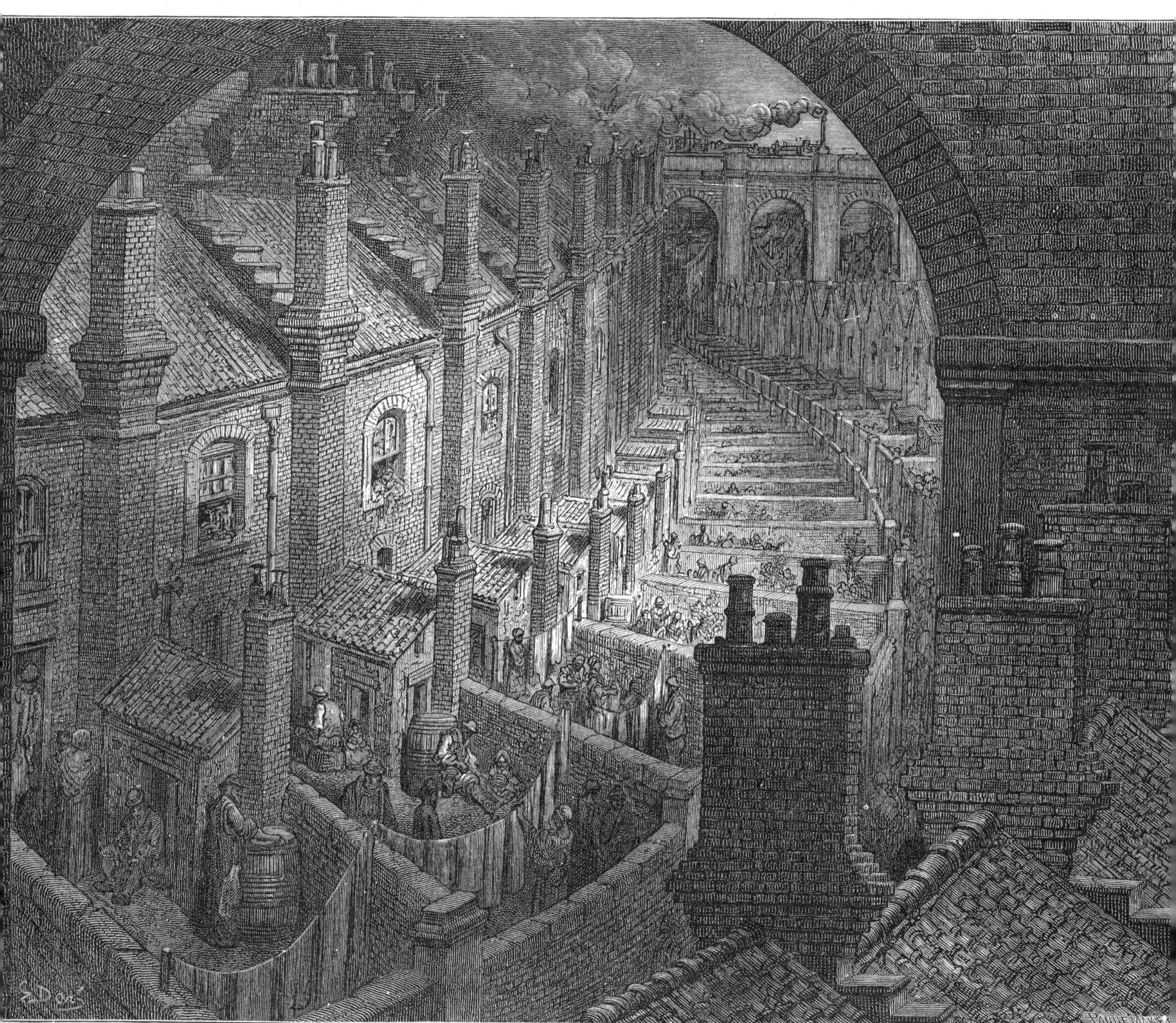

Over London by Rail, 1872

Page 120, *London, A Pilgrimage*, Blanchard Jerrold
• Engraver: A.F. Pannemaker (1822–1900)

This scene uses architectural contours to show the plight of the London poor, housed in endless rows of tiny shacks behind factories that were 'so full of children you can hardly shut the door'. Doré's 180 engravings have become iconic images of Victorian London.

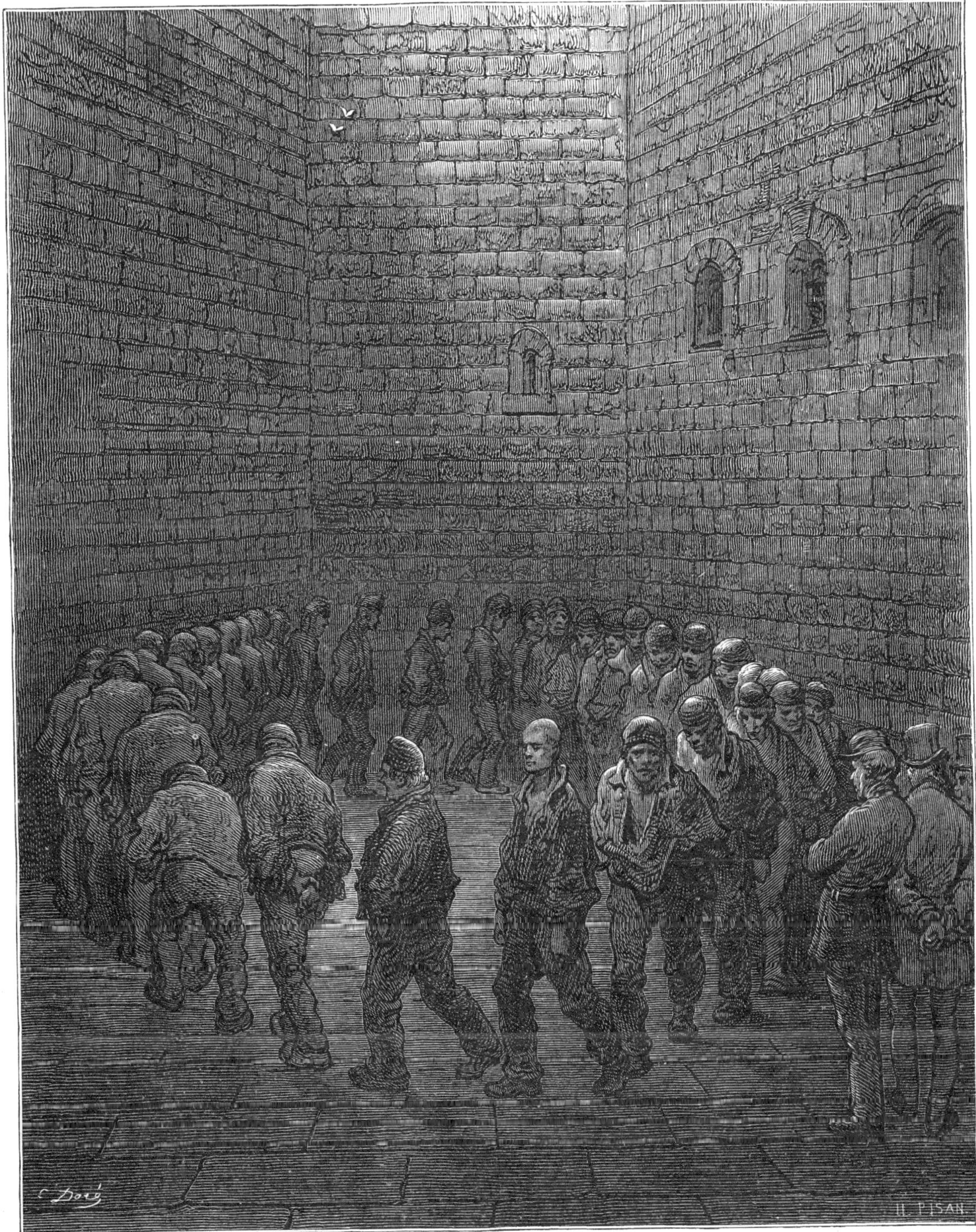

Newgate Exercise Yard, 1872

Page 136, *London, A Pilgrimage*, Blanchard Jerrold

• Engraver: Heliodore Pisan (1822–1900)

Newgate Prison's inmate exercise consisted of endlessly walking around in circles in a room with high stone walls. Vincent van Gogh made it into a painting, *Prisoners Exercising (after Doré)*, now in the Pushkin Museum, Russia. It has been used for scenes in several movies, including *A Clockwork Orange* (1971).

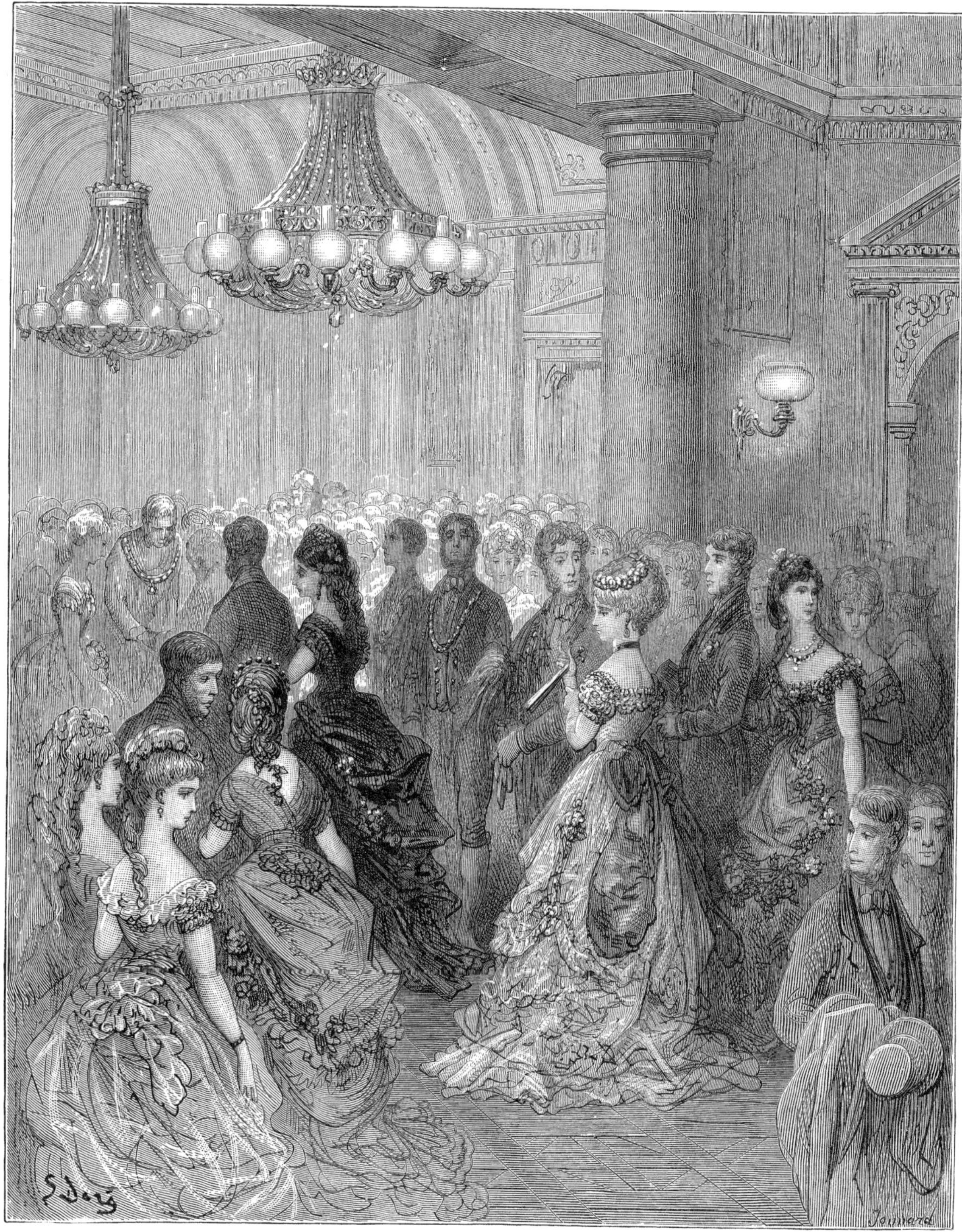

Mansion House Ball, 1872
Page 174, *London, A Pilgrimage,* Blanchard Jerrold
• Engraver: Paul Jonnard (1840–1902)

Most people thought that this folio was going to depict wealthy Londoners wearing their best gowns at a high-fashion social gathering, so many critics were very irritated by Doré's minor tribute to high society but major emphasis on the working classes and living conditions of the poor.

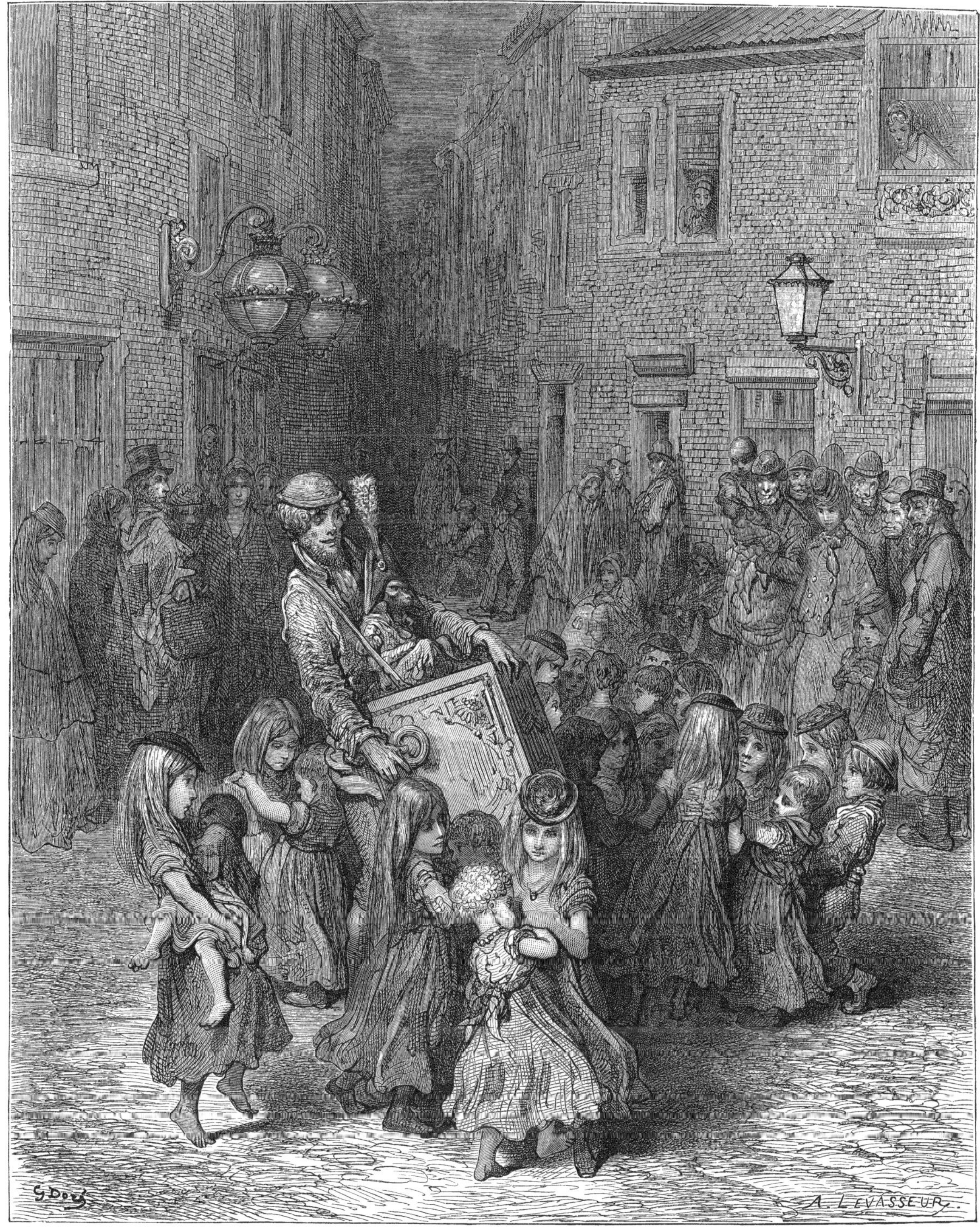

The Organ Grinder, 1872

Page 176, *London, A Pilgrimage*, Blanchard Jerrold

• Engraver: A. Levasseur (dates unknown)

One of the few moments of pure pleasure, as throngs of little girls dance around a barrel organ – 'the opera of the street folk' – in a narrow street. The many Doré scenes depicting the life of the London poor have been used for numerous Dickensian films, such as *Oliver Twist* (2005), directed by Roman Polanski.

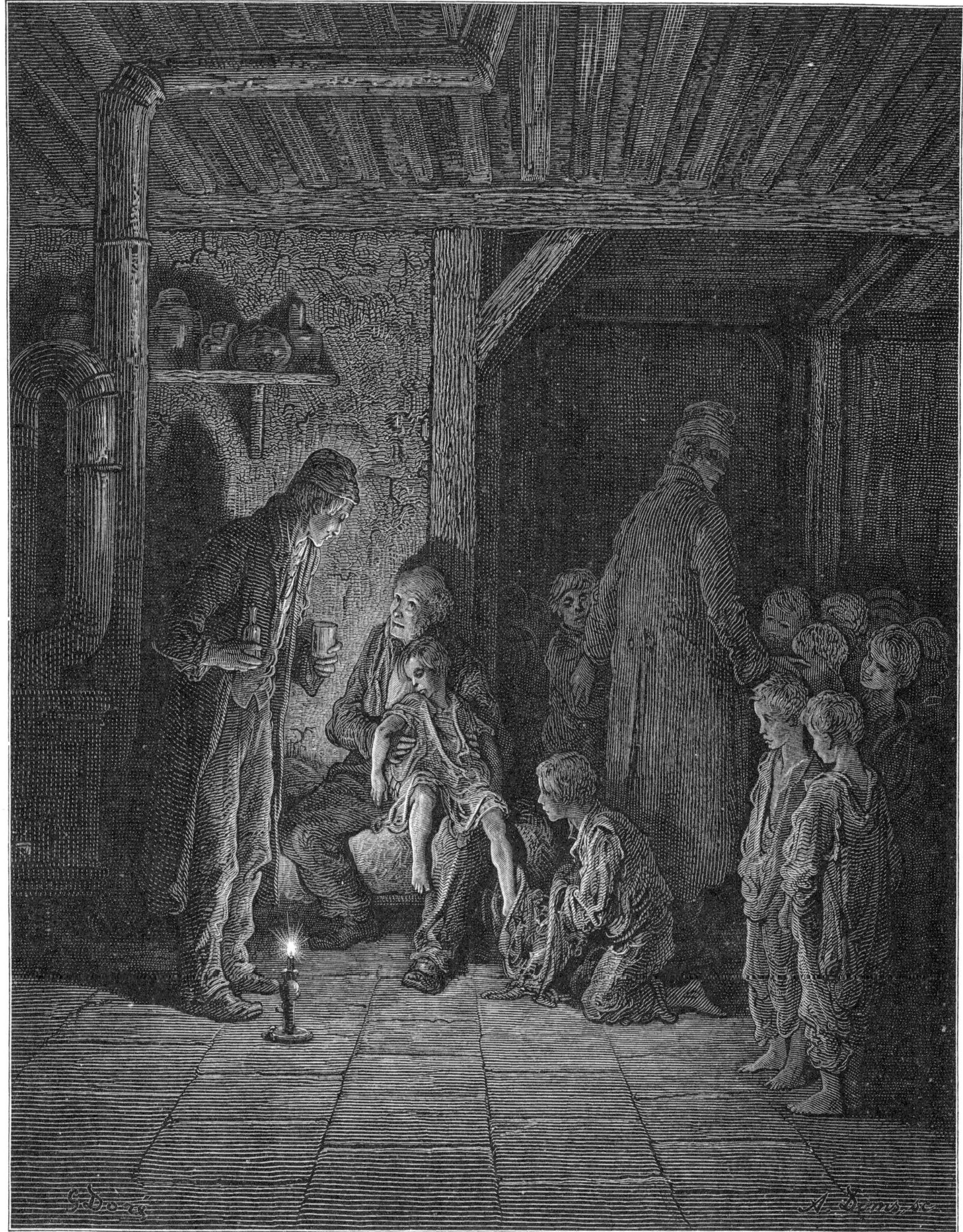

Found in the Street, 1872

Page 184, *London, A Pilgrimage*, Blanchard Jerrold

• Engraver: A. Doms (dates unknown, student of Pannemaker)

A charity takes in a boy found dying in the street. One of Doré's most pathetic and personal images, the entire scene is in white-on-black, illuminated by a single candle on the floor. It was used for a 1970s charity promotional poster for a children's hospital.

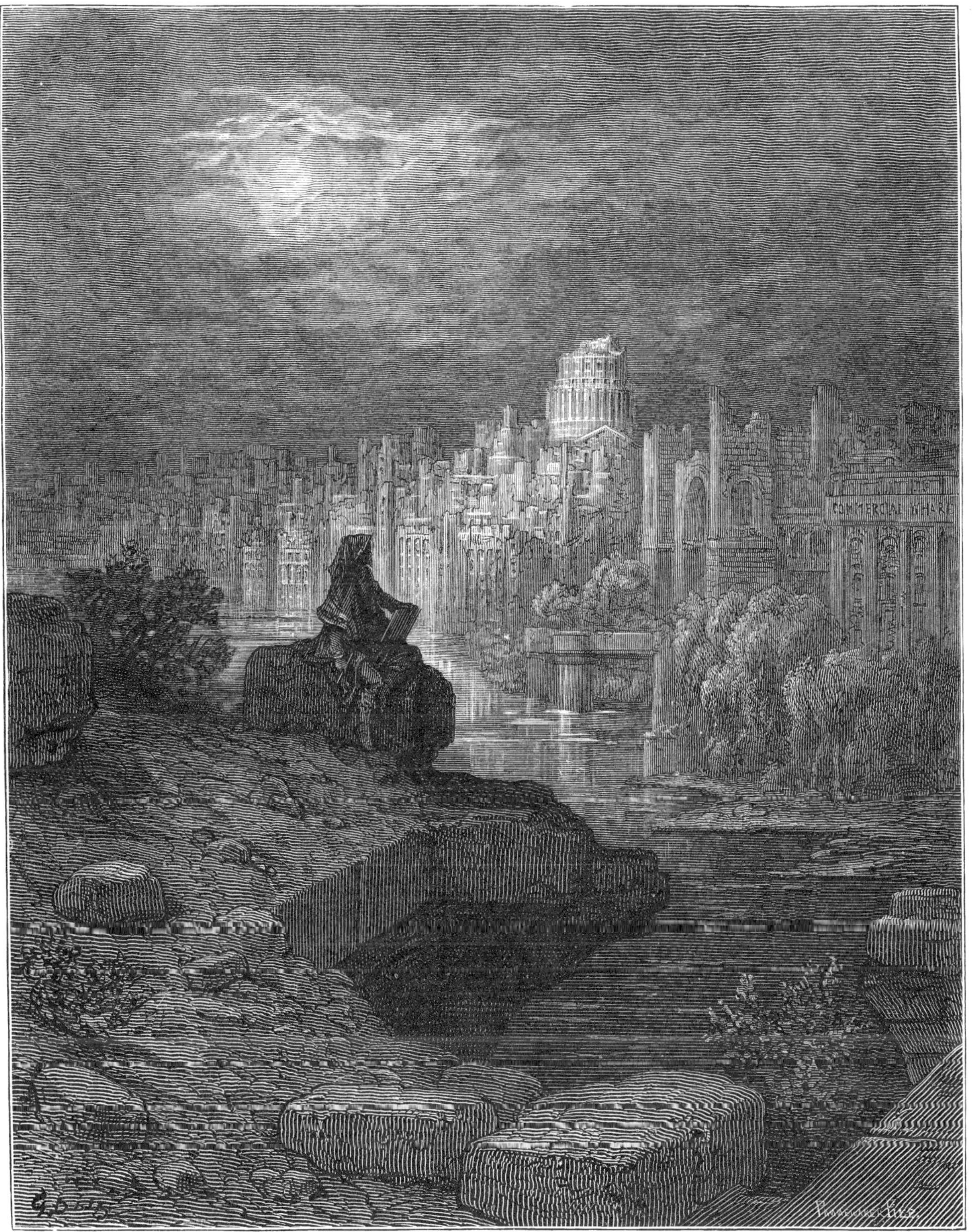

The New Zealander, 1872

Page 186, *London, A Pilgrimage*, Blanchard Jerrold

• Engraver: Stéphane Pannemaker (1847–1930)

In one of Doré's most prophetic images, envisioning the 1940 Blitz, a future traveller from New Zealand sketches the ruins of London. The 1872 folio quotes from Thomas Macaulay (1840), but Doré changes some details. This image has been reprinted on the cover of many books and is still heavily debated today.

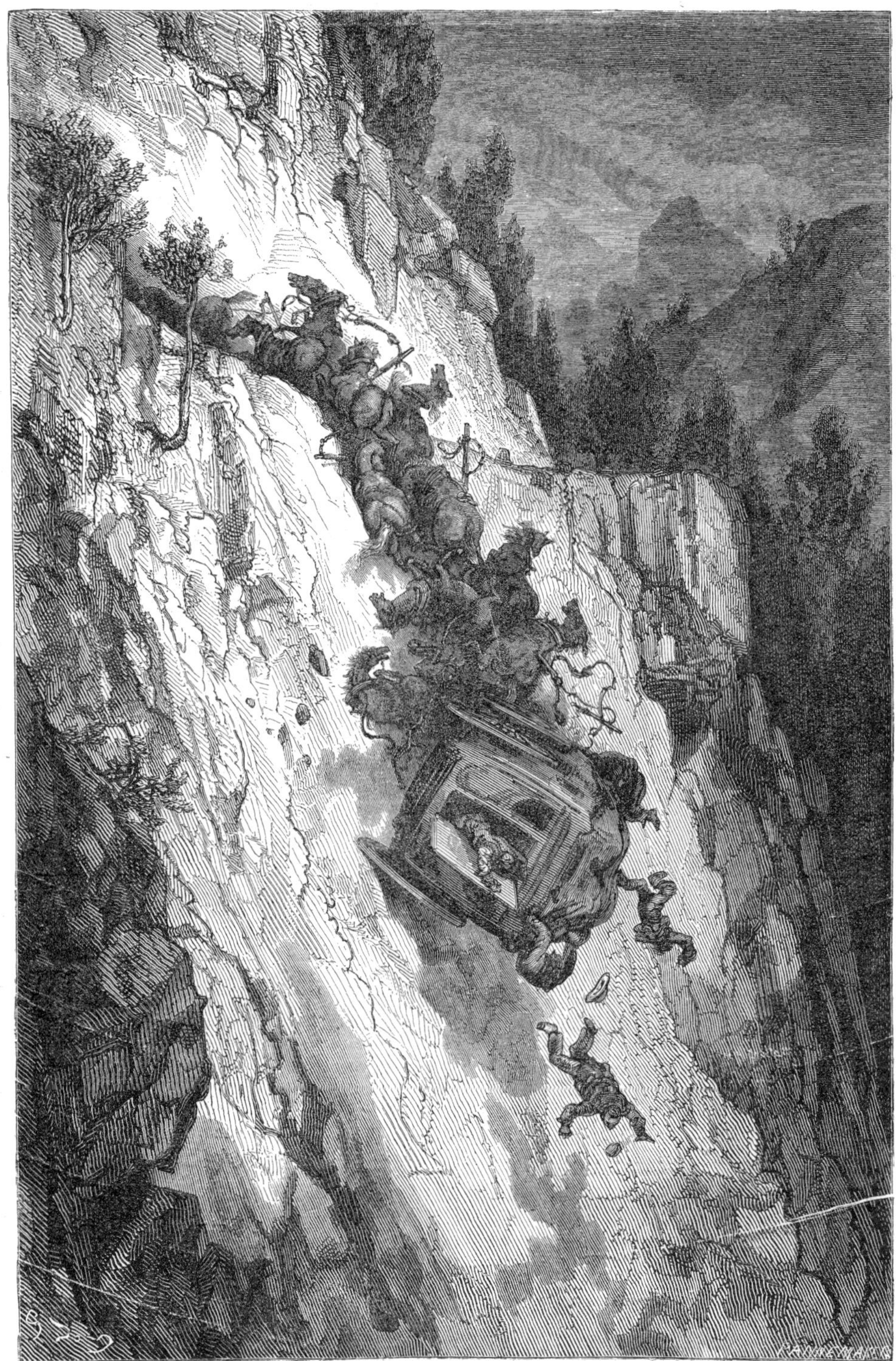

Coach Falling over Cliff, 1874

Chapter 1, *Spain*, Baron Charles Davillier

• Engraver: A.F. Pannemaker (1822–1900)

A coach on a narrow mountainous Spanish pathway has fallen over the edge of the cliff. Doré loved action frozen at a most dramatic point, showing men falling out of the vehicle in mid-air. Doré's 1874 folio book edition was a reprint of a serial running from 1860 to 1873 in *Tour du Monde*.

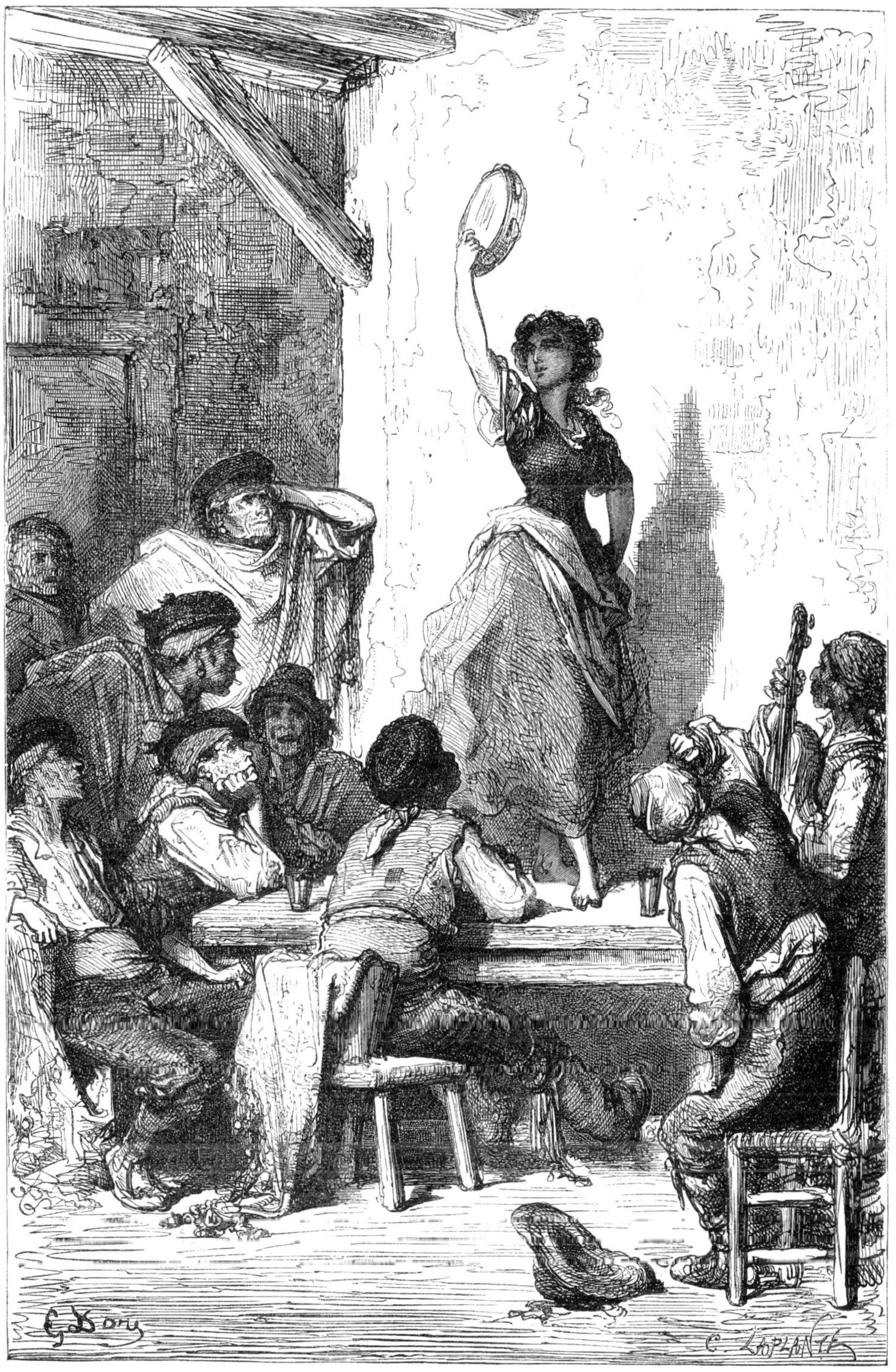

Gypsy Girl Dancing the Vito, 1874
Chapter 14, *Spain*, Baron Charles Davillier
• Engraver: Charles Laplante (1837–1903)

A barefoot gypsy girl with a tambourine dances on a table, mesmerizing a group of men. This is Doré's most famous print from *Spain*, which was a major influence on Georges Bizet's *Carmen*. One of the most famous posters for that opera is an almost-exact reproduction of this engraving.

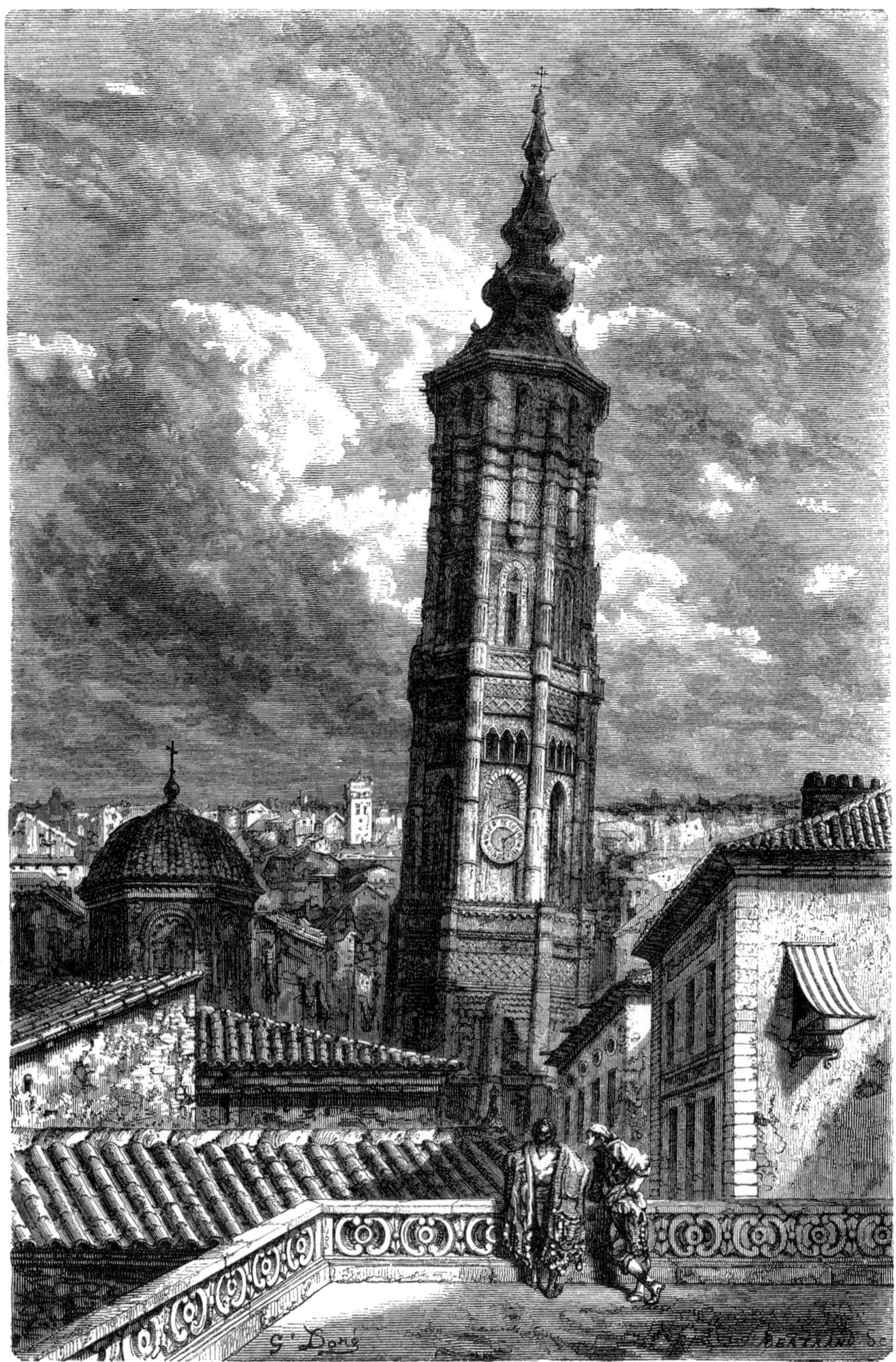

The Leaning Tower of Saragossa, 1874
Chapter 26, *Spain*, Baron Charles Davillier
• Engraver: Antoine Bertrand (1828–88)

Unlike *London, A Pilgrimage*, *Spain* contained very little social commentary. It was Doré's travel book, showing the breadth of Spanish landscape, people and architecture, such as the country's leaning tower. Doré did over 700 engravings set in Spain (for this folio and *Don Quixote*), all highly regarded.

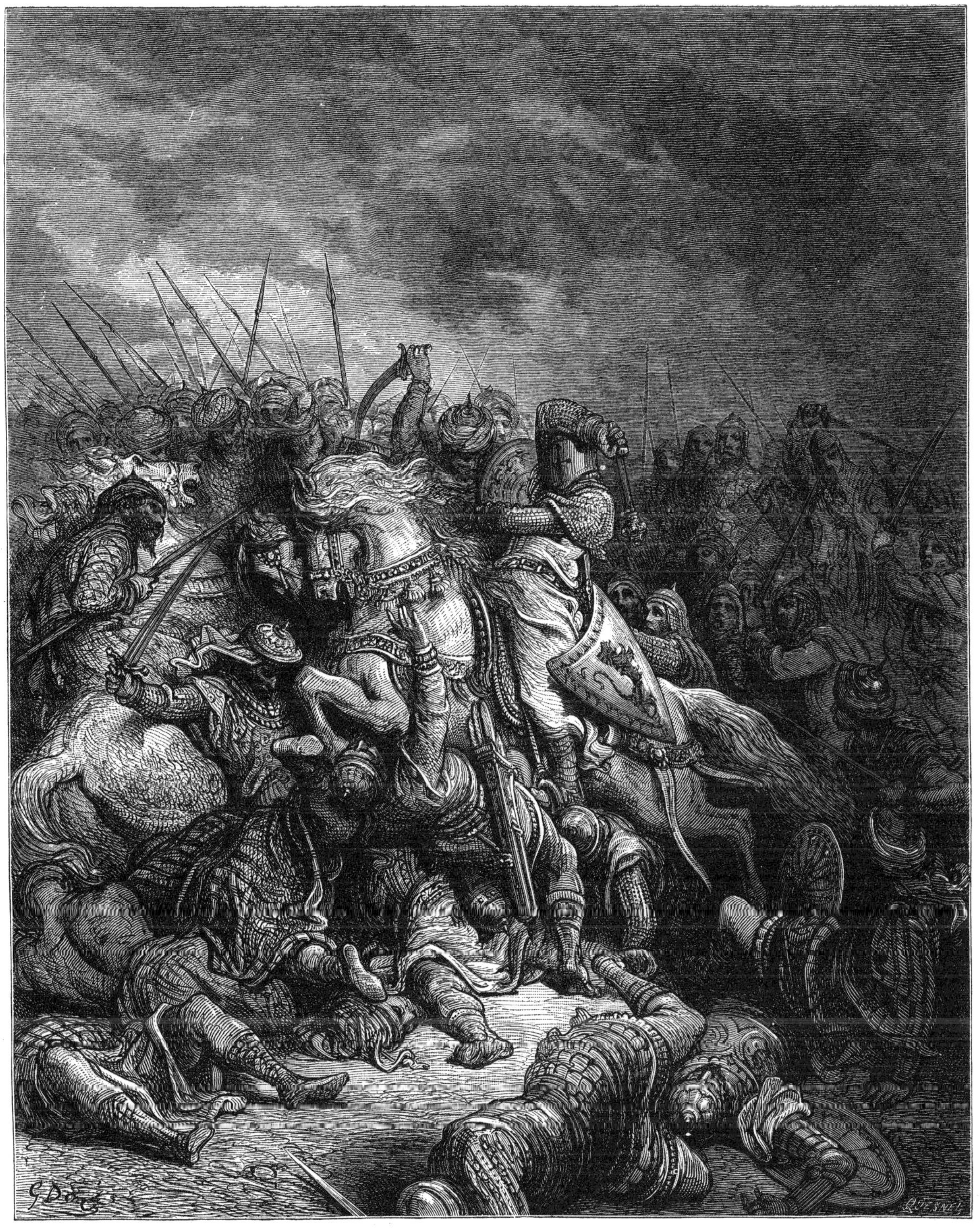

Richard the Lionheart and Saladin, 1877

Plate 45, *The Crusades*, Joseph Michaud

• Engraver: Mathieu Quesnel (1843–1915)

This is perhaps the central scene in the Crusades folio and depicts the Battle of Arsuf. Doré was very proficient at capturing the chaotic melee of battle, starting with hundreds of engravings of the Crimean War. But there are flaws in this scene: Richard is shown with a very small weapon – and how could those horses even move?

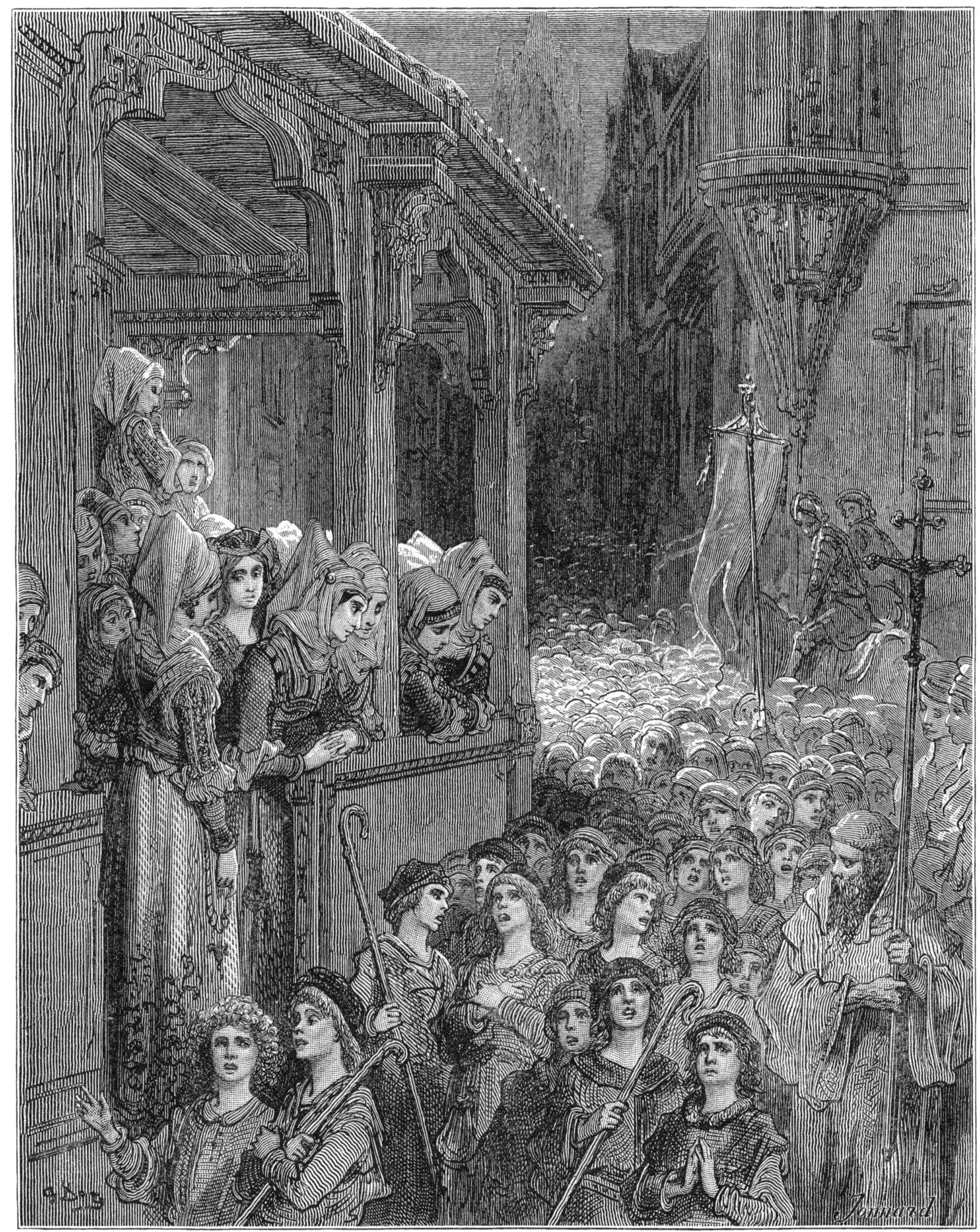

The Children's Crusade, 1877

Plate 53, *The Crusades*, Joseph Michaud
• Engraver: Paul Jonnard (1840-1902)

A pathetic element of the Crusades was thousands of naïve unarmed young people thinking they could go to the Holy Land and achieve something. Doré depicted local women puzzled by the endless parade of dreamy young people, many of whom would end up dead or sold into slavery. A 2008 Gary Dickson book on the subject features this Doré print on the front cover and in the introduction.

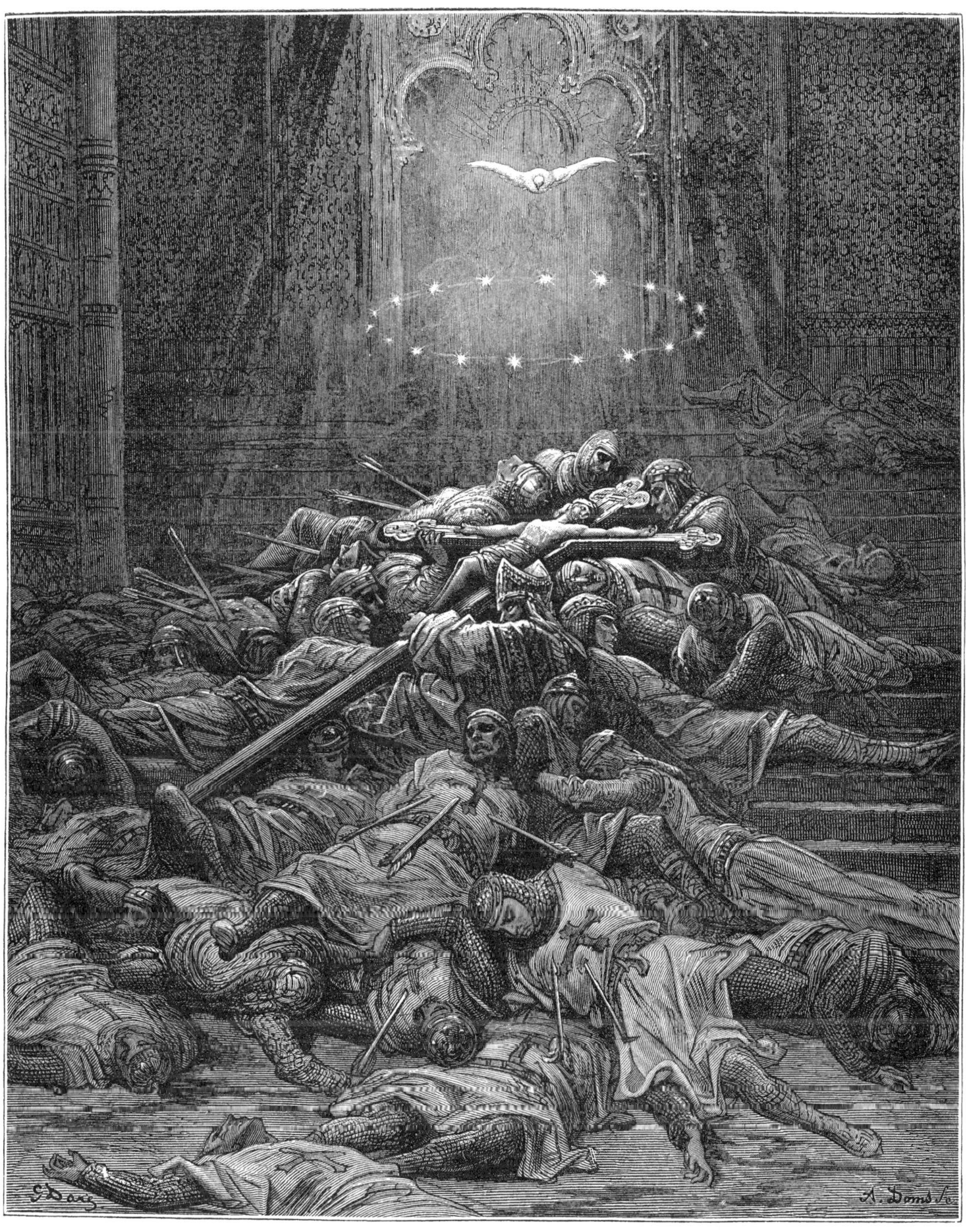

Celestial Light, 1877

Plate 74, *The Crusades*, Joseph Michaud

• Engraver: A. Doms (dates unknown, student of Pannemaker)

Doré adds mystical elements to a group of dead Crusaders killed by arrows at the Battle of Sefed: a large crucifix blankets their bodies, while a celestial light, with stars and a dove, hovers over them. Doré does not portray the Crusades as a victory.

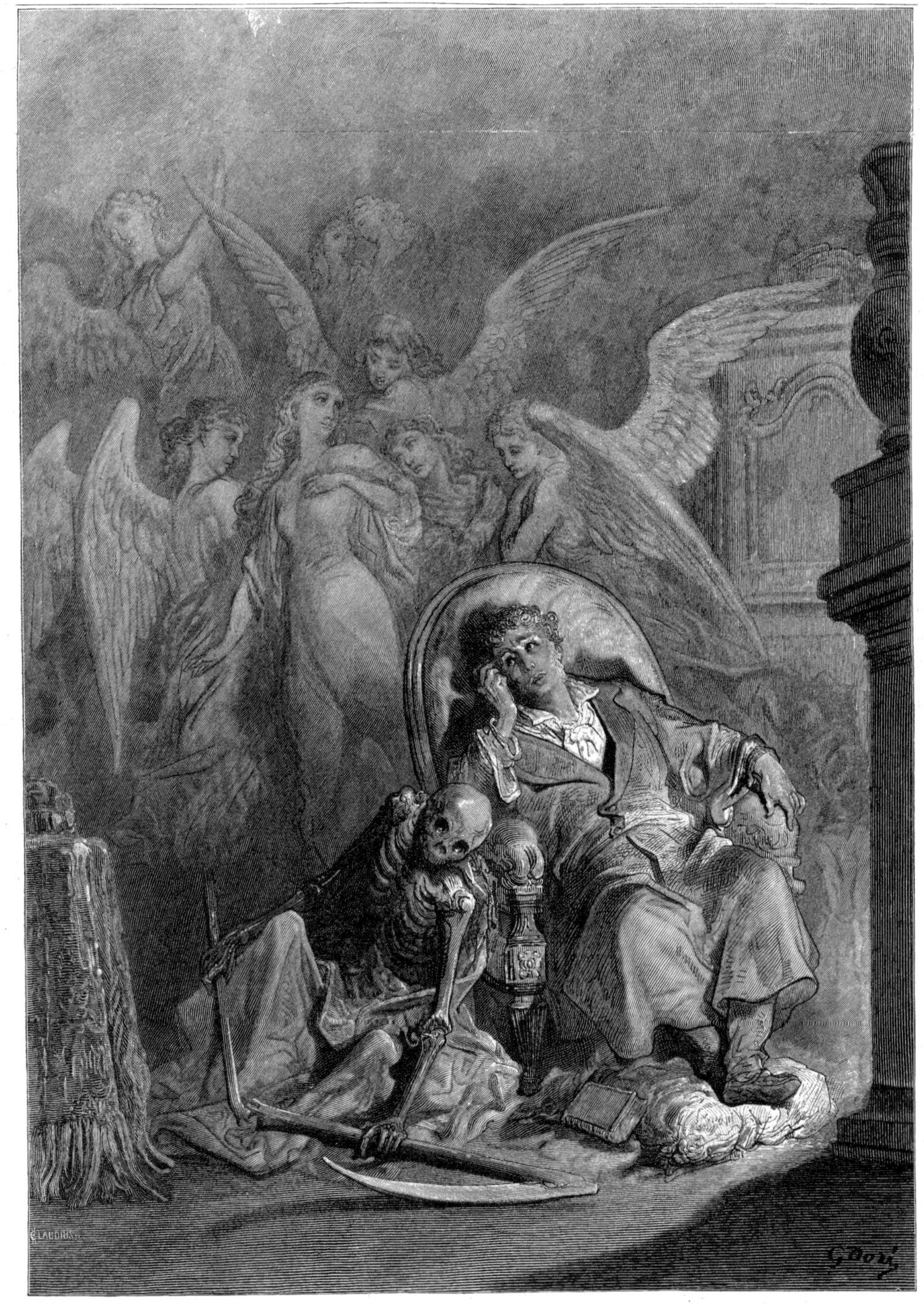

Sorrow for the Lost Lenore, 1883

Plate 4, *The Raven*, Edgar Allan Poe

• Engraver: H. Claudius (dates unknown)

The light from the fireplace shines on the writer, as the ethereal Lenore and the angels hover behind him, while Death bends over with a broken scythe. This is Doré's most powerful image of *The Raven*, representing all the elements of Poe's famous poem.

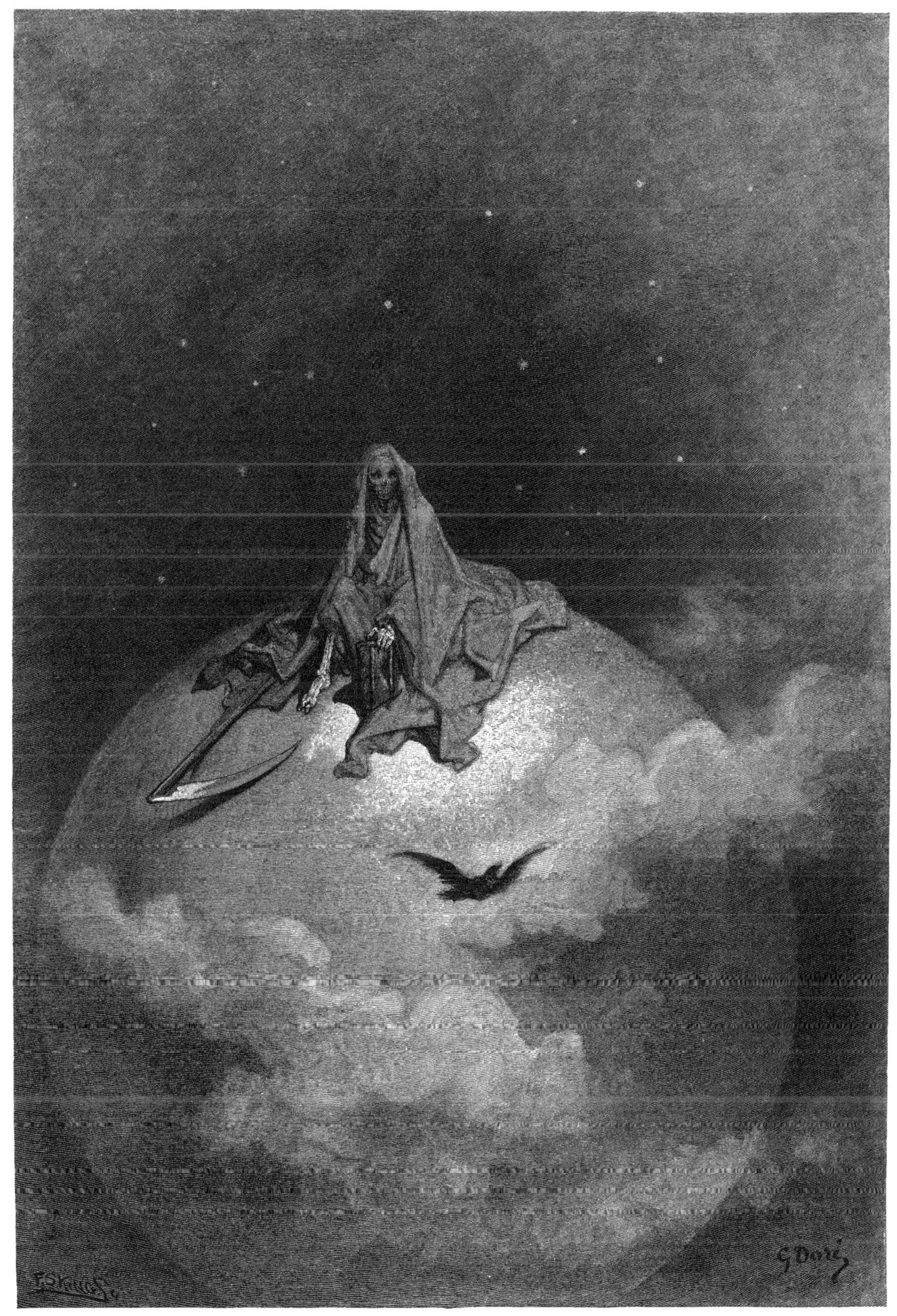

Death on the Globe, 1883

Plate 9, *The Raven*, Edgar Allan Poe

• Engraver: F.S. King (1850–1913)

Doré's imagination often went beyond the author's text. In another prophetic image, Death sits, holding a scythe, on the globe and sends out the raven. Sixty years later, this would become an artistic symbol of worldwide warfare in the Second World War and then for the 1960s Vietnam War anti-war posters.

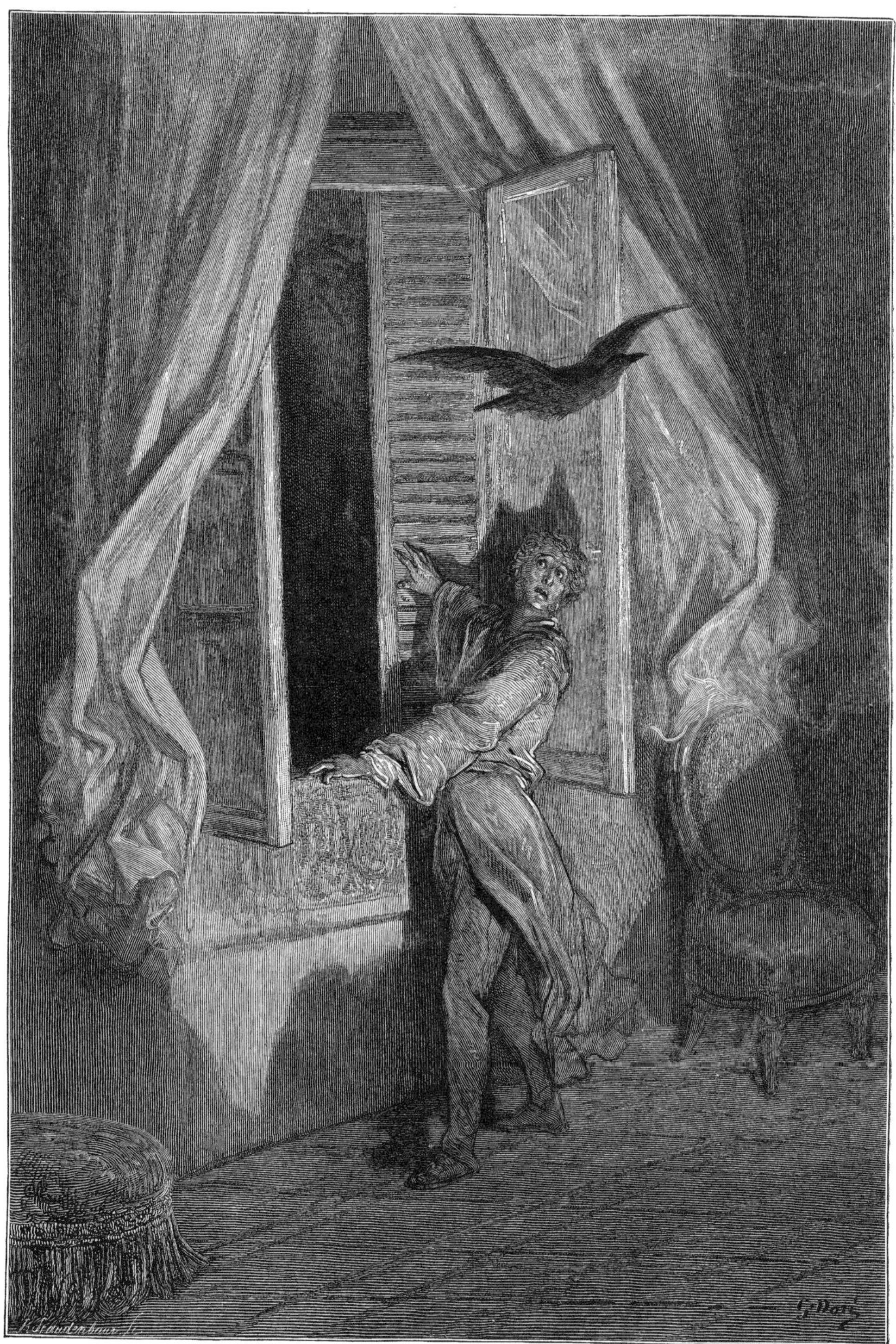

Raven Flies in Window, 1883

Plate 12, *The Raven*, Edgar Allan Poe

• Engraver: R. Staudenbaur (dates unknown)

The curtains are blown aside as a black bird makes its entrance into the melancholia of the room; Doré's image bears comparison to Edouard Manet's 1875 lithograph of the same scene. The two artists were chosen to present a petition to the Emperor, which led to the 1863 Salon des Refusés and the birth of Impressionism.

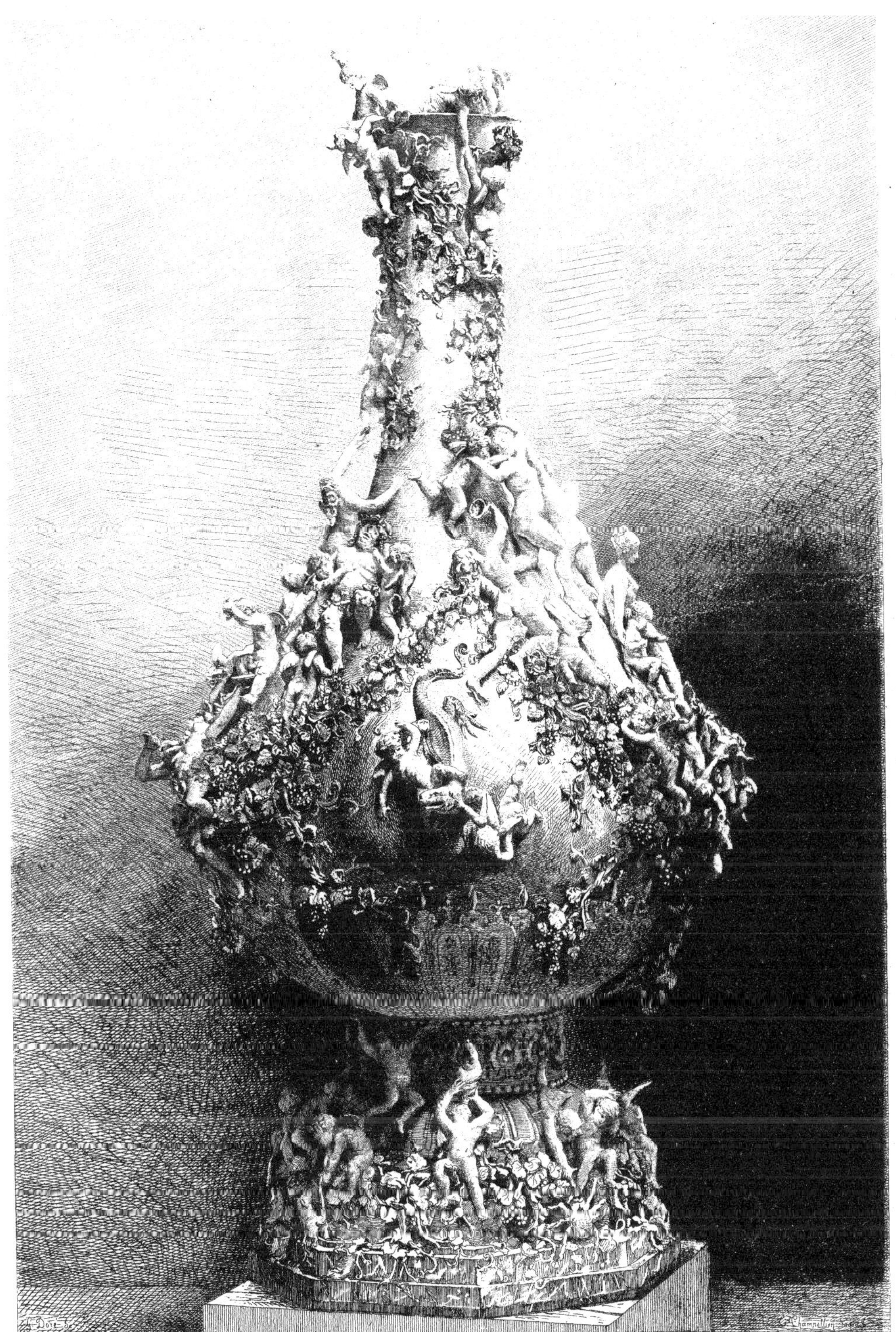

The Doré Vase, or The Poem of the Vine, 1878
Etching of bronze sculpture • Etching by E.A. Champollion
(1848–1901); original sculpture, 3.7 m (12 ft),
in M.H. de Young Museum, San Francisco

Nearly 100 creatures frolic amidst the vines of an Italian wine bottle. Doré's tribute to the wine industry is by far his most famous work of sculpture. It was at the centre of a great conflict, and then travelled thousands of miles to many countries to eventually find a home and the glory it deserved.

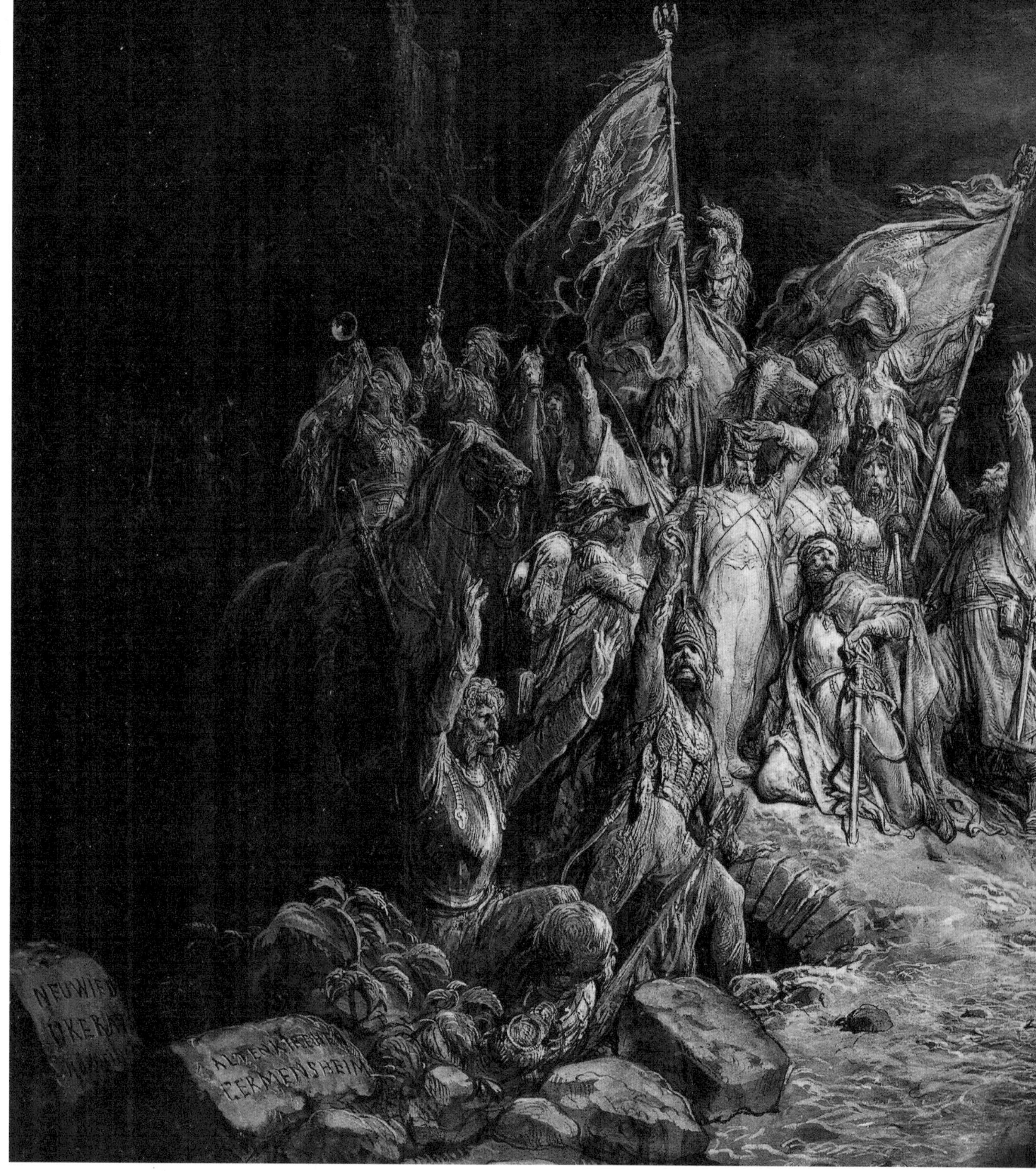

To the Rhine, 1879
Photogravure of gouache, ink and wash painting • Goupil & Cie,
Gustave Doré… by René Delorme; original painting
73 x 99 cm (28¾ x 39 in), 1870, in MAMC, Strasbourg

As the French march off to battle the Germans, the spirits of past war heroes come up out of their graves to salute the soldiers and cheer them on to certain victory, in the spirit of Napoleon. But the spirit of Napoleon III was far different from the spirit of Napoleon I, and disaster was only weeks away.

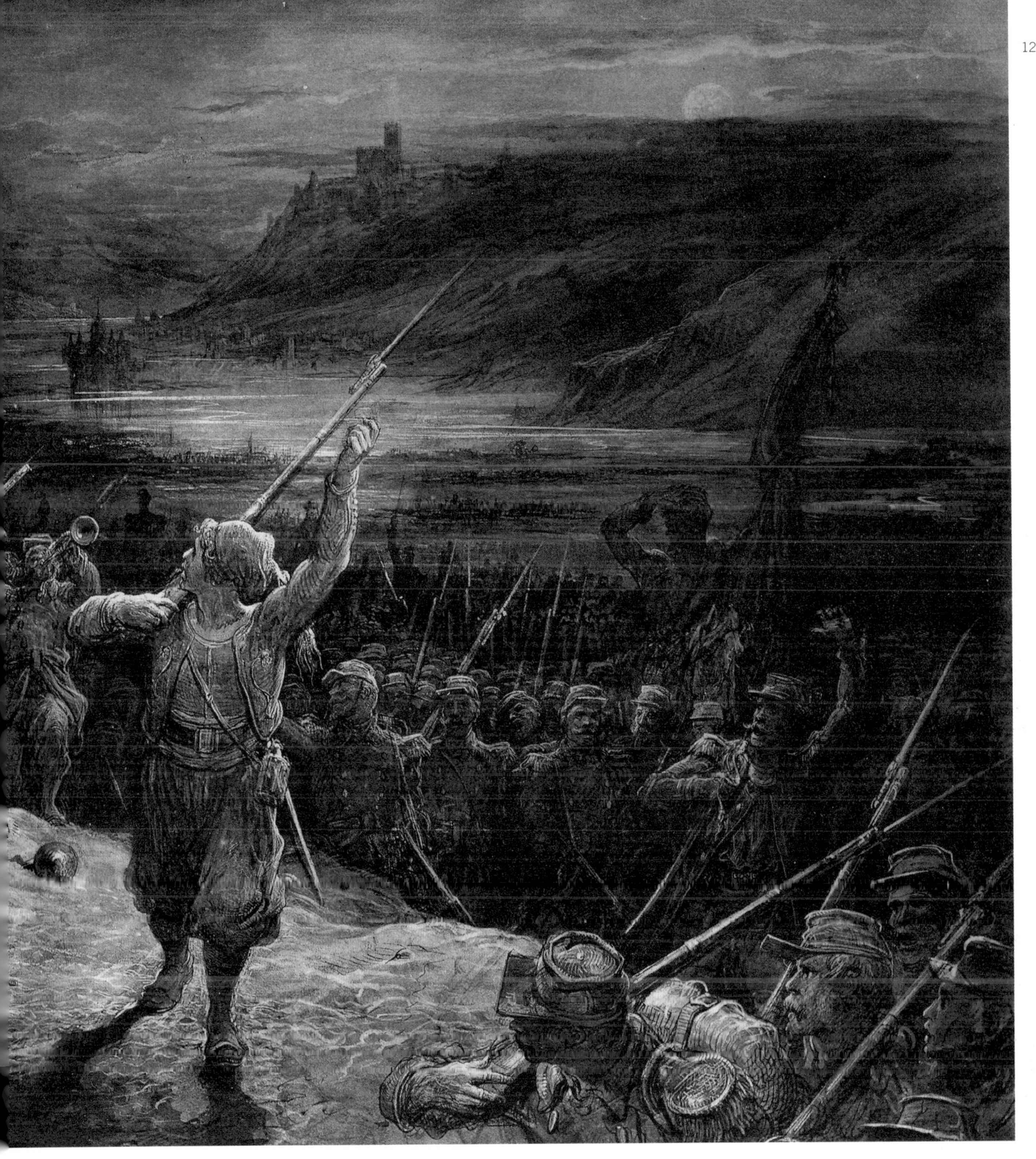

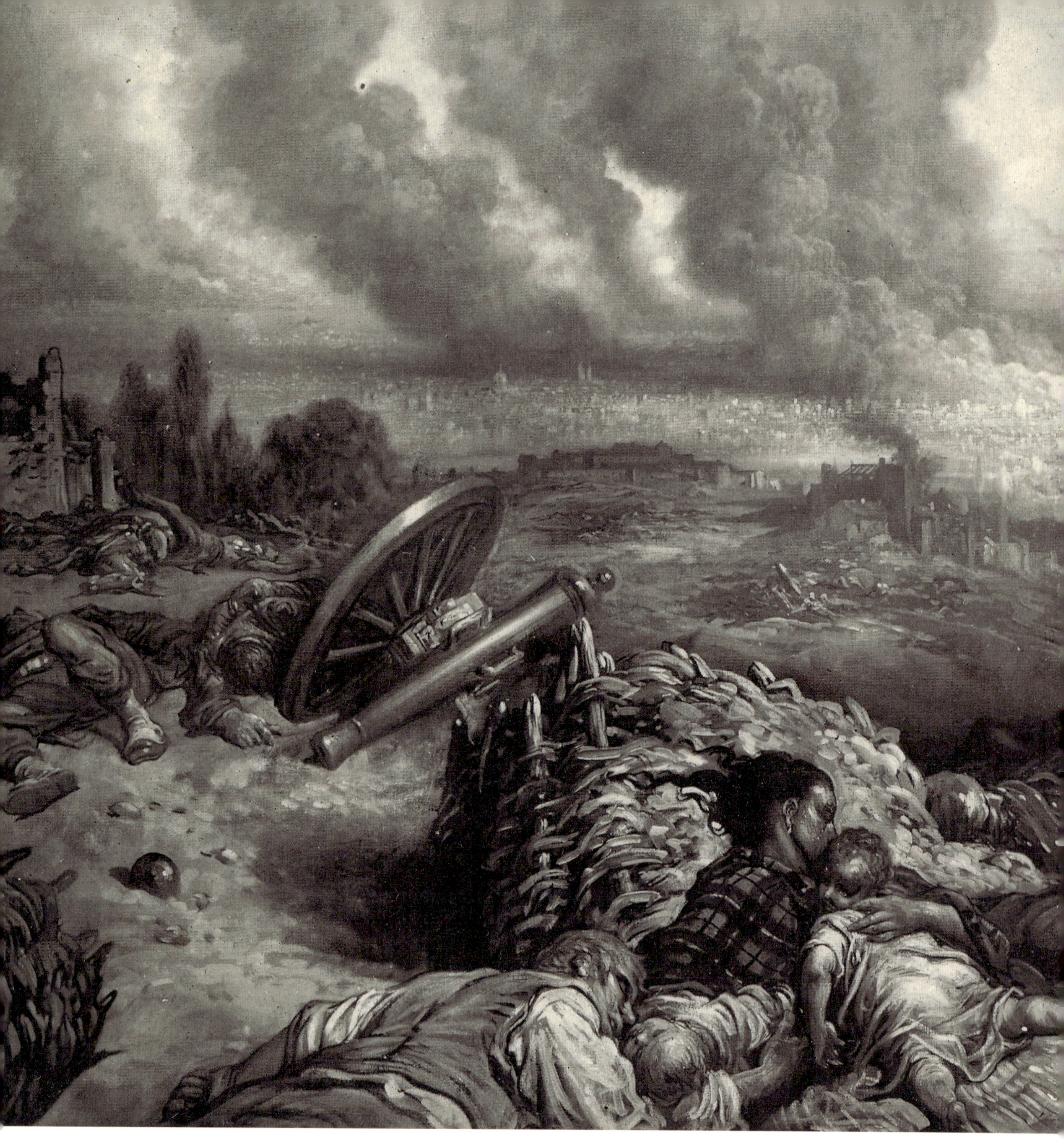

The Enigma, or The Horrors of War, 1879
Photogravure of oil painting • Goupil & Cie,
Gustave Doré… by René Delorme; original painting, 1.3 x 1.9 m
(4¼ x 6¼ ft), 1871, in Musée d'Orsay, Paris

With death and destruction all around, allegorical figures struggle to understand what went so horribly wrong. Doré's visual summary may be compared to Émile Zola's textual summary in his novel, *L'Inondation (The Flood)*, (1892): 'What have we done, oh God, to be punished like this?' In the next century, millions would echo that sentiment.

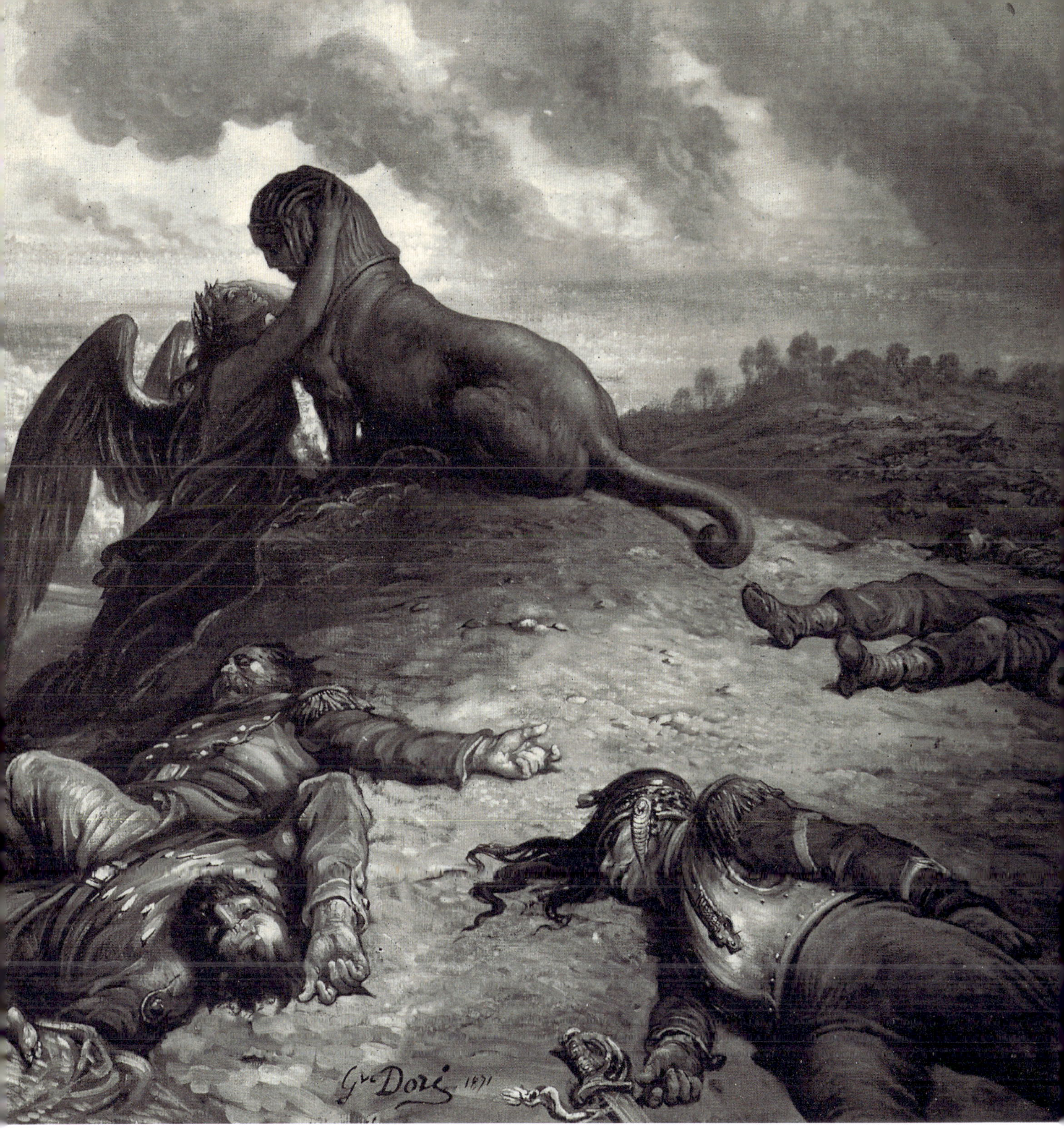

Indexes

Index of Works

Page numbers in *italics* indicate
illustration captions.

General Index

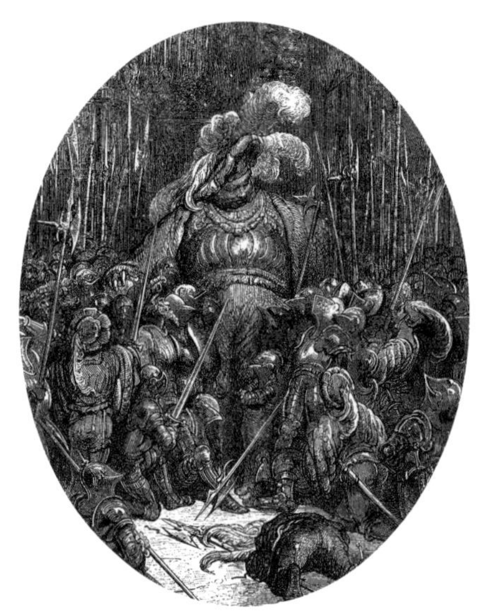

Masterpieces of Art
FLAME TREE PUBLISHING

A new series of carefully curated print and digital books covering the world's greatest art, artists and art movements.

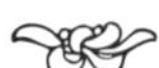

If you enjoyed this book please sign up for updates, information and offers on further titles in this series at

blog.flametreepublishing.com/art-of-fine-gifts/